Marketing to Millennials

A Wiley Brand

Marketing to Millennials

by Corey Padveen

A Wiley Brand

Marketing to Millennials For Dummies®

Published by: **John Wiley & Sons, Inc.,** 111 River Street, Hoboken, NJ 07030-5774, www.wiley.com

Copyright © 2017 by John Wiley & Sons, Inc., Hoboken, New Jersey

Published simultaneously in Canada

For general information on our other products and services, please contact our Customer Care Department within the U.S. at 877-762-2974, outside the U.S. at 317-572-3993, or fax 317-572-4002. For technical support, please visit https://hub.wiley.com/community/support/dummies.

Wiley publishes in a variety of print and electronic formats and by print-on-demand. Some material included with standard print versions of this book may not be included in e-books or in print-on-demand. If this book refers to media such as a CD or DVD that is not included in the version you purchased, you may download this material at http://booksupport.wiley.com. For more information about Wiley products, visit www.wiley.com.

Library of Congress Control Number: 2017938428

ISBN 978-1-119-36904-2 (pbk); ISBN 978-1-119-36905-9 (ePub); 978-1-119-36902-8 (ePDF)

Manufactured in the United States of America

10 9 8 7 6 5 4 3 2 1

Contents at a Glance

Table of Contents

Introduction

Millennials aren't magical, elusive consumers, but marketers have had a great deal of difficulty figuring them out. Millennials are defined as individuals born between the years 1980 and 2000, and they make up the largest audience of consumers in the world. Although they're defined by their age, Millennials are essentially prototypes for the modern consumer. Importantly, they're poised to inherit the largest transfer of wealth ever recorded in human history!

A seismic shift has taken place regarding buying behavior, and it's up to the marketers of the world to find new ways to reach customers. There is no one-size-fits-all model for reaching this coveted demographic. Every consumer is an individual and will uniquely respond to different brands, campaigns, and content.

Marketing to Millennials For Dummies is written to provide you with a framework to develop an effective Millennial marketing strategy. It's filled with information that you can use to craft programs that are right for your brand.

About This Book

I wrote this book to provide guidelines that marketers in virtually any field can leverage. Whether you're working in a business-to-business setting selling raw materials to manufacturers or developing consumer-oriented communications strategies to sell discounted school supplies to an incoming class of mobile-oriented college freshmen, there's something in this book that can help you.

The methods outlined in this book don't preclude any level of marketing professional from participating. Whether you're a seasoned veteran who is looking for new ways to spice up your brand's communications strategies or a new marketer wondering how to tackle certain types of campaigns, you'll be able to develop your strategies.

Foolish Assumptions

First and foremost, I assume that you're either a business owner who handles your own company's marketing, or you work in the marketing department of a brand, organization, government, or other entity. I assume that you're already familiar with certain marketing strategies and tools. Therefore, you can use what I cover in this book to expand that knowledge. I also assume that

» You're familiar with some of the business applications of social networks, like Facebook and Twitter.

» You've already created content and other assets for channels — for example, blogs and branded social platforms.

» You or your staff have worked on marketing campaigns in the past and are familiar with some of the more general processes involved in marketing a product or service.

» You recognize that Millennials are regular consumers with unique traits and habits and should not be looked at in a vacuum.

» You're willing to work with hard data and take the time to analyze and optimize your campaigns and strategies based on what these data are telling you (admittedly, not the most exciting thing in the world).

Icons Used in This Book

Throughout the margins in this book, you see little pictures that point out important information. The following list tells you what those icons mean:

TIP

The Tip icon marks tips (duh!) and shortcuts that you can use to expedite processes or improve the results of your campaigns in a shorter time frame.

REMEMBER

The Remember icon marks the information that's especially important to keep top of mind.

TECHNICAL STUFF

The Technical Stuff icon marks information of a highly technical nature or something related to the specifics of a particular network or industry that is being reviewed.

WARNING

The Warning icon tells you to watch out! It marks critical information that may save you headaches and identifies common mistakes or mix-ups that can easily trap marketers.

Beyond the Book

In addition to what you're reading right now, this product also comes with a free access-anywhere Cheat Sheet that gives you pointers on the topic of marketing to Millennials. To get this Cheat Sheet, simply go to www.dummies.com and search for "*Marketing to Millennials For Dummies* Cheat Sheet" in the Search box.

Where to Go from Here

You can read this book in any order. The chapters don't have a linear structure. Cross-references throughout the book refer you to important concepts in other chapters.

If you're wondering which chapter to start with, I strongly recommend Chapter 2. Chapter 2 is designed to provide you with an outline of how modern marketers see Millennials and how the view of Millennials needs to change to foster lasting relationships.

Part 2 focuses largely on strategies that take different media and practices into account to create a Millennial-facing program. Part 3 dives into some of the more specific markets and economies that Millennials occupy in significant numbers. Any chapter or section you choose to read, however, will provide you with the steps and information necessary to create effective communications strategies that cater to the increasingly relevant and influential Millennial audience.

1

Getting Started with Marketing to Millennials

IN THIS PART . . .

Discover the importance of Millennials in terms of their economic impact and their influence.

Provide a clear definition of Millennials that stretches beyond simple age brackets.

Build out segmented, detailed audience pockets and analyze the behaviors of audience members.

Chapter **1**

Getting to Know Millennials

Familiarizing oneself with the intricacies of Millennials is one of the most crucial steps a marketer can take. Today, personalization is the name of the game. The tailored experience that you want to create starts with getting to know the Millennial mind: how they operate and why they matter so much to your business.

In this chapter, you discover the short and long-term value Millennials bring to your organization. You see how they interact with brands across various media. You also find out ways you can connect with them.

Millennials are consumers, just like the generations that have come before them. However, circumstances, technology, and a changing global landscape have created a unique Millennial mindset.

Discovering Why Millennials Matter

Millennials are valuable because they now make up a major part of the global economy. Therefore, marketers need to focus on this group to develop effective, successful strategies that reach, engage, and convert Millennial consumers.

For our purposes, the term *Millennial* refers to consumers born between 1980 to 2000. The term Millennial can extend far beyond those age barriers, though, as I discuss in more detail in Chapter 2.

TIP

When creating a marketing plan, it can be quite effective to not define Millennials strictly by age. However, you'll want to make this distinction when analyzing the physical size of the market

There is power in numbers

In 2015, Millennials edged out Baby Boomers as the largest demographic in the United States. Immediately, without any additional information about the demographic, they become important to your business. Volume alone makes them a highly coveted group. They're all independent consumers, and the vast majority have a steady income. There are very few brands that wouldn't be interested in marketing to the largest group of consumers in the country.

The Millennial cohort provides plenty of opportunities for marketers. As the largest demographic in the American economy, you ignore Millennials at your own peril. Millennials currently have tremendous buying power and over time will become wealthier.

Here are several reasons why the size of the market is a particularly important consideration:

>> **Economic influence:** As older generations shrink, Millennials have a growing share of the consumer base. This results in the transfer of wealth. If you don't develop products that appeal to them today, then you risk your business becoming obsolete.

>> **Trend setting:** Some trends are set intentionally, such as popular challenges that pop up on social media. One example is the Ice Bucket Challenge, which asked individuals to pour a bucket of ice over their heads to raise awareness for Amyotrophic Lateral Sclerosis (ALS). Other trends occur because of the sheer size of this demographic. Thanks to the availability of web data on Millennials, marketers can spot naturally occurring trends. (For more information on the analysis and implementation of data, see Chapter 4.)

>> **Fast sharing:** The volume of data available and the rate at which it's shared creates a changing landscape for marketers. You can currently find more online data about Millennials than any poll, questionnaire, survey, or census could collect. Therefore, marketers need to be ready to adapt to the information revealed by thousands of data points.

>> **Brand advocacy:** The Millennial market has the power to make or break a brand overnight. The power of the people has never been stronger than it is now. Brands need to be transparent and respond to the demands of activist Millennial consumers. You can't ignore Millennials who work together to aid or defeat a brand. One such example took place during the original Pokémon Go craze, where a small ice cream shop in Washington state was set to close its doors for good. Millennial players stumbled upon the shop, thanks to the game, and then began campaigning to save the business online. These efforts drove enough foot traffic to triple sales and keep the business alive.

Millennials influence the economy

Millennials have a tremendous influence over the national and global economy. The Fung Business Intelligence Centre (www.funggroup.com/eng/knowledge/research.php) estimates that by 2020, Millennials will control 30 percent of retail spending in the United States, up from 13.5 percent in 2013. That 30 percent, according to Standard & Poor's, accounts for about $1.4 trillion per year — and that number will undoubtedly grow.

Millennials are poised to receive the greatest transfer of wealth in economic history. Estimates from major American financial institutions, like Morgan Stanley, and research firms suggest that over the next several decades, Millennials will receive somewhere near $30 trillion from the generations that preceded them. That is a startling figure, and one that undoubtedly whets the appetite of marketers in any field.

To determine where that money is likely going to go, marketers should become aware of the spending habits of Millennials. This knowledge will help them build effectively targeted campaigns.

Goldman Sachs has provided key information about Millennials' traits that you can see at www.goldmansachs.com/our-thinking/pages/millennials.

Some of the factors that affect their behavior are as follows:

>> **Money is coming in, but it isn't necessarily going out.** Mean income for young Millennials has gone down over the last decade. Millennials are working, but the cost of living has significantly increased. Income indicators like average national minimum wage have gone down. So, while Millennials are currently a significant portion of the national population, their disposable income isn't significant. This may have a big impact on buying behaviors, even after the transfer of wealth.

>> **Millennials carry a huge amount of debt.** The cost of education is a big one for Millennials and has a major impact on what they are willing to spend. In the last decade, according to the Federal Reserve, mean student loan balance has more than doubled for young Millennials. This counts as a form of *long-term debt*. (That is, debt that is not set to be repaid over the next five years.) This has a significant impact on Millennials' decision-making processes. Because of this debt, buying decisions are methodical and based largely on utility. A significant part of that utility is rooted in the extraneous benefits of a purchase. For example, on top of the usefulness of a product or service, is there more to be gained from the brand or ownership in the long-run? This is one of the reasons why creating relationships with Millennials and establishing yourself as a trusted brand are so important to both acquiring new customers from this market and keeping them committed over the course of their consumption lifetime.

>> **Ownership is not a priority.** Major, long-term financial commitments are not as important to Millennials as they were to previous generations. In a world where the share economy and on-demand services have exploded, ownership is less important than access. The sharing economy (see Chapter 12) plays a major role in the Millennial consumer cycle.

The sharing economy, which is covered in detail in Chapter 12, is the market for shared goods and services, giving participants in the economy access over ownership. Millennials have gone through the stages of consumer maturation during a recession era, which has led to significant financial conservatism. Companies or products that fall into the share economy, such as Uber or Airbnb, allow Millennials to access the goods and services they need, when they need them, without requiring them to pay the price of ownership.

>> **Millennials are willing to play the waiting game.** Just because ownership is not as important to Millennials doesn't mean that it isn't on their radar screen. Millennials are more patient and willing to wait for the right time to buy. This, once again, is because of the accessibility granted by both the sharing economy and on-demand services. Almost everything is accessible at the touch of a virtual button, so the necessity to own isn't quite what it used to be.

>> **Brand loyalty goes deep.** Previously, when making a sale, recognition and a strong brand were all that mattered. Now, it's the relationship between the Millennial and the brand. Also, referrals matter more than ever. Millennials care what their friends and family say. Customers trust referrals more than traditional advertising.

>> **Quality matters more than price.** Millennials are a particularly price-sensitive bunch primarily because they became consumers during the Great Recession of 2008. Price sensitivity combined with a heavy education debt load means that they are cautious spenders. When they do decide to make a purchase, the focus is much less on price than it is on quality. Millennials want a product that lasts as well as a long-term relationship with the brand in question.

They're a connected generation

REMEMBER

Millennials are the most connected generation ever, and they use that connectedness as a tool in the buying process. If you don't find a way to leverage that characteristic in your communications, your chances of long-run survival are slim.

You need to be aware of certain characteristics to take advantage of Millennials' communications habits:

>> **Millennials are over-sharers.** Millennials share everything they do, want, or think, which is great for marketers. It provides a wealth of data and information that you can use to construct highly targeted, personalized marketing messages and campaigns.

>> **You learn more by studying Millennials than you do from asking them.** Thanks to the over-sharing nature of Millennial consumers, you can find answers to any questions you have or didn't know you had by analyzing your data. (For information on effectively analyzing your data, see Chapter 4.)

>> **They trust each other more than they trust you.** Every year, worldwide public relations and consulting firm Edelman releases the Trust Barometer, indicating consumer trust levels in different groups. For the past several years (after the Great Recession), the highest level of trust is placed in peers, friends and family, and industry experts. That means that brand is not on top of the list of resources consumers look to when they need a trustworthy answer. This statement is particularly true of Millennials. They want to hear unbiased, honest opinions from people in their inner circles, likely on social media.

>> **The buying cycle is not linear.** The buying cycle has an endless number of touchpoints. You have control over some of them while the audience creates others. The key is to note where your prospects connect with your brand so that you can plan to be there. (Chapter 9 covers a complete omni-channel marketing strategy.)

   Touchpoints refer to the various interactions that a consumer has with a brand throughout the buying cycle. Touchpoints can vary by medium, creative design, and content type, such as images or video. In traditional media, such as television or print, far fewer touchpoints are in the buyer's journey. When you consider new media, like social networks, mobile, and other digital platforms, the number of touchpoints can skyrocket over the course of the buyer journey.

>> **Mobile matters most.** Mobile is where Millennials spend the majority of their time. They connect with each other and connect with brands. If you don't have a mobile strategy, you'll lose out on the tremendous potential it provides and likely face extinction in the near future. The generation that dictates how markets operate is telling you to think mobile first, and you need to listen. (I cover the details of creating an effective mobile strategy in Chapter 10.)

Leveraging Millennial Influence

The connectedness of the Millennial market may require you to create more complex, interwoven communications strategies than you're used to. It also means that you have a new marketing tool at your disposal — the consumers themselves. Taking advantage of influencers and utilizing your brand advocates is a powerful strategy.

TIP

The 2016 Edelman Trust Barometer reveals that Millennials trust "a person like yourself" and industry or academic experts over virtually any organizational operator, such as the CEO of a company. This kind of influence is crucial in making buying decisions, and it's something that marketers need to be both aware of and ready to use.

Influencers are consumers who have amassed large, loyal followings on various social platforms. High star power actors are one form of influencer, but for Millennials, those that hold the most power are consumers who have built organic followings by sharing great content. An example of a modern Millennial influencer would be a consumer who has built a YouTube following by sharing reviews of a particular line of products. The influencer gains trust above the brand because of the implicit honesty and integrity of these reviews.

Identifying key influencers

Consumers aren't as interested in traditional advertising messages as they once were. Of course, paid campaigns still serve a major role in the consumer buying cycle, but identifying influencers within your existing audience is more important.

The following sections offer a few helpful tactics for finding influencers.

Create a loyalty program

Loyalty can't be bought, but it can be encouraged. Establishing a loyalty program is an excellent way to

>> Encourage repeat business

>> Increase customer lifetime value (CLV)

>> Build a relationship with your Millennial audience

Because relationships are crucial to the survival of your brand, a loyalty program will help build those relationships. Hopefully, those relationships will lead to the cultivation of brand advocates. Those advocates can then help build your brand by introducing it to new circles of consumers.

Customer lifetime value is defined as the net profit generated by your brand based on the entire relationship of transactions with a customer.

Identify your brand advocates and brand defenders

The goal of any brand should be to turn prospects into customers and customers into brand defenders. A *brand defender* is a customer who not only advocates on behalf of your brand and acts as a pseudo-sales agent, but also defends your brand in times of crisis.

TIP

A *pseudo-sales agent* is a consumer who acts as a brand advocate. She works to spread your message without the need for an incentive. An *affiliate* shares your message and product in exchange for some form of payment or revenue. A pseudo-sales agent works to spread your brand's name throughout her social circles strictly because of her relationship with your brand.

BRAND ADVOCACY CYCLE

The easiest way to understand the brand advocacy cycle, shown in the figure, is with an example. Assume that a consumer — I'll call her Jane — is in the market to purchase a new phone. Jane has never owned a phone, so she has a completely objective viewpoint of every brand in the market. This point in the cycle is the *awareness stage*.

As Jane begins to learn more about each brand by reading reviews, asking friends, and visiting brand websites, she moves into the *understanding phase* and onto *interest* as she narrows her choices. She decides on an iPhone in the *trial* period, sees what it can do and how powerful the product is, and moves in to *belief*.

As Jane continues using the product and becomes more enamored with what it can do, she moves into *affinity*. Next time she needs a phone, she goes with the iPhone without a thought. That's the *loyalty stage*. It's hugely valuable to a brand to get customers to this point. Loyal customers mean greater lifetime value, and it's far less expensive to keep a customer than it is to convert a new one.

(continued)

(continued)

But when Jane begins telling her friends about the iPhone or writing about how much she loves it, thereby becoming a brand advocate, the value increases enormously. And when she goes to the next stage, actually coming to the brand's defense when other consumers speak negatively about it, that's when the greatest value can be reaped from the consumer.

Brand defenders are not only loyal consumers who will advocate on your behalf as pseudo-sales agents, but they will also help you handle a crisis if one ever comes up.

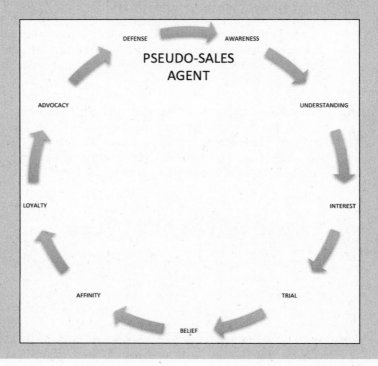

One of the best examples of brand defenders in action was evident during Apple's notorious Bendgate affair when the newly released iPhone 6 phones were bending in owners' back pockets. Despite a clear issue with the product, Apple's brand defenders rushed to their side. They insisted that the root of the problem was consumer misuse rather than a product defect. It's rare that a brand reaches this level of advocacy. But, if you can cultivate brand defenders by identifying and nurturing your existing brand advocates, your long-run success is assured.

Implement an employee advocacy program

Employees are consumers, too, and marketers often forget about the power of activating their Millennial employees. They relay positive experiences with your products and share them with their social circles. This word-of-mouth marketing helps you take advantage of the massive social reach existing right within your organization.

Encouraging and perhaps incentivizing employees to share content is a powerful way to build your presence, foster brand awareness, and prompt adoption from a new user base.

Communicate with your detractors

It's all too easy to brush off criticism and focus on new customer acquisition. But communicating with detractors shows that you care.

Often, when customers complain, their goal is to be heard rather than to remedy a bad situation. Attempting to improve these transactions goes a long way toward creating new brand advocates and defenders. In addition, addressing an issue quickly and effectively can prevent it from spiraling out of control and becoming a costly mistake.

Nurturing relationships

Millennials see relationships as a significant part of the buying process. The irony of this is that this demographic is more price sensitive than its predecessors, yet Millennial consumers are willing to pay a slightly higher price if they have a relationship with the higher-priced brand. This mindset isn't one that marketers are familiar with. However, marketing to Millennials doesn't require a completely new paradigm. It simply requires marketers to dig much deeper into the mind of the Millennial consumer.

Brand familiarity is not the driving force behind a Millennial consumer's decision to purchase; quality matters considerably more than the brand name or logo. Reaching Millennials requires careful planning.

Here are several ways to nurture a relationship with a Millennial consumer:

>> **Personalization:** The key to successful relationships with Millennials is personalization. (For more on relationship building, see Chapter 3.) The modern product and service market seems to endlessly expand, which means that there is virtually no product on the market for which there isn't an alternative. Therefore, after you have the attention of your wider audience,

tailoring your content to the tastes and preferences of the individual will help build loyalty.

>> **Brand experience:** What kind of brand do you want to be? Are you authoritative or neighborly? Is your content factual or conversational? Building a brand persona is an important step in the process because it helps you shape the consumer's experience with your brand. That experience, which is covered in detail in Chapter 11, will be a driving force behind establishing a relationship and will work toward building loyalty with your target Millennial audience.

>> **Cause alignment:** Millennial consumers connect deeply with brands that associate themselves with causes. Just because Millennials possess this consumer trait doesn't mean that you should exploit causes for the purpose of building relationships with Millennials. However, if your brand does support a cause, it's certainly a means of connecting more deeply with certain segments of your Millennial audience.

>> **Responsiveness:** Traditionally, a curtain has been in front of the big, powerful brand. Now that curtain has been lifted, thanks in large part to social media. Communication with a brand is easier than ever before. A certain sense of satisfaction comes from receiving a response from a brand. Therefore, responding to your audience members when they reach out can go a very long way toward nurturing budding relationships.

Meeting Millennials Where They Are

Billions of interactions and engagements take place online every single day. Joining a conversation in progress is always going to be much easier than trying to create your own.

Millennials are engaged on various platforms with content, brands, and each other. Your responsibility as a marketer is to find new and creative ways to become a part of those exchanges. To reach these individuals, you need to understand

>> How they communicate

>> How they share content

>> How they decide to make purchases

Communication

It may seem like the only way for brands to reach Millennial consumers is via social media. But the reality is that Millennials use a broad number of communication platforms, including traditional media. Familiarizing yourself with these media is going to play a crucial role in communicating with your audience. (Chapter 5 covers the use of traditional media.)

Traditional means of advertising, such as television and print, were once restricted to brands willing to spend the big bucks. Now new methods that meld the digital world with the offline world allow virtually any brand to connect with Millennial consumers. (Chapter 6 covers multiple kinds of new media and details how marketers can take advantage of both organic and paid initiatives to communicate with and convert Millennials into long-run customers.)

Organic initiatives and strategies are those that don't rely on paid advertising to reach a specific audience segment. Organic engagement is powerful and a key component to the success of a marketing program. However, building these kinds of audiences takes significantly longer. A well-thought-out mix of the two — paid and organic — will be useful in helping you build out your brand on both traditional and new media.

While Millennials aren't a monolithic group, many Millennials have certain traits in common:

>> **They use various media to communicate.** Millennials don't confine themselves to one particular medium. The average Millennial is active on multiple social accounts, messaging platforms, and devices. You don't necessarily need to plan to be active or even discoverable on every one of these media. That would be too costly. But you should get to know your audience and familiarize yourself with their preferred means of communicating. Then you can identify those media that stand to generate the greatest return for your brand.

>> **Mobile is the primary communications tool.** Whatever Millennials do, they prefer to do it on mobile. The explosive growth of mobile is unprecedented. Marketers have had to make a dramatic shift in the way they do business. Millennials are on the go and wherever they go, their mobile devices go with them. Essentially, ignoring mobile means ignoring your audience, and that is a recipe for disaster. (Marketing to Millennials on mobile is covered in Chapter 8.)

>> **Personalities differ from one platform to another.** The average Millennial may be active on four or five kinds of digital media. If they're active on several media, it doesn't mean that your brand will necessarily find success marketing to them in the same way on each platform. Millennials use different media in unique ways. To communicate effectively, analyze your audience on each platform.

Sharing

Sharing means a lot more than it used to, thanks in large part to new media like Facebook, Twitter, and Airbnb. You can look at the concept of sharing from two perspectives.

First is the content and information approach. Millennials share more with each other and with brands than any generation that came before them. Unlike Baby Boomers, Millennials have indicated that they are willing to share personal information with brands. This willingness to share has led to the explosion of data-gathering methods, such as social sign-in. *Social sign-in* allows users to sign in with a single click via Google or Facebook.

Thanks to social sign-in, your brand can collect a significant amount of data without having to directly questioning your audience. The desire for simplicity and convenience on the part of the Millennial consumers means that they're likely to use this option. It's less cumbersome than creating stand-alone profiles for each platform and limiting the information they share with brands. Data is crucial to the creation and improvement of your Millennial marketing strategy. The willingness of Millennials to share via social sign-in means that those processes are made significantly easier.

The second concept of sharing relates to the rise of the sharing economy (covered in detail in Chapter 12). Millennial consumers agree that access to goods and services is more important than ownership. Brands like Airbnb (`https://airbnb.com`) and Uber (`https://uber.com`) recognized this fact and built multibillion-dollar businesses to capitalize on it. The priorities and measurements of success have changed for Millennials. The sharing economy has facilitated this transformation. (Chapter 12 covers the sharing economy.)

Decision-making

Impulsivity and ownership are no longer the names of the game when it comes to making purchasing decisions. Millennials have access to a wealth of information that can help them make informed, educated, and trusted decisions, and they don't hurry the process.

The Edelman Trust Barometer showed that industry and academic experts and peers rank above brands as trusted advisors. Review sites like *Yelp!*, shown in Figure 1-1, make peer reviews readily available for virtually any type of product or service. Millennials use these kinds of sites when making a buying decision.

FIGURE 1-1:
Yelp! allows
consumers to
provide reviews.

As the availability of trustworthy, verifiable information, such as reviews, has increased, their impact has been noticeable across all markets. A 2015 study by Forbes found that only about 1 percent of Millennial consumers would trust a brand more as a result of traditional advertising. Roughly, a third of Millennials review blogs and review sites before making a purchase. Authenticity is what matters most to these prospects, and that outweighs even the quality of content.

This trend has leveled the playing field for smaller brands. Of course, big budgets open doors and opportunities not available to smaller companies, but now they have the opportunity to compete for the same business as larger organizations.

Chapter **2**

Creating a Modern View of Millennials

Building an effective strategy for Millennial consumers begins with a clear understanding of their unique characteristics. Some marketers miss the basics. Millennials, like any generation, are defined as a group of consumers that fall into a certain age bracket. But, in some cases marketing to Millennials requires you to look beyond age. For this reason, you need to develop a deep understanding of this market so that you don't misunderstand its complex nature.

In this chapter, you start thinking about Millennials as prototypes for the next generation of consumers. They're not simply soon-to-be-wealthy 20-somethings that are difficult to reach. They represent a seismic shift in the world of marketing.

Understanding the Marketer's Perception of Millennials

If you ask the average marketer to define the term *Millennial*, he or she would almost certainly start by stating that Millennials are consumers born between the years 1980 and 2000. While, demographically this is a fact, the reality is that the term Millennial embodies so much more. That said, marketers still hold certain prevailing notions when it comes to defining this important group.

Examining standard definitions that marketers use

The date ranges vary from one demographer to the next, but for the sake of simplicity, the generally accepted starting point for the Millennial generation is 1980. While the latter point of the date range varies considerably, it's safe to say that an accepted cutoff point would be 2000. Some demographers are interested in only designating those who reach the end of high school age by 2000 as Millennials. Others define the generation as reaching consumer maturity in the mid-2010s. Whichever range you choose to use, Millennials are the largest, most influential group of consumers in the world (see Chapter 1).

To gain some insight about Millennials, the Pew Research Center asked Millennials to describe themselves, as shown in Figure 2-1. As you can see in Figure 2-1, Millennials have a very particular perception of themselves that sometimes conflicts with other people's perceptions. Forty-nine percent of respondents indicate that they feel Millennials are wasteful, while 40 percent believe that Millennials are environmentally conscious. You may also find it a little hard to imagine someone being both cynical and idealistic, yet 39 percent of the Millennials who answered this survey felt that the general demographic is idealistic, while 31 percent believe that the generation is cynical. Clearly, you need to understand your particular niche audience so that you target the right characteristics.

Millennials do have a few personality traits on which the majority of marketers agree. The following sections outline the assumptions that marketers most often make when it comes to Millennial consumers. Some of these are correct, and some are misguided, as we discuss later in the chapter. A better understanding of them will help you develop content and advertising strategies that appeal to the true nature of Millennials.

Tech savvy

Millennials have been born into the digital age. They have grown up not knowing a world without extensive connectivity. Smartphones are standard equipment, and nearly the entire Millennial population of the United States has access to the web.

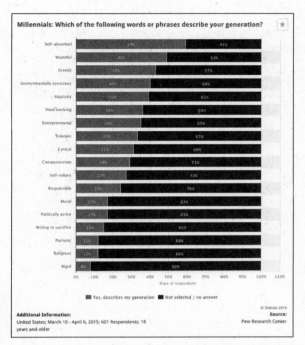

Millennials: Which of the following words or phrases describe your generation?

	Yes, describes my generation	Not selected / no answer
Self-absorbed	59%	41%
Wasteful	49%	51%
Greedy	43%	57%
Environmentally conscious	40%	60%
Idealistic	39%	61%
Hard working	36%	64%
Entrepreneurial	35%	65%
Tolerant	33%	67%
Cynical	31%	69%
Compassionate	29%	71%
Self-reliant	27%	73%
Responsible	24%	76%
Moral	17%	83%
Politically active	17%	83%
Willing to sacrifice	15%	85%
Patriotic	12%	88%
Religious	12%	88%
Rigid	8%	92%

Share of respondents

© Statista 2016

Additional Information:
United States; March 10 - April 6, 2015; 601 Respondents; 18 years and older

Source:
Pew Research Center

http://www.pewresearch.org/fact-tank/2015/03/19/how-millennials-compare-with-their-grandparents/ft_millennials-education_031715.

FIGURE 2-1: Terms Millennials use to describe themselves.

Millennials have been instrumental in the expansion of such services as social networking and helped simplify web and application development tools. If marketers can assign one characteristic to Millennials and be right, it's that Millennials are the most technologically advanced demographic in the world.

Mobile

In addition to being the most populous generation in the United States, Millennials are also the most mobile. The number of connected mobile devices associated with Millennials almost exactly matches the size of the generation.

The way Millennials use mobile devices (see Chapter 10) and their dependence on them tells a much more important story. Millennials don't separate from their mobile devices. In fact, most Millennials admit to never allowing their smartphone to leave their side.

Self-absorbed

You may or may not have heard of Millennials referred to as the Selfie Generation. High definition, front-facing mobile phone cameras and mobile applications such as Snapchat (www.snapchat.com) have normalized the self-portraits known as *selfies*. Marketers associate this behavior with self-absorption.

In 2013, *Time* published an article by Joel Stein called "The Me Me Me Generation.". Stein wrote that while Millennials may be self-assured, determined, and, in some cases, even selfish, there is much more to them than that.

Lazy

Marketers have watched the rise of the on-demand economy (see Chapter 14) and assumed that its success has come from the inherent laziness of the Millennial generation. The rationalization for that assumption is that Millennials would rather use a mobile application to order what they need than go out and run errands.

Antisocial

Millennials love using social media and sharing their thoughts with the world from behind a screen. Traditional marketers see Millennials walking down the street with their heads buried in a phone and assume that they're antisocial.

Educated

Marketers know better than to try to dupe Millennials with dated, cunning advertising tactics. That is because they recognize that Millennials are smarter than that.

Entitled

Millennials are viewed as a group that demands a lot from previous generations without offering much in return. This perception is rooted largely in the availability of content, resources, information, and necessities available free online. Since the launch of social networking sites and share-based resources (see Chapter 12), marketers assume that Millennials feel they deserve a lot because they have gotten so much free online.

Informed

When it comes to making buying decisions, Millennials have access to a plethora of information that previous generations did not have. The buying process used to rely largely on the word of the brand via traditional advertising channels. Now Millennials talk to one another and receive honest reviews about a product, service, or brand before making a purchasing decision. Trust in brands, executives, and even government has significantly decreased in recent years, which has coincided with a rise in the trust consumers put in experts and peers. This increased reliance on others means that marketers need to recognize the importance of relationships and the brand experience.

Lacking in loyalty

At one time, the name of a brand would guarantee a certain amount of loyalty. Now, marketers see Millennials chasing something that can be difficult to pinpoint. Whatever it is, marketers assume that brand loyalty has gone out the window. They believe that Millennials prioritize budgets over brands.

Price sensitive

Marketers believe that the lack of loyalty Millennials display is due to price sensitivity. There is irony in the fact that Millennials seem to insist on getting what they want, when they want it, but are apparently willing to wait to make any purchase until a price is found that meets a certain criteria.

Private

With hacks, data breaches, and the fear of Big Brother monitoring their every move, Millennials want to keep their information private. Even with their high degree of oversharing on social media, marketers assume that Millennials don't want to share with brands for fear of exploitation.

Reviewing what marketers get right

Some of the assumptions marketers make about Millennials are accurate, with the data and research to back them up:

>> **Educated and informed consumers:** The majority of Millennial consumers review blogs and review sites before making a purchase. According to data from Bazaarvoice, an online retail shopper network (http://blog.bazaarvoice.com/2012/01/24/infographic-millennials-will-change-the-way-you-sell), 84 percent of Millennials say that user-generated content has an influence on what they buy. The brand experience is extremely important to Millennials. They believe that they can find good information in the unbiased accounts of other consumers. Tailoring the experience to the Millennial audience segment is crucial. This connected consumer base has more power than even the most rich and powerful brands.

>> **Price sensitive, but will spend:** Millennials became consumers during the greatest economic downfall that the United States experienced in nearly a century. Combine that with a high amount of student debt, and you have a generation of consumers that thinks before it buys.

REMEMBER

The important thing to note is that Millennials will buy. Quality matters more than price, so if they find value in a product or service, they will spend more. Also, don't be fooled by their cautious approach to spending; Millennials are impulsive. This impulsiveness may be attributable to the fast-paced nature of buying online.

>> **Highly tech-savvy and living mobile-first**: Millennials live online and, more importantly, on their mobile devices. They are constantly connecting and communicating. Any brand that doesn't take this particular trait into account and recognize that mobile is the new norm won't survive in an increasingly competitive marketplace.

Looking at what marketers get wrong

When you make assumptions about an entire demographic, you risk getting some things wrong. (Chapter 3 covers analyzing audience segments.) Here are some of the false assumptions marketers make:

>> **Millennials are not loyal.** Millennials are, in fact, very loyal. The difference with Millennial loyalty is that it relies much more on the relationship rather than brand recognition. Identifying the traits of audience segments, developing content that caters specifically to those traits, and building lasting relationships are what drive Millennials to be loyal.

>> **Millennials protect their privacy.** In reality, millennials are willing to share more than any other generation. It may appear that they're very private, but less than half of Millennials set strict online privacy settings.

>> **The group is lazy and entitled:** Millennials are quite the opposite of lazy. In fact, many Millennials work more than one job to pay bills and debts. What marketers miss is that on-demand services provide access and convenience, not laziness or self-entitlement. Millennials don't want to interrupt their work to run errands; they can have things like food delivered to them. This change signals a shift in consumer norms rather than providing evidence of a negative trait.

>> **Millennials are antisocial and self-absorbed.** Self-absorption is actually a byproduct of shifting communications practices. Millennials receive a constant stream of personalized messages. Marketers know that personalized messages are more likely to catch a Millennial's attention, so they become the norm. Therefore, Millennials aren't so much self-absorbed as they're used to responding to messages that specifically cater to their needs.

Recognizing common flaws in marketing campaigns

When you apply certain false assumptions to the strategy behind a campaign, the results can be underwhelming. To avoid getting disappointing results, don't make these common marketing mistakes:

» **Providing generalized, umbrella content with no specific target audience:** You need to analyze your audience segments and develop tailored, personalized content to deliver to specific targeted groups. Sending generic content without the customization that Millennials look for leads to failed campaigns.

» **Targeting Millennials by age and age alone:** Millennials are more than an age range; they're the new generation of consumers. When you think about Millennials as a mindset as opposed to a group of consumers restricted by an age range, you expand your potential audience and position yourself for long-term success.

» **Duplicating content across all media:** All consumers varies their use of media, so you can't apply the same strategy to each of them and hope to be successful. You need to understand your audience on each of the platforms you frequent (see Chapters 6, 7, and 8). Then you can develop effective strategies for each audience and media type.

» **Making assumptions without analyzing data to back it up:** Data needs to be at the core of everything you do. So much of it is readily available to fuel your success, so make sure that you use it. (For more about the analysis and applications of data, see Chapter 4.)

Finding the roots of the most common mistakes

The mistakes listed in the previous section are common for one reason: They generally come from the same four roots. These roots are

» **Inattention to data:** Data needs to be the driving force behind your decisions. If you're developing strategies that don't rely on data, you'll likely be disappointed with the results. You have no reason to rely on gut instinct. Data insights are simply too accessible.

>> **Broad generalizations applied to your audience:** With so much information about Millennials, it doesn't make sense to run on assumptions alone. Take some time to analyze and get to know your audience so that you can develop content and campaigns that really resonate with them.

>> **A lack of testing:** Everything you do should be tested. One of the greatest powers of new media is the ability to test, analyze, optimize, and implement all in a matter of hours. The ability to react in real-time is powerful and should not be ignored.

TECHNICAL STUFF

The term *new media* describes primarily digital, social, or mobile media. Traditional media, such as print, radio, and even television, have seen declines in consumer use, marketing value, and adoption.

>> **Refusing to adapt to changing audiences:** The audience you've cultivated and analyzed for today's campaign may not be the same audience you'll find when you're ready to run your next initiative. Auditing and analyzing your audience can be a tedious process, but it's an important one if you want to maintain relationships and find long-term success. (Running an audit on your audience and strategies is covered in Chapter 11.)

The Millennial Mindset

If you think about your Millennial audience without the constraints of age, you begin to understand that in some ways the term Millennial is becoming synonymous with consumer. The traits exhibited by Millennials, the largest and most influential demographic of consumers in the United States, are traits that marketers can apply to individuals across a multitude of demographics. Understanding and adapting to a new age of consumer habits and traits will set you up for long-term success.

Defining the Millennial

If you look beyond the scope of age, how would you define Millennial consumers? Giving them a singular definition would be dangerous because it significantly limits the audience. You need two definitions when discussing Millennials so that you can properly analyze them:

>> **Age:** The first definition of Millennial consumers has to do with age range. Use this definition when discussing data about the consumers. Demographers, sociologists, social anthropologists, and marketers use age to conduct studies and collect data. (Most hard data collected applies age restrictions to this group.)

>> **Interests and behaviors:** The second definition for the Millennial consumer is much more broad. Instead of focusing on age range data, you need to turn your attention to interests and behaviors. In these audience segments, the definition of Millennial extends far beyond age restrictions. Here, you look at like-minded consumers that fit a series of behavioral criteria. You can broadly define this category of Millennials as being tech-savvy, price-sensitive consumers who place their trust in peers and experts over brands. They digest information at a rapid rate and look for tailored, personalized brand experiences. Brand familiarity is less important to these consumers than relationships. When they form these relationships, they're fiercely loyal.

TIP

You can find out more about building segmented groups and developing more detailed definitions of your targeted Millennial audience in Chapter 3.

Identifying preferred Millennial media

When compared to a generation ago, you can have a presence on an endless array of media. Ideally, having such a vast presence also means you have a strategy and a budget. To maximize your budget, you need to find and target the specific platforms your audience uses. Here are some points to keep in mind, when you begin to identify your audience's preferred media:

>> **Start with Facebook.** The majority of online Millennials say they are active on Facebook. This means that you're almost certain to find some of your Millennial audience on Facebook. Despite what marketers and news outlets have said, Facebook is far from being irrelevant to Millennials. In fact, Facebook and its products have become so commonplace that Millennials don't even realize how inextricably linked to it they are. Facebook is a great place to begin the process of analyzing your audience.

>> **Match email lists before building strategies.** Before you begin building a strategy for a particular channel, you should either run an email match audience analysis or extract data using an ad platform. This step will help you determine whether a channel is worth investing in for the purpose of acquiring and retaining Millennial consumers.

TECHNICAL
STUFF

Running an *email match audience analysis* is the process of uploading an owned email database to match emails with users on a given network and then analyzing aggregated data in order to identify marketing opportunities within a network or audience. (See Chapter 3 for more on this topic.)

>> **Identify top interests in your audience analysis.** When conducting your audience analysis, you should pay close attention to topics of specific interest to Millennials. Certain content makes some media more attractive for investment than others. (For more details on this type of analysis and the types of content most effectively used on certain media, check out Chapters 5 and 6.)

>> **Evaluate content requirements and access.** If your brand isn't built for specific channels like Instagram (https://instagram.com) or Snapchat (https://snapchat.com), which are predominantly visual and entirely mobile, then making the investment to use them may not be worth it.

TIP

Finding a way to be relevant on these kinds of media is ideal, but if you don't fit, your investment will go to waste. It makes more sense to focus on platforms that are ideally suited for your brand and content.

Grasping the importance of relationships

One of the overarching themes of Millennial engagement is the value placed on relationships. The importance of relationships is something that transcends media, brand recognition, and even quality of some products or services. Millennials engage primarily in impersonal spaces, so when a real, genuine connection is felt with an organization, it lasts a long time and can lead to loyalty and even brand advocacy.

One long-term goal of any organization should be to cultivate brand advocates from within their Millennial market. Brand advocates help promote your brand and expand your horizons. Advocates decrease marketing costs and open up new doors for marketing and advertising.

To begin cultivating brand advocates, you need to find common ground and nurture these relationships. Over time, that common ground leads to personalized communications that ultimately lead to new customer acquisition.

The retention of these new Millennial customers, however, is where the real value lies. Retaining and reactivating existing customers is far less expensive than acquiring new ones. With the help of brand advocates or pseudo-sales agents, keeping and acquiring customers becomes much less burdensome and much more affordable.

Chapter **3**

Creating Your Target Audience

Millennials have unique personalities on each of the social media platforms. Recognizing these differences will go a long way toward building lasting relationships with this coveted demographic. When it comes to Millennials, it's important to recognize that the same individual may have a very different response to your brand's message based entirely on the platform they're on. So, if Johnny Millennial is highly engaged with your brand on Twitter, he may not be as receptive to the same content on Facebook or Instagram.

In this chapter, you find out about various Millennial audience idiosyncrasies that exist on each of the different media platforms. You also see why you need to respect and plan to leverage traditional media as well as social networks.

Considering These Questions

Before diving into the various media platforms to see how to create targeted Millennial audiences, think about the following questions, which are designed to facilitate the audience development process:

>> What are your objectives by media type?

>> What does your ideal Millennial audience member look like?

>> How will the customer journey connect across various media?

>> How do you prioritize target demographics and psychographics?

>> Can you define some of the segmented audience pocket umbrella categories right away?

What are your objectives by media type?

Not all media are alike. Every platform offers up something unique and valuable. For this reason, Millennials use them in very different ways. Take time at the out-set of your campaigns to understand how Millennials use these media platforms and what objectives are best suited for each one. This will assist you in the creation of targeted Millennial audience goals in the shortest possible time.

What does your ideal Millennial audience member look like?

Use an analytical process to build your Millennial audience, which will help you build a targeted series of audience clusters or segments. Asking what your ideal audience member looks like will provide you with a working road map. It will also help you determine whether something is wrong with your clusters or whether the data has presented a new opportunity.

Here are a few key elements that you'll want to address to develop your ideal audience profile:

>> **Age range:** Age range limits the audience to users between a certain set of ages.

>> **Education:** Education looks at users that have either completed or are in the process of completing a certain level of education, such as high school or college.

>> **Income:** Income will focus on an audience that earns a certain range of income each year. This income range is determined by Facebook based on a series of criteria including self-reported job title and career field.

>> **Location:** Location settings will target your ad to audience members in a given location.

>> **General interests:** Interest categories and topics are selected in an effort to reach Facebook users that have expressed an interest in a particular field or subject.

>> **Employment field:** Employment field limits the focus to users that have indicated they work in a particular field by self-reporting this data.

>> **Buying behavior:** Buying behavior can include aspects such as the number of touchpoints a user will need before making a decision

>> **Brand engagement tendencies:** Engagement tendencies tell you whether a user prefers to click on an ad or like it on Facebook. It can also be as broad as Very Often or Rarely.

Use this list as a guide and add any additional ones that you decide are important to you.

How will the customer journey connect across various media?

Millennials are interested in a cohesive omni-channel experience. The *omni-channel experience* refers to the modern customer journey that includes interaction with several media and platforms in the buying process.

As you develop your target audience, you want to consider how every touchpoint and every medium connect. For example, when Millennial audience members leave your Facebook page, how do you ensure that the brand experience isn't broken when they reconnect with you over email?

The omni-channel experience is an important concept for which you need to plan. (See Chapter 9 for a detailed discussion about the omni-channel strategy.) No longer does a buying decision rely solely on brand recognition or proximity to a product. Millennials have access to vast amounts of information that is viewed on many different channels. Building a strategy that provides an optimal brand experience across all these channels is important.

You need to determine beforehand how you'll track and measure every touchpoint and what your success metrics or key performance indicators will be.

How do you prioritize target demographics and psychographics?

After you determine the important demographics and psychographics of your ideal Millennial persona, you need to prioritize each of the characteristics that has been laid out. For example, if you've indicated that you want your audience to be interested in electronics and live within a five-state region, you need to decide whether the location (demographics) is more important to you than their interest in electronics (psychographics).

From this prioritized list, you can create audience pockets or segments. Then you can rank those pockets according to their value to your brand and business objectives.

TECHNICAL STUFF

When developing a Millennial persona, you want to consider the ideal Millennial customer, both in terms of demographics and psychographics (interests and behaviors) that you would like to target for a specific campaign. Narrow this list down to specifics that extend beyond basic age range and interests. The Millennial persona needs to be as detailed as possible. (For more on this process, see the section "Creating Segmented Audience Pockets," later in this chapter.)

Can you define some of the segmented audience pocket umbrella categories right away?

At the initial stage, before diving into real-world information, you'll want to focus on the categorization process. Thinking up these categories without first looking at the data may be difficult, so here are a few category suggestions to help get you started:

>> **Region:** This category focuses on users in a particular part of the country or world.

>> **Technology:** If you plan on catering to Millennials based on the types of technology they use — for example, Apple or Android — then you may want to consider grouping them together.

>> **Behavior:** A few examples of this category may be tech early adopters versus late adopters, mobile users versus desktop users, fast turnaround versus long nurturing period, and so on.

>> **Content receptiveness:** Not all Millennials will be willing to engage with branded content as it appears in their social feeds. In some cases, your

messaging will need to differ in order to drive up engagement. You'll need to create different content and advertising strategies and target different audience clusters.

>> **Socioeconomics:** This category is another case where your content is going to differ from one group to the next. Socioeconomic conditions (see Chapter 1) are hugely important with regards to shaping the mindset of a Millennial. Therefore, your content will need to shift in order to maintain your benchmark level of engagement with every member of the audience.

Engaging Audiences on Different Media

Every media platform serves a purpose, which is why you to need to ask yourself how the customer journey connects across all the channels. To get your strategy of engaging and converting Millennials into lifelong customers to work, you'll need to determine where they are — and that could be anywhere.

You'll want to study two primary categories of media in more detail: traditional media and new media.

As you've probably guessed, *traditional media* encompasses most nondigital or early digital platforms like radio, print, telephone, and television. Also, for Millennials, email is considered traditional media.

On *new media* platforms, communication takes place significantly faster, sometimes even in real time. These platforms open the lines of communication between the brand and the audience as opposed to being used as a one-way broadcast platform. Millennials prefer these platforms. This category includes social media, blogs, and chat products, such as WhatsApp or Facebook Messenger.

TIP

Audiences on traditional media are considered to complement those on the more affordable social media platforms.

Traditional media

Traditional media is expensive. The majority of brands are simply not going to be able to take direct advantage of traditional media.

However, you can use some creative thinking and strategizing to reach a Millennial audience elsewhere without losing the potential benefits offered by traditional media. Following are three strategies that you can take advantage of to leverage traditional media:

>> Newsjacking

>> Second-screen engagement

>> Content-media alignment

Newsjacking

The term *newsjacking* refers to the practice of leveraging news and reports on traditional media outlets for your own benefit on your owned media. (*Owned media* are all the media and channels over which you have complete control — for example, your website.) Renowned marketer David Meerman Scott coined the term and wrote about it in his book, *Newsjacking: How to Inject your Ideas into a Breaking News Story and Generate Tons of Media Coverage* (Amazon Digital Services, 2011).

To take full advantage of any newsjacking opportunities that may come up on traditional media, you need to have a carefully laid-out plan ahead of time. This way, you'll know what to do when the opportunity presents itself.

Here are three initial actions you can take when developing your newsjacking plan:

>> Set up alerts across the web for key industry terms

>> Develop a series of guidelines for the types of stories that are worthy of newsjacking

>> Create a generic content template that you can easily adapt

SET UP ALERTS ACROSS THE WEB FOR KEY INDUSTRY TERMS

Setting up alerts for key industry terms allows you to track what traditional media outlets are publishing in and around your industry. One of the keys to successful newsjacking is the ability to capitalize on news while it's still relevant and turn the story into a brand opportunity. You can most easily seize these brand opportunities when you're tracking your industry for hot stories. You can use several online tools to track your industry:

>> **Google Alerts** (http://alerts.google.com): This free tool allows you to set up notifications any time specific terms or brands are mentioned across the web, as shown in Figure 3-1.

>> **Salesforce Marketing Cloud** (www.marketingcloud.com): This paid tool was originally known as Radian6 and is an enterprise-level web and social monitoring platform (see Figure 3-2).

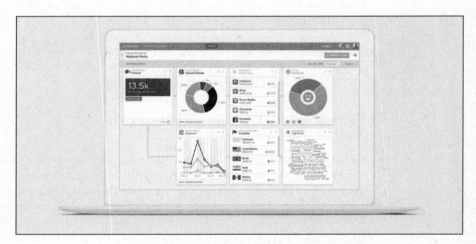

FIGURE 3-2:
Salesforce
Marketing Cloud.

>> **Brandwatch** (http://brandwatch.com): Brandwatch is a powerful keyword tracking and data analysis tool for brands (see Figure 3-3).

DEVELOP A SERIES OF GUIDELINES FOR THE TYPES OF STORIES THAT ARE WORTHY OF NEWSJACKING

A common mistake made by brands is attempting to implement a newsjacking strategy using stories that don't quite fit with the brand or may be inappropriate. This approach is almost certain to backfire. Start with a series of guidelines to avoid this pitfall.

REMEMBER

One way to prevent yourself from landing in a sticky newsjacking situation is to completely avoid sensitive subjects. These subjects can include death, politics, social issues, or other potentially divisive areas.

CREATE A GENERIC CONTENT TEMPLATE THAT YOU CAN EASILY ADAPT

Creating a generic content template can expedite the process of writing newsjacking stories when the time comes. You don't necessarily need to have all your content ready, but some basic skeletal frameworks will serve you well when the time comes to share content and take advantage of a hot developing story.

Second-screen engagement

Millennials engage on their mobile devices while also engaging with traditional broadcast media, such as television. Taking advantage of this *second-screen experience* is an excellent way to leverage the power of real-time, traditional broadcast media without the enormous expense of paying for advertising.

Here are a few key points you'll want to keep top of mind:

>> **Take advantage of the second screen:** Millennials are most likely to activate second screens like Twitter when engaging with traditional media. This audience is engaging in real-time, and you need to be a part of the conversation where it's happening as opposed to trying to bring the conversation to your owned channels.

>> **Keep content relevant and short:** This is a real-time environment, so long-winded content will likely be ignored. Keep it short and to the point.

>> **Be part of the conversation, not an intrusive ad:** This is a conversation that your brand is joining. If it was the place for advertising, then others would be sharing ads, and Millennials would most likely not participate. Instead, use this space to develop a relationship with your target audience.

Content-media alignment

The content–media alignment strategy ties in closely with both newsjacking and the second screen. On traditional media, the message is linear and direct. On new media, multiple messages may be fed to users at the same time. For this reason, you want to ensure that the content you create to reach your target Millennial audience directly relates to the content they're digesting on traditional media.

In addition to message alignment, you want to clearly distinguish the content you share on social media platforms versus traditional platforms. When you spot an opportunity, you can leverage it on traditional media and determine where the audience is going to be. Then determine the type of content that best fits that audience and the media platform on which they can be found. This approach will help you drive up your engagement rates and improve the receptiveness of the audience to your content.

New media

When it comes to Millennials, new media is going to be your bread and butter. When building your target audience, you need to know how Millennials interact with each of the major social networks. Specifically you want to know three important things:

>> How they are engaging with one another

>> How they are engaging with brands on blogs and forums

>> Where real-time chat applications factor in the mix

Knowing these things will make the process of developing targeted Millennial segments significantly easier.

Millennials frequent five major social media platforms. The platforms where Millennials are most active and, perhaps more important, where they regularly engage with brands like yours are

>> Facebook

>> Twitter

>> YouTube

>> Instagram

>> Snapchat

While there are other new media platforms, these five are the ones where Millennials spend the majority of their time. That is especially true when it comes to brand engagement. Understanding how Millennials interact on these platforms makes the process of building your target audience much easier and leads to a more successful overall program.

Facebook

Facebook is the most used social network by Millennials by a fairly strong margin. According to data from Fluent, an ad-serving marketing company:

>> Of younger Millennials, born between 1990 and 1997, 36 percent say that they use it most often.

>> Of older Millennials, born between 1980 and 1990, 50 percent say that they use it most often.

So why are Millennials so active on Facebook? There are the obvious, personal reasons like keeping up with friends, the Fear Of Missing Out (FOMO), the accessibility to relevant information, and the ease of connecting with brands.

From a business standpoint, Millennials choose to engage with brands on Facebook to support a brand and get regular updates.

REMEMBER

Facebook is a place where a Millennial's life is on display. In order to drive engagement with a member of this audience, you need to develop content that caters to their tastes and preferences.

Twitter

A Millennial active on both Facebook and Twitter may operate entirely differently and respond to a brand in a very unique way from one network to another. A study at the University of Massachusetts Darmouth found that on Twitter, one of the main reasons Millennials engage with a brand is for the opportunity to collect and redeem coupons and discounts. The next most popular response falls in line with Facebook; users want to support a brand.

TIP

Though Facebook is a much more personal space where relationships are at the root of engagement, you still need to develop a connection to Millennials on Twitter to build your follower base.

YouTube

The most important thing to remember when it comes to content for Millennials is that it needs to provide some degree of utility. Millennials have a short attention span, and they'll only be retained if they can find some degree of value in the content. (The use of video content is discussed in more detail in Chapter 6.)

A few types of video content can significantly drive up engagement and retention:

>> **Tips and tricks:** You can share short tidbits of insider information that help viewers accomplish tasks faster. One of the qualities that video viewers are looking for is value. Tips that make life even a little bit easier is exactly the kind of information your audience is seeking.

>> **How-tos or tutorials:** Much like tips and tricks, how-to and tutorial videos provide value to your audience. These types of videos can be a little longer than short tip videos. Viewers want to learn the steps of a process, so you can go into detail and showcase your expertise while providing relevant, useful information.

>> **Questions and answers:** Q&A videos are a great way to drive up audience engagement and participation. Encouraging your audience to submit questions and then creating short video answers shows that you

- Care about helping your audience
- Have expertise as a thought leader
- Can tell them where to find additional resources

>> **Humor:** Everyone likes to laugh. That has been proven consistently with the popularity of everything from TV shows like "America's Funniest Videos" to YouTube viral sensations like "David After Dentist."

Instagram

When it comes to Millennials, more women than men are on Instagram. This fact is largely due to the visual nature of the platform. On all social platforms that offer an entirely visual experience, the audiences swing heavily female. On Instagram, which is completely native, some of the most popular categories are fashion, food, and beauty, which all tend to favor female audiences.

TECHNICAL STUFF

When a platform is referred to as *native*, it means that the medium exists almost exclusively on mobile devices. Of course, websites exist for networks like Instagram and Snapchat, but use of the network exists within a mobile realm. This trend has been particularly successful with Millennial consumers and is covered in detail in Chapter 10.

Millennials on Instagram have the following characteristics:

>> **Users want to stay within the Instagram app.** Millennials you target on Instagram aren't going to want to leave the app and visit a web page, so keep that in mind when focusing on an audience here.

>> **Think visual first.** As you can probably imagine, Instagram is all about the imagery. That means that if you're trying to reach an audience on this network, you're going to need to focus on the creative aspects rather than deliver a sales pitch.

>> **Users love brands with personality.** This holds true for Millennials on most social networks, but it's particularly true on Instagram. Millennials are more than willing to engage with brands, if the brand personality is genuine and cultivated. Reaching that point takes some time, but it's what builds lasting relationships.

Snapchat

Snapchat is a favorite among younger Millennials, ages 18 to 24. A huge number of these users access the network daily — over 80 percent, in fact — and share billions of snaps every day. Snapchat also provides a very personal user experience, so once again building a relationship is crucial if you want to retain a loyal following of Millennials on Snapchat.

Here are some characteristics of Millennial users on Snapchat:

>> They're eager to connect with one another.

>> They have a genuine interest in what is taking place in their network.

>> They have a high willingness to share content.

>> They're interested in engaging with brands on a much more personal level.

>> Daily active users visit the app several times in a day in order to retrieve new updates.

REMEMBER

Snapchat, though highly engaging, is a very particular platform with a specific audience that will not necessarily fit in with every brand's Millennial marketing strategy. (Chapter 6 covers more on the topic of using new media as part of your Millennial acquisition strategy.)

Running an Interest-Identification Audience Analysis

The most valuable practice that you can implement to build your target audience(s) is to run an *Interest Identification Audience Analysis* (IIAA). This process leverages the huge amount of data that is both self-reported by users and inferred by networks like Facebook based on audience activity in order to develop audiences that are well defined. These audiences are understood based on their similar interests and can be targeted with more relevant content, which leads to greater engagement and the faster growth of relationships with your brand.

The advent of social media has led to a significant increase in the availability of user data. This data, while often unavailable on an individual level due to privacy concerns, is available at the cluster or segment level. By running this kind of analysis within a certain cluster in your database, you can learn a tremendous amount about specific groups in your audience. Then you can more quickly reach those users with highly targeted, relevant, and engaging content that builds lasting relationships.

While you can use a few different tools to run an IIAA, the most common and readily accessible one is the Facebook Insights tool and your email databases.

If you truly want to better understand your audience(s), it is crucial for you to have a segmented email database. In fact, you should already have this best practice in place. If you haven't yet segmented your email lists according to certain parameters, then you'll want to take the time to get some basic segmentation done.

TIP

An example of segmentation would be to group emails by their respective sources or even something as simple as determining whether the email comes from an existing client or a prospect.

When you segment your lists, you don't need to create new ones. You can use email list building tools, such as Constant Contact (www.constantcontact.com), to add tags to your unfiltered list, as shown in Figure 3-4.

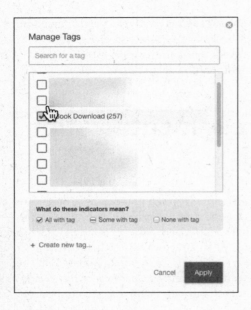

FIGURE 3-4: Add tags to your unfiltered email list in Constant Contact.

Another email list building tool you can use to tag your lists is MailChimp, (www.mailchimp.com). You can add tags to selections of email addresses, which is the easiest way to segment a database after the unsegmented emails have already been added (see Figure 3-5).

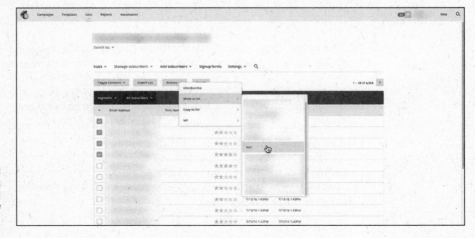

FIGURE 3-5: MailChimp offers an option to add tags to clusters of email addresses.

Using the Facebook Insights tool

The following steps walk you through the process of using the Facebook Insights tool. These steps assume that you have already created a Facebook ad account. If you don't have one and are a Facebook Page owner, you can create a free ad account in Facebook.

TIP

You don't need to create any ads or load your credit card in order to use the Audience Insights tool. You simply need to create an ad account, which you can use for advertising purposes at a later time if you choose to run a campaign.

1. **Select the Audiences dashboard in your Facebook Business Manager.**

   When you access the Facebook Business Manager (https://business. facebook.com), you select the Audiences dashboard from the menu available under the three-bar icon on the top left, as shown in Figure 3-6.

FIGURE 3-6:
Select the Audiences dashboard from your main Business Manager screen.

2. **Click the blue Create Audience button and choose a Custom Audience.**

   In Figure 3-7, you can see a snapshot of your Asset Library. The blue button at the top of the list of assets gives you the option to create an audience. Click on that button and choose the option to create a Custom Audience.

3. **Choose to load a customer file as an Audience.**

   This step allows Facebook to cross-match a particular customer or email database and build a custom audience for your use. Upon clicking on this option, you can load your email list or link your MailChimp account to create a new audience, as shown in Figure 3-8.

FIGURE 3-7:
From your asset library, click on the Custom Audience button to create a new audience.

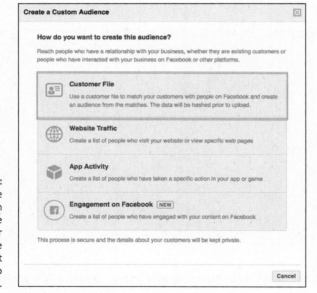

Create a Custom Audience

How do you want to create this audience?

Reach people who have a relationship with your business, whether they are existing customers or people who have interacted with your business on Facebook or other platforms.

Customer File
Use a customer file to match your customers with people on Facebook and create an audience from the matches. The data will be hashed prior to upload.

Website Traffic
Create a list of people who visit your website or view specific web pages

App Activity
Create a list of people who have taken a specific action in your app or game

Engagement on Facebook [NEW]
Create a list of people who have engaged with your content on Facebook

This process is secure and the details about your customers will be kept private.

Cancel

FIGURE 3-8:
Choose to create an audience from a customer file and then either copy and paste emails or connect your MailChimp account.

TECHNICAL STUFF

Facebook doesn't keep your uploaded customer data. This is a simple matching process. The data you load is used to reference Facebook users by email address or another indicator to build an audience within the social network. After the matching process is complete, the data is purged from Facebook's system, which means that there is no security risk to your customer data.

4. **Open Audience Insights in your Facebook Ads dashboard.**

   From your ad account, open the drop-down menu once again in order to access the Audience Insights tool, as shown in Figure 3-9.

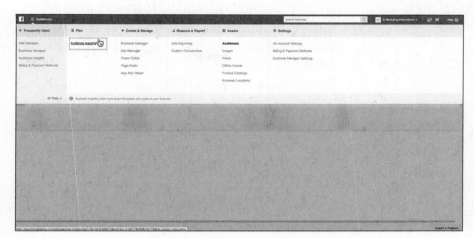

FIGURE 3-9:
Access Audience
Insights from
the menu.

5. Choose the option to run an analysis on a custom audience and select one of your new audiences.

You can see the options that exist when you first open the Audience Insights dashboard, as shown in Figure 3-10. These options automatically populate when you access this dashboard. You want to run your insights analysis on a custom audience.

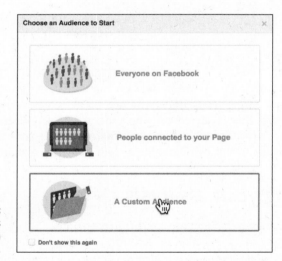

FIGURE 3-10:
Run an analysis
on a custom
audience.

REMEMBER

It can take up to 72 hours before the data associated with your audience members populates in the backend of your dashboard. Don't be discouraged if you aren't seeing a lot of information at first. After a few days, all of the available data will be accessible for a new audience.

6. **Select an age range for Millennial (24 to 35, for example) in order to obtain insights into a particular segment of your selected Custom Audience**

If your goal is to focus on Millennials, which is the intent behind this particular strategy, start by toggling the age parameters, as shown in Figure 3-11. This step isolates the data for a particular set of users — in this case, Millennials — and you can begin analyzing your Millennial audience in more detail without additional data from outside customers interfering with the findings for Millennials.

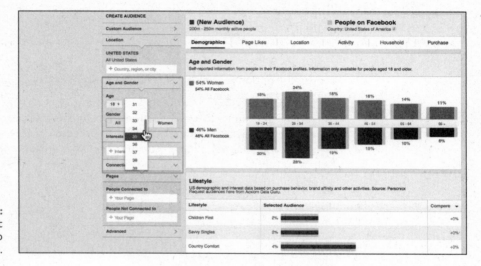

FIGURE 3-11: Select the specific age range to analyze.

REMEMBER

Marketers cannot target users under the age of 18 to view advertisements on Facebook. Because this is an advertising tool, the lower limit of your target Millennial audience will be 18. This means that you can't analyze the youngest remaining members of this demographic in your Audience Insights analysis.

Analyzing your analysis

After you run the analysis, here are some things to note:

>> **Review key audience interest indicators within the target audience selected:** A lot of data populates when a large enough audience is loaded into the Audience Insights tool. This data is all very valuable, but certain insights will be more valuable when it comes to developing audience clusters and targeted content. Your focus should be on the categories of Lifestyle, Page Likes, Activity, Household, and Purchase, as highlighted in Figure 3-12.

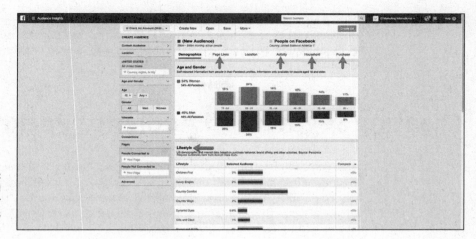

FIGURE 3-12:
Highlighted
sections in your
Audience Insights
analysis.

>> **Take note of the insights that go beyond Facebook averages in order to prioritize your target audience clusters.** When a particular aspect of your audience analysis reveals that the Millennials you're studying behave in a way that outperforms the average audience on Facebook, you have a very valuable indicator. It tells you that audience will have a high responsiveness to content. Figure 3-13 highlights how this might appear in your analysis.

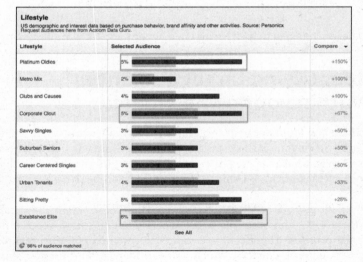

FIGURE 3-13:
The selected
audience may
present an
opportunity
for higher
engagement.

Each of your email lists may generate different findings that help in the creation of your audience clusters. While you can also conduct interest identification analyses with Millennials on networks like Twitter, the sheer amount of user data on

Facebook makes it an ideal starting point. After running this analysis, you can begin to create audience pockets that you can target with specific types of content.

Creating Segmented Audience Pockets

After you complete your IIAA (see preceding section), you'll have a much better understanding of the small details that make your Millennial audience members tick. You'll likely notice after conducting this analysis that not all of these individuals are exactly alike. Your Millennial audience analysis will uncover several subsets within the overall age demographic.

Each of these audience clusters possesses its own set of characteristics and will respond very differently to various types of messages, campaigns, and images. With this in mind, you want to create even more narrowed audience pockets that take these idiosyncrasies into account. You can do this by

>> Developing strategies that reach Millennials on your owned platforms in public media spaces

>> Determining where brand awareness opportunities exist with other Millennial audiences that have not yet been directly identified

These strategies help drive up engagement and build more lasting relationships.

Identifying target audiences within your owned media

When you build out your target Millennial audiences, your owned media is likely going to be your easiest starting point. So, while you don't necessarily have control over what is posted on a news website like *The New York Times,* you do have complete control over your own website or Facebook page.

On your owned media, you have a wealth of information about your audience that doesn't exist on other platforms where you don't have access to expanded audience profiles. Therefore, you can consider incorporating several elements into your audience clusters, which you can identify and group using a mix of your audience analysis and the data available within your owned audiences. These elements, which you can find in your Audience Insights analysis, include

- **Millennial:** Targets age range segments, which are primarily users between the ages of 18 to 35

- **Gender:** Choose either male or female users

- **Location:** Can be as broad as a country or as narrow as a zip code

- **Lifestyle subsection:** Identified from your audience analysis

- **Interest categories:** Can be broad and all-encompassing

- **Interest topics:** Select from a range of interests that your audience members have indicated matter to them, based on their profiles

- **Buying behavior:** Based on various findings in your audience analysis

- **Liked pages categorization:** Choose the kinds of branded Facebook Pages that your audience has indicated it's interested in

- **Branded content engagement propensity:** Helps you dictate the types of content (subtle or overtly branded) to develop for each one of your audience segments

- **Household details:** May include income, home value, and whether a targeted user lives alone or with others

- **Education level:** Select the level of education that your audience has received, from high school to post-graduate

- **Employment status and field of employment:** Can target users based on the fields in which they work, their employer, or even by their job title

- **Marital or relationship status:** Can segment based on relationship status as well, which can be particularly valuable when you are promoting a product or service — for example, that caters more to individuals who are married or who are planning a wedding

Categorizing target audiences within online public forums

The digital and social spheres of the web are filled with an endless number of conversations. The vast majority of them are publicly available and readily accessible. You should take advantage of this fact and leverage these conversations to refine your target audiences and identify new opportunities.

TIP

Monitoring tools like Brandwatch and Salesforce Marketing Cloud track conversations that take place online about your brand and your industry. You can take this tactic a step further and use it as a way to analyze the audiences talking about your industry in order to identify new opportunities.

Many of these social listening tools pull data from public profiles to provide brands with insights into the demographics of users talking online. You can isolate these bits of information d by age range and study them further to add to existing audience segment descriptions, or you can create entirely new ones.

These tools were originally designed with one type of objective in mind — for example, conducting social care and customer service by listening to conversations online. However, there exists a world of opportunity when they're used in unique ways. One opportunity is to develop new audience clusters and content strategies based on new web discussions.

With the help of these technologies, you can

>> Identify new audiences that fit into your target demographics

>> Discover an audience you ignored because its members were not traditionally in your target audience

>> Identify unknown targets that were previously underutilized or missed entirely

Finding Millennials for brand awareness targeting

While the majority of the campaigns you develop will be geared toward driving some form of action, one campaign type you'll still want to consider is the ever-important brand awareness campaign. Although returns on brand awareness campaigns may not be as tangible as action-oriented ones, you should still aim to identify Millennial audiences and strive to expose them to your strategically developed content.

Considering the vast number of conversations that are consistently taking place online, it's always easier to join an existing conversation for the purposes of brand awareness. It's fruitless to try and pull Millennials away to your channel from a conversation in which they're already engaged.

REMEMBER

By focusing entirely on industry and industry-adjacent keyword analyses using the powerful tools like Brandwatch and Google Alerts, you'll be able to segment your Millennial audience and identify both user profile themes as well as media types where Millennials are already having conversations about your industry.

Once that brand awareness connection is made, the action-objective campaigns will see lowered barriers to success, as well as improved conversion rates and lowered costs per conversion.

TECHNICAL STUFF

An *action-objective campaign* is one that establishes a campaign-specific goal, which can only be accomplished when an audience member takes a particular action. This is a common structure for singular, seasonal, or topical campaigns that do not run forever.

2

Creating Your Millennial Marketing Strategy

Establish the foundation of your strategy through the strategic discovery and analysis of data.

Connect with Millennials on both traditional and new media in creative ways.

Build a strategy that unifies every utilized type of media, both online and offline.

Create a mobile strategy that connects with Millennials on the move.

Audit your individual initiatives and overall strategies in order to measure their effectiveness.

Chapter **4**

Using Data to Build a Strategy

D
ata is all around you. With the advent of social media and broadcast platforms like Facebook and Twitter, data has become more powerful than ever, especially for Millennials. The amount of data that exists about them is unprecedented.

In this chapter, you develop a better understanding of the many forms in which you can extract, manipulate, and analyze data.

Recognizing the Value of Data

Data is everywhere, and as such, it's extremely important. While the data may be overwhelming at times, when used correctly, it's a valuable source of information that you can use in your marketing efforts.

REMEMBER

Keep in mind that data can often be industry and audience agnostic. By *agnostic*, it's meant that that raw data can apply to any or all situations and demographics and isn't necessarily limited by a particular group or scenario. This means that the lessons, tips, and processes covered in this chapter may not be limited to Millennials.

In the following sections, I describe several different types of data that you can use in your marketing efforts.

Raw data

Raw data is information in its purest form. Raw data is data extracted at the source but not yet processed. While raw data can be daunting when you first come across it, it's completely malleable, which makes it one of the most valuable data types. An example of raw data sorted in a Microsoft Excel spreadsheet is shown in Figure 4-1.

Cooked data

The industry reference to cooked data relates directly to raw data. *Cooked data* is what marketers get when raw data has been manipulated in some way in order to highlight a particular segment, finding, or aspect of the unadulterated information.

Figure 4-2 shows you an example of cooked data.

Social media user data

When it comes to social media, you can leverage a treasure trove of user information to create your marketing strategy. For example, Millennials may share answers to questions on their social feed that you never thought to ask.

Analyzing your social audience user data can be as simple as reviewing your Facebook Insights data, as shown in Figure 4-3. This data can lead to some significant breakthroughs. (I discuss how to collect Facebook Insights data in Chapter 3.)

FIGURE 4-2:
Cooked data
is the result
of some
manipulation of
raw information.

	A	B	C	D	E
1		Column 1	Column 2	Column 3	Column 4
2	Column 1	1			
3	Column 2	0.9801522	1		
4	Column 3	0.7005677	0.70967484	1	
5	Column 4	0.75343644	0.7648072	0.98399868	1

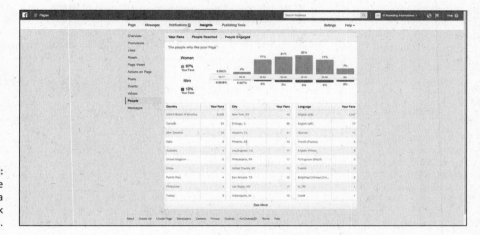

FIGURE 4-3:
You can find free
social user data
using Facebook
Insights.

Customer lifetime engagement data

When a customer engages with your brand across multiple channels, a story is being told. At every touchpoint, or chapter of the story, data is collected, and you can analyze it to improve your marketing efforts.

Millennials have a preference for a single sign-in, where they have the ability to use a Facebook or Google profile to sign into all accounts, tools, websites, or online stores. With that single sign-in, information about the customer journey is collected at every step of the way, and that data is hugely valuable for improving the customer experience.

Brand profile data

You can usually find the jackpot of user data in the brand profile. This user data relates specifically to your organization. Every bit of information you extract directly informs how you might shift your marketing efforts, your sales tactics, or even some of your internal operations to improve efficiency.

Figure 4-4 shows you an example of Amazon's recommendations. Tracking user profiles and searches and using advanced algorithms that learn about user tastes and preferences, Amazon can make customized recommendations to its customers.

Over time, this robust profile data provides a company like Amazon with the ability to build a well-rounded view of each customer at every stage of the buying process.

Visualized data

Just as with cooked data, *visualized information* is a representation of some sort of manipulated data in a visual framework. Plenty of tools exist to help users analyze and manipulate data to depict it in visual form.

Tableau (www.tableau.com), shown in Figure 4-5, is one such tool.

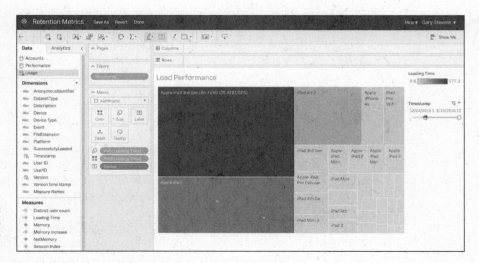

Big data

Big data means exactly what you might think it does. It's a large amount of data collected from a variety of sources. You can analyze this data to make predictions, identify trends, improve pricing, optimize customer buying paths, and optimize products. While you can find plenty of other areas where big data may be of use, these are some of the most popular cases.

TIP

Showcasing only big data is a disservice to small and medium business marketing teams. The real value for marketers rests on how you can segment and use this data on a smaller scale.

Small data

Small data results when you conduct an in-depth analysis of smaller segments of your complete data sets. When your data is condensed into smaller groups, it becomes significantly easier to analyze and more opportunities can be discovered. Diving into your small data can help improve your efforts with such things as

>> **Message targeting:** Creating tailored messages for small groups of your Millennial audience leads to much higher engagement and conversion. Small data presents opportunities for improved targeting.

>> **Content and creative split testing and optimization:** When you dive into your small data, you can identify minute details that allow you to optimize your campaign. This again can lead to some pretty dramatic improvements in your results.

>> **Rolling ad budget optimization**: Improving the performance of your budget means making your ad dollars go further. When you analyze your small data, you can identify new information that leads you to change small details. These details include such things as maximum bids or placements of your ads, and they impact the performance of your campaign as a whole.

The opportunities with small data extend even further when you consider the fact that data is always full of surprises. Keep an open mind and analyze every possible angle of your small data subsets. Doing so can lead to major improvements in your campaigns.

TIP

If you have a strategy, a target audience, content, and a series of objectives, the small data you analyze may present findings that would have otherwise gone unnoticed. This can lead to a significant expansion and improvement of your strategies and the overall growth of your business both on and offline.

Competitive data

You can learn quite a bit when you analyze publicly available competitive data. Your competitors are most likely trying to achieve the same objectives you are. Taking cues and learning lessons from both their successes and missteps will serve you well. What you learn from this process will help you achieve your objectives in a shorter time frame and avoid some pitfalls that were costly for your competitors.

Several tools exist for the purposes of competitive data analysis and tracking. The following four are easy to use:

>> **Alexa:** In Figure 4-6, you can see some of the data that Alexa pulls from a competitor's website and digital presence when using the Pro version. The product provides users with insights into the online performance of sites across the web.

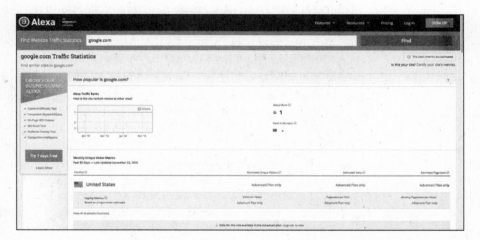

FIGURE 4-6:
Alexa.

>> **BuzzSumo:** When it comes to tracking your competitors' social presence, you have dozens of additional options. Figure 4-7 showcases BuzzSumo, which provides insights into the performance of content on social media and assists with the development of effective content strategies.

>> **TrackMaven:** TrackMaven, shown in Figure 4-8, has some great features like content optimization capabilities, integrated social networks including paid ad optimization, and some pretty extensive insights into the performance of your marketing efforts.

FIGURE 4-7:
BuzzSumo.

FIGURE 4-8:
TrackMaven.

TIP

Other good products are SimilarWeb (www.similarweb.com), Rival IQ (www.rivaliq.com), and SEM Rush (www.semrush.com).

All of the preceding tools can help you

>> **Identify responsive audiences:** Identify audiences that have been most responsive to your competitors' content on both websites and social channels.

>> **Create effective content strategies:** Craft content strategies that have a higher likelihood of driving engagement from your intended audience based on content that has succeeded in your competitors' campaigns.

>> **Discover pain points:** Pinpoint missteps and pitfalls that your competitors have suffered or are currently dealing with in order to avoid facing the same issues.

>> **Uncover industry insights:** You can use several tools to discover industry insights. (See Chapter 3 for more details.) Another, more advanced example of a product that highlights industry insights is Crimson Hexagon (www.crimson hexagon.com), which is shown in Figure 4-9.

FIGURE 4-9:
Crimson Hexagon is an advanced, enterprise-grade industry analysis tool.

You can also achieve the following objectives with the strategic use of industry insights:

>> Development of a new or expanded content strategy

>> Expansion into new media and new platforms based on engagement from your target audiences

>> Development of new short- and long-term objectives

>> Identification of trends that indicate how an additional investment may be beneficial

Transactional data

Transactional data are the insights gleaned from your customer transactions. If your organization has digitized its client records or if you sell products via an ecommerce platform, then transactional data will be very useful to you. Perhaps the most notable reason why you'll want to leverage transactional data is for the purpose of improving the buyer journey, thereby shortening the path to conversion and decreasing your internal costs that go into the customer experience and marketing timeline.

Transactional data can also be extremely useful to you when allocating your marketing budget. Within a transaction, assuming that your tracking has been properly developed and implemented, you can monitor each touchpoint reached by your customer. Identifying the most valuable touchpoints across hundreds or even thousands of transactions will allow you to optimize the resources to which your budgets are allocated.

Pinpointing Key Indicators in Your Data

Although data comes in many different types, all data exhibits certain universal indicators. By monitoring these indicators, you can get a better sense of what your data is telling you and how to use it.

The following sections describe some of the more common indicators.

Outliers

Outliers are data points that sit outside of the normal range that you may expect to see when looking at a particular performance indicator, such as engagement. For example, if you generally expect to see 10 clicks on a link and a specific post receives 50 clicks, then that data point would be an outlier as it falls far outside the range that you normally see with regards to clicks and engagement. Outliers are perhaps the most valuable indicator of importance within your data sets. You can see a graphical representation of this phenomenon in Figure 4-10.

TECHNICAL STUFF

When extracting raw data, running a simple linear regression and analyzing your data for outliers, generally within a 5 to 10 percent margin of error, will give you some great insights into what is working and what is not. A *linear regression* is a statistical analysis whereby a curve, expressed in this case by the formula $y=ax+b$ is calculated and placed to fit over a given data set. This straight line is the closest representation of a linear progression through the data, and the proximity of your data point to this line — or curve — indicates how well a particular point fits the average. The points that fall far outside this curve are your outliers.

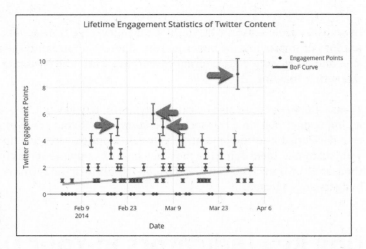

FIGURE 4-10:
An example of an outlier in a data set.

You can find the steps for running a linear regression using a source like Statistics Solutions (www.statisticssolutions.com). You can also use a free tool like Plotly (www.plot.ly), which is shown in Figure 4-11. The data used for these kinds of analyses can range from engagement metrics to conversions to clicks. You can analyze virtually any isolated data set using this extremely powerful method.

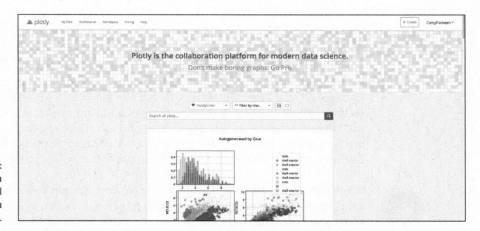

FIGURE 4-11:
Plotly is a powerful free tool that makes data analysis simple.

Peaks and valleys

As with outliers, you're looking for *anomalies* (things that are unusual) in your data when identifying *peaks* and *valleys* (highs and lows) within a given set.

Run through highs and lows with specific performance indicators, such as traffic from a particular social network, and determine what commonalities exist at each high point and each low point. You can compare periods of analysis, for example, a week or a month. Take what you've found and integrate those findings in your everyday strategy. For example, if you see on the first of every month that an unusually high amount of traffic comes from Facebook, and upon further analysis, you see that on the first you tend to share a particularly inspiring quote accompanied by a link to a landing page, use those findings to expand on this strategy and use it more frequently. Repeat this process for all your identified peaks and valleys, where it is applicable.

Correlations

When analyzing data of a particular type (whether it's audience data or post-level data), you want to pay close attention to any correlations, either positive or negative, that exist.

Your Facebook Page's *post-level data* are the insights gathered and exported about your individual posts, rather than general data about your Page and audience. The value in analyzing post-level data is that it aggregates insights about the most valuable kinds of engagement, such as clicks to your website or shares on Facebook. It provides you with the necessary information to build a robust content strategy.

While it is not absolutely necessary to run a *Pearson product-moment correlation test*, which is an advanced statistical analysis to measure the mutual dependence of two variables, and while it may not be possible based on the available data, it certainly helps. In cases where it's not possible, you'll want to simply review your data in order to identify whether similarities arise in a particular cluster, as shown in Figures 4-12, 4-13, and 4-14.

For example, if you analyze high-performing posts shared on Facebook, ask yourself whether these posts share similarities such as the time they were posted, an abundance of a certain color, or length. You can then use these indicators to develop new content that will ensure a significantly higher engagement rate.

Industry trends

Using an industry monitoring technology (see Chapter 3) has several benefits. One of the greatest is undoubtedly the ability to spot conversational trends within your industry before the competition does.

When using an industry monitoring tool, pay close attention to upward-trending conversation topics within your audience segments. Identifying these trends can be extremely beneficial when developing your next campaign or creating new, relevant content.

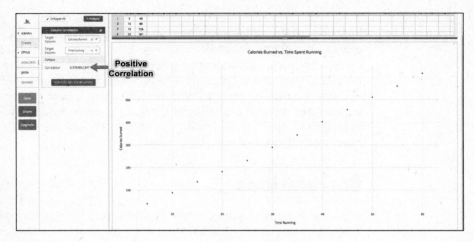

FIGURE 4-12:
This graph shows an example of a positive correlation.

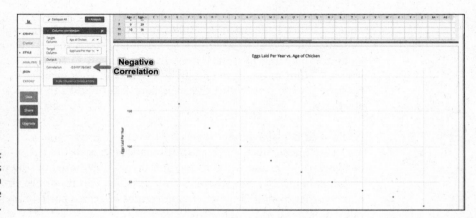

FIGURE 4-13:
This graph shows an example of a negative correlations.

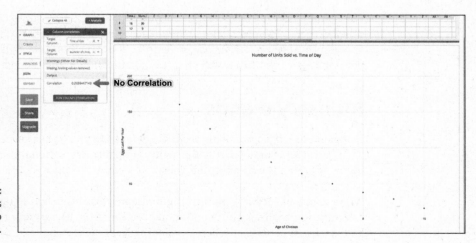

FIGURE 4-14:
This graph shows an example of no correlation.

Waste

When you want to optimize your budget and improve operational efficiency, *waste* is a powerful indicator. In this case, waste refers to ad spends put toward ads that yield little to no results. You know you have waste if you find these two primary indicators:

>> A higher than average number of touchpoints in a particular sales cycle, which may indicate inefficiencies with the cycle flow.

>> A significantly greater cost-per-conversion or cost-per-action, which may indicate flaws or discrepancies between the product and the Millennial audience you've targeted.

REMEMBER

Essentially, as with outliers, you want to take the time to analyze certain outstanding data points. Determine whether they're indicative of some form of budgetary or time waste. Then make the necessary adjustments in order to optimize your processes.

Using Your Data as the Foundation of Your Strategy

Millennials, more so than any generation before them, have populated the web with a seemingly endless amount of data. As a result, everything you choose to do from building audiences (see Chapter 3) to developing social ad campaigns (see Chapter 6) will be completely rooted in data.

Following are five steps you can take — before employing any strategy or starting any campaign — to ensure that you have data to justify every one of your decisions:

1. **Review all the data sources to which you have access.**

The following section covers specific sources, but you'll effectively review all your owned, earned, and paid media data sources in order to pinpoint all the data to which you have access.

2. **Segment your data in order to focus entirely on Millennials.**

After you access all your data, filter out anything that isn't relevant to Millennials. Begin with age ranges and then expand to include those that possess the Millennial mindset. (See Chapter 2 for more detail.)

3. **Establish your objectives.**

   Of course, establishing objectives is a standard practice with every campaign you run. But in this case, you justify your objectives with actual data.

4. **Refine your objectives through the use of your data.**

   You can now analyze the information that you have filtered in order to elaborate or change some of the more universal objectives that you have outlined for a given campaign.

5. **Set your benchmarks and key performance indicators.**

   What is most important about this step is the fact that any one of your benchmarks and all your indicators should be measurable. That measurability will result from your ongoing data analysis.

REMEMBER

It's crucial that before executing a campaign, every one of your objectives has measurement criteria. After all, how can you know whether your campaign is a success if you haven't defined how it will be measured?

Data is agnostic. That means that for every campaign you run, you'll be able to implement these five simple steps. You'll be able to support every one of your actions with numbers and justify every decision with the statistics needed to back it up. Implement this process each time you plan on launching something new, and the entire process will be simpler and more successful.

Identifying Data Sources

Data can come from virtually everywhere. Millennials leave small bits of information everywhere they go. To develop your Millennial marketing strategy, you use three types of data:

>> Data from your owned media channels like your website

>> Data from social media channels like Facebook, Twitter, and YouTube

>> Data from public channels

Data from your owned media

Perhaps the richest center of owned data is available from the backend on your website. Because the vast majority of businesses track their web data using Google

Analytics, shown in Figure 4-15, the points I make in this section come from Google Analytics.

FIGURE 4-15:
The Google
Analytics
audience
dashboard.

Within Google Analytics, you can segment data according to a variety of elements. One is the ability to segment by age.

Creating a segmented dashboard is simple and is useful when you want to isolate a specific cluster of data for deeper analysis. Simply follow these steps:

1. **Create a new view in order to avoid filtering other data.**

A mistake that marketers often make is applying segments or filters to general Google Analytics data. Google doesn't save data that it doesn't collect, so when you filter out data from your general dashboard, it's gone forever. Instead, create a new view in your admin dashboard and title it something specific, such as Millennial Web Data.

2. **Add a segment in your audience dashboard.**

Select the option to add a new segment in your audience dashboard, as shown in Figure 4-16.

3. **Select a new segment and filter by age.**

You can also filter by other criteria, but for the purposes of Millennials, you need to add only an age filter, as shown in Figure 4-17.

After you do this step, the data pulled into this segmented view will be only the data that fits the applied filters. Now, all the data you analyze in the backend of your website will relate specifically to the actions taken by Millennials visiting your website.

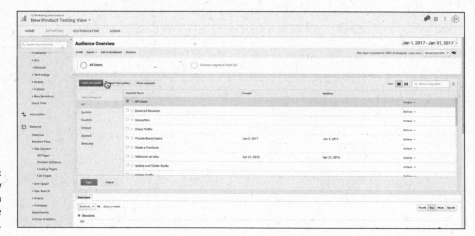

FIGURE 4-16:
Create a new
segment from
your audience
dashboard.

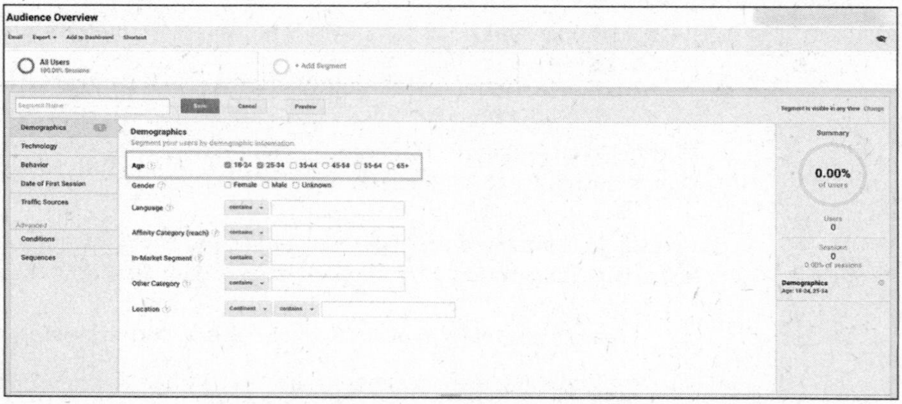

FIGURE 4-17:
Select the age
range filter.

You can utilize the information you collect to develop new strategies for content and marketing. For example, in the analysis of your website's content, you can identify what posts and pages Millennials are most attracted to. Using this information, you can develop Millennial-oriented content strategies. If you're working in an ecommerce space, you can analyze the products that are most frequently viewed or purchased by Millennials. Then you can allocate more of your marketing dollars to these high performers and eliminate some of the waste that might go to ad dollars spent on less popular products.

Another area of focus in the backend of Google Analytics will be your acquisition dashboard. Here, you'll be able to identify the channels and campaigns that have driven the most Millennial engagement. This information allows you to optimize ad dollar spending and marketing budget allocation for the different networks. You don't want to be spending money on a channel that isn't sending viable Millennial traffic.

Data from social media

When it comes to publicly available, accessible data on Millennial consumers' habits and interests, you can't find many places with such a comprehensive amount of information as social media. Millennials share everything, and you can access that data on several media platforms in order to leverage it:

>> Facebook

>> Twitter

>> YouTube

Though you can extract profile and user data from many other platforms, these three sources cover the most valuable social media platforms and provide the most insightful information about your users.

Facebook

The backend of your Facebook Page contains a world of information about your audience. Simply clicking on the Insights tab, as shown in Figure 4-18, will reveal an abundance of data about your overall audience on the Page.

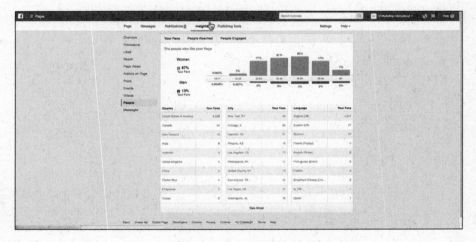

FIGURE 4-18:
Access free Page insights on Facebook.

While you may not be able to segment your audience specifically by age on Facebook, like you can on your website, your audience will largely fall into the category of users that fit the Millennial mindset. This means that the observed habits that you identify in the backend and the content you analyze will be largely applicable to your Facebook content strategy.

Within Facebook, you can also export page and post-level data for further, more in-depth analysis. This data is exported pseudo-raw, which means that it's segmented but not manipulated. You can manipulate this information using a variety of tactics or tools in order to discover new opportunities.

Twitter

Twitter also offers a fairly robust backend to gather insights, which you can see in Figure 4-19. This dashboard is available when you create an ad account, and can be found by visiting `https://analytics.twitter.com`, though you don't need to be running any ads in order to access this data. While the data is somewhat more limited than it is with Facebook, you can gather many valuable insights about audience interests, engagement rates, and details about your content. By aggregating this Twitter insight data, your content strategies can become significantly more refined, and you can develop content that leads to action.

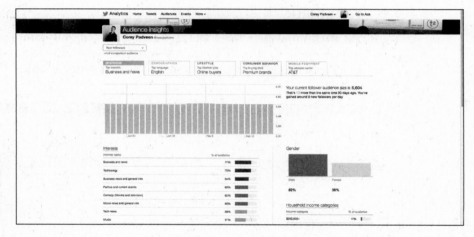

FIGURE 4-19: Twitter provides some good insight into both content and audiences.

YouTube

Much like Google Analytics age and user data, YouTube links your content with profiles of the users watching your videos. This powerful approach provides you with a better understanding of your audience's viewing habits so that you can develop even more successful video content. It also helps you create channel and content strategies that appeal to the Millennials watching your videos.

Some of the details of YouTube view data include Watch time, Average view duration, and Views, as shown in Figure 4-20.

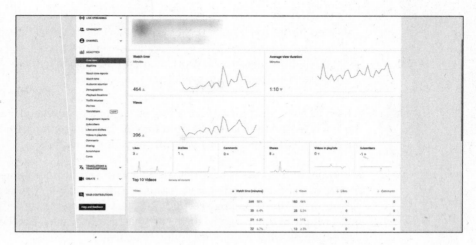

FIGURE 4-20:
User viewing
habits data in
YouTube.

Data from public channels

You can find plenty of publicly available databases related to Millennials across the web. To manually sift through billions of public posts and bits of information would be impossible, so you'll want to use tools that are designed to do that. Many of these products peruse tens if not hundreds of millions of online sources including blogs, forums, social networks, and ecommerce websites.

These tools are designed to scour any readily available data on the web for keywords, phrases, and brand names in order to provide you with the most accurate view of what the conversation looks like. These data are then visualized in an easy-to-analyze format, which allows you to quickly and efficiently identify opportunities so that you can statistically justify your strategies.

The following list of tools have some of the highest user satisfaction reviews on the market. Each has the ability to filter your user data by age range, which will allow for the analysis of all publicly available information about Millennials across your industry.

>> **AgoraPulse** (www.agorapulse.com): AgoraPulse offers a fairly broad range of services within its platform, from insights to management to engagement. Reporting with AgoraPulse is top quality, and it's very affordable. (As of this writing, prices start at $49 per month.)

>> **Brandwatch** (www.brandwatch.com): Brandwatch falls on the more costly side of the spectrum of data analysis tools, but the detailed data reports make it worthwhile. You can quickly analyze your brand from all angles and measure your performance across the web compared to your competitors. You can also drill down pretty deep into the data, which can be particularly useful when it comes to identifying new campaign opportunities.

>> **Mention** (https://mention.com): Mention is a simple yet powerful listening tool that offers some great insights into the conversations taking place within your industry and around your brand. You can analyze trends at the keyword level and use that data to exploit new opportunities.

REMEMBER

A high user satisfaction rate for a tool or technology is a good starting point, but the key is to find the tool that's right for you. Do your research and make sure that the investment in technology pays off for your company.

A *keyword* in this case is a particular term with significance related to the subject matter of your audience's conversations. If, for example, you're analyzing conversations in the technology sector, a keyword of interest may be "machine learning," while another term, such as "real estate," may not be as important, depending on what it is you're trying to analyze.

Analyzing Your Data on a Regular Basis

After you look at the key indicators that you need to analyze to get the most out of your data, you need to determine what steps you need to take to maximize the benefits from the strategic use of your data. (See Chapter 11 for more details on the overall audit of your strategy and substrategies.)

Following is a step-by-step auditing process that you can easily implement on a regular basis using the tools and processes discussed earlier in this chapter:

1. **Establish an auditing schedule.**

   At the outset of your auditing process, you need to develop a schedule to ensure that you're regularly keeping up-to-date with your process review.

TIP

   Generally, for smaller organizations, a monthly review is all you need. If, however, you're a very data-driven organization, then you'll want to review your data, benchmarks, and objectives either every two weeks or even weekly.

2. **Pinpoint the factors that indicate an opportunity.**

   Outliers and correlations can be indicative of opportunities within your Millennial audience. In addition, you can look at things like upward trending conversation topics or spikes in audience segment participation.

3. **Establish benchmarks for the newly created opportunities and review benchmarks for ongoing initiatives.**

   You may need to establish new benchmarks each time you conduct an audit. Remember, Millennial habits may shift from one period to the next; they don't necessarily have long attention spans when it comes to content and campaigns.

4. **Review your key indicators in order to identify new opportunities.**

   Just as you review your key indicators to establish benchmarks and make the necessary adjustments, you need to review your data's key indicators to discover new opportunities.

REMEMBER

When looking for new opportunities, keep an open mind and look for anything out of the ordinary. These data points occur organically, so no road map can necessarily detail exactly what you should be looking for. Anything that seems new or interesting is worth investigating, because you never know what you may find.

Chapter **5**

Connecting with Millennials on Traditional Media

Television and other traditional media has had a great impact on prior generations. With the advent of new media technology comes new uses for these traditional channels. While they no longer function in the same way that they once did, traditional channels can still be valuable assets in your outreach strategy. This is particularly true when you leverage the ways that Millennials use these channels to enhance your new media strategies. (Chapter 6 covers this topic in more detail.)

In this chapter, you get a better understanding of where traditional media fits when it comes to reaching Millennials. At first glance, traditional media doesn't seem like something that is of much interest or readily accessible to a Millennial demographic. After all, this audience lives online and engages with brands primarily through more conversational channels, like Twitter and Facebook. Even though this is true, traditional media still has a place in your Millennial outreach and engagement strategy.

Taking Advantage of Television (With or Without the Budget)

For most marketers, television is far out of reach of their budget. Advertising on this once-prized medium and, to be fair, still prized medium, remains important for a lot of reasons.

Television is just valued today in a different way. The barriers are significant, and for small- and medium-sized brands, the risks of potential overspending and undermeasurement generally outweigh the benefits.

What's more, when you compare the metrics associated with television and social media, television is far more limited. If your goal is to reach and convert Millennials, then your natural inclination will be to invest your money online so that you can track it from start to finish. However, you can still track your investment if you leverage television strategically. The following sections look at how you can do so.

Looking at Millennial TV viewing habits

It's hardly a secret that Millennials are watching less traditional TV than any generation that has come before it. MarketingCharts (http://marketingcharts. com), a company that provides insights and charts related to the world of marketing, has analyzed Nielsen television viewing data, and aggregated the information shown in Figure 5-1. You see that since 2011, the amount of weekly time that Millennials have devoted to watching traditional TV has steadily decreased.

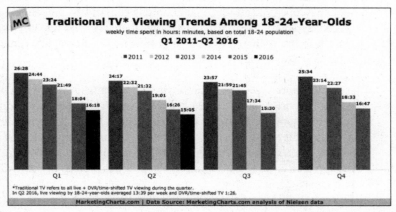

FIGURE 5-1: Millennial viewing habits have decreased in the past five years.

MarketingCharts.com.

The term *traditional TV* takes the average of live TV viewing with recorded or time-shifted viewing. It doesn't take into account new media, such as streaming, and doesn't factor in connected devices.

If you compare television viewing among other generations, you'll find that in 2016

>> Millennials watched about 20 hours per week.

>> GenXers (born between the early 1960s and mid-70s) watched 30 hours per week, which is a little over 9 hours more television per week than Millennials.

>> Boomers (born between the mid-1940s and early 1960s) watched upwards of 40 hours per week, which is double the time that Millennials watch per week.

You can see that Millennials are definitely not the most engaged when it comes to television, so marketers need to take some creative measures, such as the use of the second screen, covered in the next section, in order to effectively leverage TV.

Reaching viewers with the second screen

Have you ever watched your favorite team play your favorite sport, while all the while you're tweeting about a play or reading tweets about that last missed call by the ref? If you have, then you've engaged in what's referred to as *second screen viewing.*

According to research from Accenture (`www.accenture.com/us-en/insight-digital-video-connected-consumer`), a global professional services company, 87 percent of consumers use a second device while watching television. For Millennials, that second device often means a smartphone. (Chapter 10 covers the development of a mobile strategy.)

Essentially, you can take advantage of second screen viewing through three primary methods:

>> **Scheduled events, such as a national election or the Olympics:** Considering the nature of scheduled events or times of year, planning your second-screen strategy around this kind of an event is pretty easy. You know when the event takes place, so you can develop and prepare your content well ahead of time. Of course, because scheduled events are often live, you need to leave room for adjustments and modifications. However, you can lay out your content strategy in pretty robust detail before these kinds of events begin.

>> **Spontaneous events, such as breaking news:** When breaking news strikes, members of all generations tend to be glued to the television. For Millennials, this fascination is largely accompanied by ongoing updates on social media, particularly Twitter. With a proper strategy in place, your organic reach and engagement can skyrocket, thanks to the second screen viewing during these events.

>> **Regular programming:** While Millennials may not be watching as much television as the generations that have come before them, they still watch about 20 hours of television every week. By identifying the tastes and preferences of your audience through a data analysis (like the one I cover in Chapter 3), you can effectively reach these viewers while they're engaged with specific programming.

You can significantly leverage organic reach and engagement by using two types of second screen viewing: scheduled and spontaneous events.

Capitalizing on planned events

To see how you can capitalize on planned events, take the Olympics as an example. The Olympics consistently draw significant online engagement from Millennials around the world. The games provide an ideal setting in which you can leverage the second screen for both conversions and brand awareness. Users regularly share thoughts about the events across a multitude of social platforms. The development of a comprehensive content strategy that plays into the popularity of this conversation can lead to strong results.

When it comes to scheduled events, here are a series of actions that you can take that will help ensure that your campaign generates the kind of success you want to achieve:

>> **Identify an event or series of events that significantly engages your audience.** In the example of the Olympics, it can be something as small as identifying the events and sports that are talked about most. (Chapters 3 and 4 discuss the conversational habits of Millennials.)

>> **Establish main conversational topics around which to base your content strategy.** Several conversations will undoubtedly be taking place during these major events. While some of these conversations may be spontaneous, you can certainly predict others. Do your best to figure out these probable conversations and draft a content strategy outline that hits on these main topics.

>> **Determine the channels on which your target audience of Millennials are most likely to have these discussions.** Generally, when it comes to the second screen, the most popular conversations will be on platforms like

Twitter that they can access from their mobile devices. That said, there is always a chance that your audience is engaging on Snapchat, Instagram, or Facebook while watching an event on television. It will be up to you to determine the best platforms on which to execute your strategy and invest most of your effort and resources.

>> **Determine the tone that you'll adopt during engagement.** Everyone participating in the conversation has at least the event in common. This means that it truly is a conversation with a common theme. That means that you'll need to predetermine the level of familiarity you use and maintain it throughout the event.

Capitalizing on unforeseen events

Unforeseen circumstances are always a factor during live events. However, you can use some strategies to capitalize on the second screen. Here are a few tips to keep top of mind:

>> **Build a list for absolutely every scenario you can think of.** That way, you can limit surprises as much as possible.

>> **Determine the kinds of stories that you want to engage with and those that may be too sensitive.** Too many marketers and brands have made the mistake of inappropriately weighing in. One such story, for example, took place in 2015 when, for International Women's Day, Bic South Africa shared an ad that stated, "Look like a girl. Act like a lady. Think like a man. Work like a boss." The ad drew international criticism, and Bic was forced to rethink its strategy.

>> **Develop an easily revisable content template that you can use in most of the cases that you expect to encounter.** Again, creating content for an event that hasn't taken place yet is fairly difficult, but in the meantime, you can work on image files, video templates, and other basic design work so that you can react quickly to big news.

Using Twitter TV targeting to reach Millennials

Another type of second-screen experience that provides you with a great opportunity to engage Millennials takes place entirely on Twitter through its advertising backend. Twitter TV targeting is a mechanism that pushes your ads or sponsored content directly to consumers engaged with a particular television event while on Twitter.

Take, for example, the popular HBO series, *Game of Thrones*. During any given episode, the Millennial audience watching is engaged with fellow fans on Twitter. TV targeting allows brands to push their sponsored content into those feeds, thus making them a clear part of the conversation.

There are, of course, options that exist outside of the advertising mechanism that allow you to manually be part of the organic conversation. After all, that is what second-screen engagement during scheduled events is all about. But in this case, you get to push sponsored, intent-based content directly into the feeds of viewers, and you can do it at scale.

TECHNICAL STUFF

When a campaign is executed *at scale*, it means that it can be expanded to reach a significantly larger audience with a decreasing marginal cost. Essentially, as you build out the campaign, each new level of expansion requires less relative investment than the last. New media advertising easily allows this to take place as compared to scaled up campaigns with traditional media.

Running a campaign that leverages TV targeting on Twitter is fairly simple once you have access to the Twitter advertising backend:

1. **Access your Twitter ads dashboard.**

   Just as with Facebook, you don't need to run a campaign in order to access your ads account, which you can find at (http://ads.twitter.com).

   The Twitter ads dashboard is shown in Figure 5-2.

FIGURE 5-2:
A preview of your Twitter ads dashboard.

2. Choose the type of campaign you'd like to run.

On Twitter, several types of campaigns serve a variety of purposes. (Chapter 10 covers more about these types of campaigns.)

3. Determine the specifics of your campaign's TV targeting.

You can choose from three major types of TV targeting: by shows, networks, and genres (see Figure 5-3).

FIGURE 5-3: Three types of TV targeting.

TIP

For the highest levels of engagement, you'll most likely want to target an audience based on the shows its members are watching.

Targeting by genre or, in some very specific cases, by network may be a strong course of action. But the value in targeting an audience based on the specific program means that you'll be able to develop much more tailored content. It's likely that when you send this type of targeted content, it will reach an audience that is more receptive to it.

4. Incorporate additional targeting specifications for improved results.

To drive that engagement level even higher, a few additional targeting elements, such as gender and a more narrowed location, can be very beneficial.

REMEMBER

Millennials want a very personalized experience, so the narrower you can define your audience and the more tailored you can make your content, the higher the likelihood that your campaign will be a success.

Targeting Millennials with Print Media

For centuries, print media was the primary way to reach the masses. Most people got their news from newspapers and magazines. The development of new low-cost and readily available technologies means that print media has suffered. Nowhere is this truer than with the Millennial audience.

Now Millennials use real-time mobile apps. In fact, Pew Research (www. pewinternet.org) has reported that more than 80 percent of Millennials say that they use social media as their primary source for news.

However, you can still use some tactics to leverage print media to attract Millennials.

Reaching Millennials in magazines

Of the various types of print marketing and advertising that exist, leveraging the content in magazines can be the most readily accessible type for Millennials. Surprisingly, the level that Millennials read magazines falls very closely in line with those of Gen Xers and Baby Boomers, according to research for JWT (www.jwt.com), an advertising company based in New York. This means that there is a real opportunity to capitalize on the popularity of magazines, particularly when you know which magazines your audience is reading.

TIP

One benefit of running a Facebook Insights program (see Chapter 4) is that you can identify some of the print publications that your Millennial audience is reading. You can find this information in the section of liked pages in your audience analysis, where print publications populate as distinct pages. Identifying the magazines that are of interest to your Millennial audience will initially help you narrow down the avenues to consider leveraging on print magazines.

After you determine the publications you want to target, you have a few options worth considering:

>> **Advertorials:** Consider writing an *advertorial* to showcase your brand through written content. Unlike an ad, an advertorial is a sponsored piece of written content that highlights a product or service, but in the form of an editorial. Of course, advertorials aren't free, but in some cases, they can be very cost-effective. They offer you more space to truly define your product or service and showcase why it's better than the competition.

TIP

In some smaller industry or trade publications, an advertorial may only cost a nominal amount, if anything at all. Some trade publications are more concerned with gathering as much content as they can for a given issue and will forgo the cost to place one. If you can find a magazine that will offer you this option, it can provide you with a *pseudo-advertorial,* which isn't an explicit sales-focused advertorial but still has a self-promotional subtext. Inquire whether this option is available. It may not run you anything more than the time it takes to draft the article. But don't approach this tactic with the assumption that it will be free; if it is, think of it more as a pleasant surprise.

>> **Inclusion in an article:** Reach out to existing publication editors and staff writers in an effort to have your product or service included in an article about the topic. Unlike advertorials, your relationship with specific writers and editors largely influences your success. Reaching a point where a writer will be willing to feature your brand in her next article may take some time. But the fact that this mention is entirely organic, and therefore genuine, means that the audience reading about it will be much more receptive to what the writer is saying.

>> **Display ads:** Opt for display ads in smaller publications. Large, internationally distributed publications will simply be too expensive. Smaller publications will be more affordable and receptive to your business. In these more local or targeted publications, the audience you reach may be exactly the audience that you've defined — rather than a very large audience that also includes your targets.

Connecting with Millennials through the use of newspapers

According to the Newspaper Association of America (www.newsmediaalliance. org), 68 percent of Millennials ages 18 to 24 react to advertisements in print newspapers. This is especially true of coupons. So, while newspaper readership among Millennials may be down, engagement and responsiveness to sponsored content is still strong. So how can your brand leverage sponsored content?

Effectively leveraging newspapers in print form can be a little trickier, but one area with potential is in the use of coupons in place of your ads. Advertising in local publications can be much more affordable, and the data surrounding Millennials highlights the fact that they do respond well to coupons in newspapers. While the volume may not be significant, there is potential in small markets. If your coupon also has an online tie-in as opposed to something that people can only redeem in-store, then the potential is even greater.

TECHNICAL STUFF

When working with a coupon that connects to your online store or online offer, make sure to use a specific code that tells you the link is from a newspaper. This will come in handy when measuring the results of your various marketing efforts and will help you determine the return on your newspaper investment.

You need to evaluate whether or not you're willing to even make an investment in newspapers. Yes, you have ways of measuring return when using the coupon offer strategy, but there is still risk involved. According to research from Retale (www. retale.com), a coupon-sharing mobile application, nearly 30 percent of Millennials are simply not reading newspapers at all. With that in mind, you need to carefully consider the decision to invest in newspapers. If you can measure all aspects of the campaign and you can justify the investment based on the potential you identified in your research, then go for it!

The case for investing in print media

Print media still holds an important place in the world of marketing to Millennials. While online media has become a Millennial hotspot, this audience is still active on a variety of print platforms. This means that investing in a presence in print media is a viable option for several reasons:

>> You can increase your exposure on an ongoing basis to a Millennial audience.

>> You can tie your offline efforts to your online efforts.

>> You can reach new prospects that your brand may not have reached online.

The case for abandoning print media

While Millennials are still using a variety of print media, it's not their preferred set of channels. Millennials have grown up with the technology they use. They have evolved as consumers at the same rate as their technology. With this in mind, you need to ask yourself, "Do I want to invest in a channel that may not be viable for Millennials in a few years' time?"

For brands and organizations that have larger marketing and advertising budgets, the question is an easier one to answer. When a large budget is readily available, the decision to invest in all viable media options is clear: It has to be done. But for smaller organizations, it may not be as simple a decision.

For small- and medium-sized operations, where budget allocations are made sparingly, cutting print media out of the equation is often all too easy. Print media can be cost prohibitive, difficult to measure, and hard to predict. Those problems don't exist nearly to the same extent when it comes to social and new media. Essentially, you'll need to run an analysis on your available budgets and determine whether you have additional budget to allocate to traditional media.

TIP

Your priority should be to choose the more cost-effective channels of new media, where you have significantly more control over the specifics of a campaign.

Incorporating Email into Your Strategy

It may seem a little strange at first, but as far as Millennials are concerned, email isn't considered a new media. Email is the digital side of what is now categorized as traditional media. Millennials, therefore, use email very differently when communicating with brands. Knowing what these idiosyncrasies are and tailoring your Millennial email marketing strategy to them will help you maximize the potential of this platform.

Creating messages specifically for email

Email messages targeted to Millennials won't necessarily align with the content you create for Millennials on other channels. Instead, you need to pay close attention to the responsiveness of Millennials to specific types of emails and build your content strategy around them.

Research from email marketing company Adestra (www.adestra.com) found that the most popular reason a Millennial wants to receive an email from a brand is to receive a coupon or a discount. This preference mirrors what was seen regarding newspapers. Millennials are extremely price sensitive. (See more about the Millennial mindset in Chapter 2.)

With this in mind, you need to ask yourself how to capture the attention of Millennials in order to both justify your investment in email and keep your Millennial audience engaged. These two tips may help you capture their attention:

>> Leverage email as a component of your overall strategy as opposed to thinking about email in a silo.

>> Build subject lines and headings that capture the attention of your audience right away.

Tying email into your traditional and new media strategies

Receiving an email from an audience member is often the first indication that he wants to take the relationship with your brand a step further. While someone may like your Facebook Page or follow you on Twitter, nothing is quite as intimate as signing up for your newsletter or providing you with an email address. Personal information is seen as a form of currency by Millennials.

Email can and should tie into your Millennial marketing efforts in several ways:

>> **Segment your Millennial email lists as narrowly as possible.** In order to target your messaging to the specific behaviors and tastes of Millennials, narrow your segments. Millennials respond to personalization, and the best way to drive up conversion rates is to keep your lists segmented, and your messaging highly targeted.

>> **Leverage diverse types of email campaigns.** Of course, Millennials respond to coupons and discount offers, but email list-building tools like Constant Contact (www.constantcontact.com) provide many variations of email campaign types, as shown in Figure 5-4. Run a campaign that collects survey data or asks for some sort of action that Millennials can take within the email. You may even sell tickets or products directly from the email. These examples are both readily available and mobile-friendly, which is most likely where Millennials will be checking their email.

FIGURE 5-4:
Different types of campaigns available in Constant Contact.

>> **Cross-match email addresses on Facebook and Twitter.** You can cross-match email addresses on different platforms to better target your ads. Improving the targeting of your ads by performing this task leads to higher click-through rates, lower cost-per-click, and ultimately, increased conversion rates.

Building subject lines and headings that generate opens

When you consider how much content Millennials are bombarded with on a daily basis, it's easy to understand why Millennial email open and click-through rates have been steadily declining. (*Open* and *click-through rates* are defined as the number of your total audience that opens your emails and then clicks through to the URL they find.)

TIP

Increasing open and click-through rates starts with the subject line. That is the first thing your audience is going to see, and it can really be a make-or-break moment.

To see your open rates shoot up among Millennials, here are a few tips worth keeping top of mind when crafting your next subject line:

>> **Keep your subject line as short as possible.** The majority of your Millennial audience is checking email on a mobile device, which means less screen space for your subject. It also means that a novel-length subject line will be cut off before you even hit the main point.

>> **Personalize your subject line with personalization tokens.** A common theme across all marketing channels is the desire for a personalized experience. Personalization goes for email as well. If you have an option to personalize the subject line using a token in your email software, take advantage of it.

TECHNICAL
STUFF

Personalization tokens are small bits of code found within your email software that automatically populates a designated space either in your subject line or the email body itself. It pulls out certain personal elements from the profile of the user receiving the email. So, John's subject line will read something like "Hey, John! Collect Your Reward Now!" and Mary's subject line will swap out John's name for her own.

>> **Be clear about what recipients will see in their email.** Don't be vague or mysterious about email content. This is a quick way to get your email sent to the trash. This technique of enticing opens and clicks from your audience may

have worked when email was in its infancy, but smarter, busier, and often passive Millennial users aren't interested in mystery email. Everything they need to encourage them to open the email should be in the subject line.

>> **Use action or intent-oriented verbs in your subject line.** Much like the subject of clarity noted in the previous tip, use an active verb, such as *buy* or *register*, in your subject line to highlight what it is your audience members will need to do once they open the email.

Chapter **6**

Engaging with Millennials on New Media

Reaching Millennials on new media requires more than a simple presence. Everyone has that. You need a deep understanding of your audience and a willingness to invest in reaching them using social advertising. With this understanding, you can create a comprehensive set of content strategies.

In 2014, social audience engagement platform Crowdtap (http://crowdtap.com) conducted a study that found that Millennials are spending an average of 17.8 hours per day consuming various media. It is important to keep in mind that this number doesn't necessarily reflect total, or real hours, but rather cumulative hours on various media. So Millennials can be answering texts while scrolling through Facebook with the television on in the background. What is important to note in this study is that Millennials are always connected, and the majority of these nearly 18 hours is spent engaging with new media.

In this chapter, you see exactly how new media operates as the backbone of your overall Millennial marketing strategy.

Using Facebook at the Core of Your New Media Strategy

According to the New Media Institute, *new media* is defined as media that are primarily digital. They offer a highly interactive platform that can be manipulated and customized. *New media* is an umbrella term that comprises all the platforms and social networks where Millennials are spending the majority of their time. One new media platform that you want to make sure to include in your marketing strategy is Facebook. If you're a fan or follower of particular marketing or advertising publications on Facebook, you've almost certainly scrolled through your News Feed and seen a headline that discusses the death of Facebook and how Millennials have abandoned it. Don't let these shock-value headlines fool you. Facebook is alive and well, particularly with Millennials around the world. The misconception is that Facebook has become so ubiquitous in our daily lives that we rarely, if ever, think about using it as a special case or event. We're simply connected to it and using it more than ever.

Utilizing Facebook features

Over the past several years, Facebook has significantly expanded its product to include so many features for brands and Pages that it could serve as your base of new media marketing operations on social. The following list highlights just a few of the many features that Facebook offers its Page users:

>> Share content with fans and followers

>> Advertise to target audiences

>> Create and promote events

>> Access Facebook's Audience Network for greater reach with rich media

>> Collect user data

>> Sell products in your Shop

>> Run contests, sweepstakes, polls, and so on

Rich media content features more than simply text. It can include images, GIFs, and videos.

TECHNICAL STUFF

You can develop or customize contests, sweepstakes, and other audience participation initiatives using an easy-to-use tool like Woobox (http://woobox.com), shown in Figure 6-1.

FIGURE 6-1:
Woobox.

Over *4 million* brands trust Woobox to help them run
effective campaigns.

Analyzing your Facebook audience

After you segment your audience and run a program on Facebook to cross-match
users and identify certain defining characteristics, you can begin analyzing these
pockets to develop a content strategy that fits each one. (The process of building
your Facebook Millennial audience pockets through the use of your segmented
email lists and Facebook's Audiences product is covered in detail in Chapter 3).

When analyzing your Facebook audience pockets, follow these steps:

1. **Clearly name the audience you're analyzing.**

This step may seem trivial, but all too often, marketers lose track of the
audiences they've developed in Facebook. Not naming your audience makes it
harder to analyze your audience. It also makes building your ad campaigns
more difficult. When you segment your audiences and prepare to analyze
them, start first by naming the audience.

TIP

The name you choose shouldn't be something as simple as "Audience 1." You
should include details about the audience. For example, a name like "Female
Millennials White Paper Download June 2016" tells you that these users initially
came from a particular category. The name can always change as you identify
something unique about a given audience in your analysis process, but start
with something clear and distinct right off the bat.

2. **Start with statistical details.**

Facebook offers up a lot of details about personal attributes that stretch
beyond gender and age in the Audience Insights dashboard, shown in
Figure 6-2. Start your analysis by reviewing characteristics such as education
level, employment field, or marital status. Everything is clearly represented, so
little to no guesswork is involved in determining what these statistics are telling

you about the audience members. The Audience Insights dashboard is your simplest starting point, and it immediately helps you build a more robust picture of your audience.

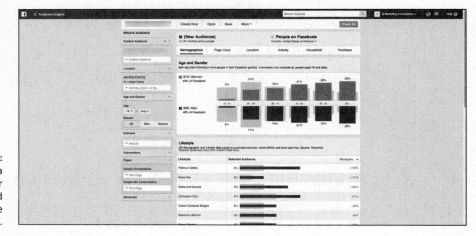

3. **Review the Lifestyle categories, but don't live by them.**

   After you review the statistics associated with your audience, you'll want to take some time to review some of the Lifestyle categories that Facebook has allocated to your audience, as shown in Figure 6-3. These categorizations can be particularly helpful when you're trying to get a feel for the kinds of lives your selected audience lives. However, relying entirely on these categorizations is a mistake. Take the time to outline a proper persona, which will give you the opportunity to uncover new details that you may have missed. These Lifestyle categories can provide some good groundwork and presumptions that you can reference as you build out the audience in more detail.

4. **Identify initial interests through Page likes.**

   Look at the breakdown of Page likes in your Audience Insights, as shown in Figure 6-3. You'll notice that they're segmented according to category. Analyze these categories by tying in the kinds of pages liked with the statistical data of Millennials and the behavioral data that is analyzed last. Tying in the data points surrounding aspects such as career and education level with the categories of interest makes aligning your message from both a content and rhetoric standpoint significantly simpler and more effective.

   TIP

   When Facebook lists the Pages below the categorical listing, you'll see a relevance score for individual Pages. This metric is another valuable one because it tells you not only how popular a Page or brand may be, but also how relevant that Page is (as determined by Facebook) to your audience based on its overall profile.

FIGURE 6-3:
Facebook
automatically
segments your
audience into
Lifestyle
categories.

5. **Analyze user activity to strategize about engagement.**

In the Activity tab in your Audience Insights dashboard, shown in Figure 6-4, you'll notice a breakdown of how the selected group of users interacts with the Pages and brands they follow. When you understand how Millennials are engaging with the content that brands are sharing, it becomes easier to craft a content strategy that caters to these habits.

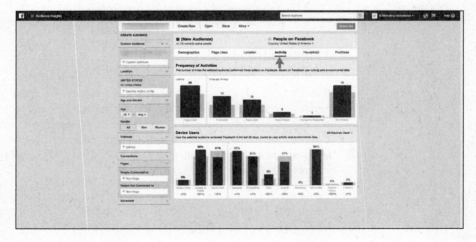

FIGURE 6-4:
The Activity tab
shows you how
your audience is
engaging with
Pages.

6. **Get to know your audience's household makeup.**

When you have a sense of your audience's income, how it spends money, and the size of its households, creating targeted messaging, again, becomes significantly easier. The more you understand about the state of mind of these Millennials, the easier it is to craft content that connects with them on a very personal level.

7. **Dive into purchasing behaviors of your audience.**

This step helps you further analyze your audience's spending habits and buying behavior. In the Purchase tab, shown in Figure 6-5, you see a fairly robust breakdown of your selected audience's spending both online and in brick-and-mortar locations. This breakdown provides you with insights into audience priorities about finances. It will further assist you in deciding how you want to structure your content and determine which points to highlight to significantly drive up engagement.

FIGURE 6-5:
Analyzing buying habits in the Purchase tab of Audience Insights on Facebook.

8. **Build out a written persona of the customer.**

A best practice you can use to analyze a selected audience pocket is to write a persona. A *persona* is a detailed written description of the personality associated with your target customer. To effectively develop content and reach your audience, outlining a detailed persona is a valuable activity. A persona should be written out in a pseudo-narrative fashion and defined in a detailed manner that gives him or her some character.

WRITING IN A PSEUDO-NARRATIVE FASHION

The term *pseudo-narrative* is used to describe the fashion in which a character description is written. Use full sentences, with each trait building off the previous one, to clearly define a character. Instead of listing line items about schooling and employment, write about the school itself, the degree earned, and how that led to your character's current job.

Think of a persona as a living person with personality and lively traits, rather than simply thinking of your customer as a set of demographics. Developing a content strategy is easier when the image of a real individual fuels your communication.

REMEMBER

Keep in mind that when it comes to new media and social interactions, Millennials want to have a conversation and develop a relationship with a brand. This desire for a relationship means that you need to talk to the audience on a personal level. Creating a lifelike persona before developing a content strategy goes a long way toward building real relationships.

Analyzing your audience takes time. Each of the clusters that you develop when creating your audience pockets will need to undergo this analysis (covered in Chapter 3).

Developing targeted content strategies

To develop highly targeted content strategies on Facebook, you have to understand what makes each of these audience pockets tick. To do so, you need to go through the public data available for each and build out a variety of persona profiles.

To facilitate this process, here are a few simple tips to keep top of mind:

>> **Keep an eye on the Facebook averages in your audience analysis.** Facebook audience averages are shown in Figure 6-6. The Facebook averages tell you whether your audience has a particular affinity or dislike for something in particular, or they tell you what ratio of an audience falls into a particular category or designation. This knowledge will significantly help with the crafting of your content strategy for the given audience.

>> **Remember that not everything is going to factor into your audience outline.** Although you'll find a lot of data about your selected audience, you don't need to use all of it right away. For example, the data that Facebook collects may include some information about whether a member of your selected audience is in the market to purchase a vehicle. That information may be irrelevant, which means you can ignore it.

>> **Think about your written persona as an actual person.** Give your character a name and a little bit of creative backstory. Marketing to a group with similar traits is effective, but may cause you to have a mechanical tone of voice. If you can truly envision the person to whom you're talking, the tone will be far more natural, and the responsiveness from your audience will be significantly higher.

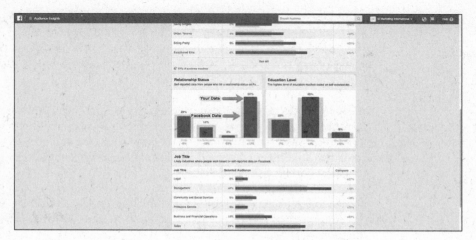

FIGURE 6-6:
Consider how your own audience data compares to Facebook averages.

Creating a Facebook Content Strategy Geared Toward Millennials

After you closely analyze the audience pockets of Millennials that you've cultivated, you can begin the process of developing a content strategy to drive engagement and action. While your content strategy may have overarching themes and a consistent tone of voice, small details will vary from one outlined audience cluster to the next. It is those small details that will consistently keep your audience engagement rates at levels significantly above Facebook averages.

TECHNICAL STUFF

While there are often different opinions about what the average branded Page and content engagement rate on Facebook is, a general consensus in the marketing industry is that the norm (as of the time of this writing) ranges between 0.5 to 1 percent. Organic reach and engagement were, at one time, significantly higher on Facebook. Those rates have declined and have leveled off at the 0.5 to 1 percent range. One reason is that the social network moved aggressively toward a pay-to-play model for brands and encouraged Page owners to pay for advertising by systematically decreasing organic reach.

Your Millennial-targeted content strategy on Facebook will contain a number of components, which are described in the following sections.

Tone of voice outline

If you want to build a loyal following among Millennials on Facebook, where they're spending the majority of their time online, then you're going to need to distinguish your brand through your voice. Building a voice takes time. While you may have started the process with one idea in mind, you may find that as you begin to execute your content strategy, that idea changes. Don't worry about that; it's all part of the process.

To build out that initial voice, you need to answer a few questions, each of which builds off of the last:

>> **Has your Facebook audience analysis uncovered universal commonalities?** When analyzing your Millennial audience pockets, you may have found one or perhaps several traits that the majority of your Millennial audience members possessed. These traits can be anything ranging from a consistently high level of education to commonalities in each group's professions. Look across each of the outlined personas that you've created and see whether you can find certain universal traits among these descriptions.

>> **Do you want to have a professional or neighborly voice?** You can choose a preliminary answer before answering the previous question regarding audience commonalities, but you may revise it once you identify those universal traits within your audience. Facebook is conversational, and Millennials will ignore a brand's robotic, formulaic, and often boring content. Just because Facebook is meant to be conversational, however, that doesn't mean that you should nix the idea of taking a more professional approach to your voice on the network. Of course, you'll want that professional voice to be one that your audience members can relate to and communicate with. A professional tone can often build credibility and generate an even higher degree of engagement.

TIP

Choosing between a professional and a friendly tone of voice will depend on some of the universal traits that your audience exhibits. Pay attention to elements such as household makeup and career fields to determine the maturity level of your audience. You should also look closely at the Pages that your Millennial audience follows and take some notes on the voice used by those organizations on Facebook.

>> **Are you self-involved or community-oriented?** Regarding the content you share and the comments you make in your posts, your tone of voice will change dramatically depending on which direction you choose. In this particular case, the term *self-involved* is not a negative one. It relates to the direction of the conversation. Are you going to focus inward, linking your posts and comments to your website to highlight your expertise? Or will you be looking outward focusing on the conversation on Facebook to encourage additional comments? The answer to this question will help guide the development of your content.

Editorial calendar structure

Content moves quickly. At the drop of a hat, you may find yourself in a situation that requires the immediate development of new content to address a major news story or a brand crisis. But just because things are happening in real-time doesn't mean you can't appropriately prepare content ahead of time according to a well-outlined editorial calendar.

A well-cultivated brand voice means that certain identifiable characteristics are in your content. Your Millennial audience should be able to recognize your posts in the blink of an eye. After all, that's about as much time as they give to each piece of content they come across. Producing a steady stream of certain types of content, themes, and staples in your weekly or monthly Facebook posts will go a long way toward building recognition for your brand. Of course, this isn't to say that your editorial calendar will remain the same month after month. Your audience's tastes and preferences may change on a fairly regular basis, so your editorial calendar will have to change with them. This process ties in closely with your audience analysis and audit (see Chapter 3).

An editorial calendar structure doesn't need to be terribly complex. Figure 6-7 shows an example of what a fairly basic editorial calendar designed in Microsoft Excel might look like.

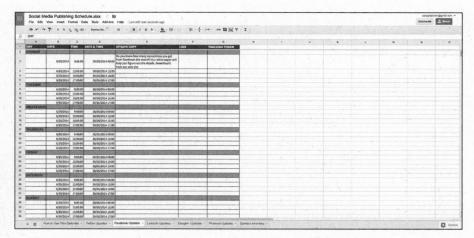

FIGURE 6-7:
An example of a simple editorial calendar designed in Microsoft Excel.

While you don't necessarily need to plan for daily content, it is worthwhile to consider the topic of weekly or monthly content staples. These regular posts on Facebook become sources of strong engagement, particularly when they're based on the expressed interests identified in your Millennial audience clusters. The following sections describe a few post types to consider.

Audience activation

Audience activation posts are designed to drive up engagement with your Facebook audience. Of course, these posts will be seen by everyone, not just Millennials. But a targeted boost specifically to Millennials (in your saved audiences on Facebook) will ensure that the users you're trying to activate will see the content.

Essentially, audience activation posts are pieces of content designed to push a user to take action. It can be a simple question, a weekly opinion poll, or virtually any other post that encourages engagement on Facebook itself. This question serves two purposes:

>> Driving up engagement on your Page and with your Millennial audience (the more obvious goal)

>> *Gaming,* or manipulating, the Facebook algorithm, which heavily favors content from Pages that have strong engagement rates, to work in your favor

The more your Millennial audience regularly engages with your content, the higher the likelihood that your Page content will appear organically in its News Feeds. This reality on Facebook means that the small amount of ad dollars you initially spend can stop completely as the organic engagement steadily rises.

Spotlight

A *spotlight post* features one particular aspect and falls under the more self-promotional marketing content types.

TIP

Spotlight posts should be used sparingly — no more than twice per month when targeting a Millennial audience.

FACEBOOK ALGORITHM

The Facebook algorithm determines what a user sees in her News Feed. The content you see on Facebook is neither linear nor chronological. You see content deemed to be most relevant to you based on a number of factors. In fact, while the Facebook algorithm was relatively simple to analyze, it has now grown to include well over 100 factors. Of these factors, only some hints have been given about how they can be manipulated. Though the practices are not perfect, it's well known that engagement factors heavily influence what is seen in a Page's News Feed.

Millennials may react differently to marketing messaging than the generational cohorts that preceded them. That doesn't mean that an opportunity to explicitly market to Millennials doesn't exist. It simply needs to be done in a way that doesn't make them feel bombarded or annoyed by your message. Through the use of strategically placed spotlight posts on Facebook, you can showcase your brand and your product. Because your Millennial audience has become accustomed to your content strategy and editorial calendar, it will be far more receptive to the message.

This is not to say that your spotlight content should aggressively push the audience to take action. Remember that social and new media are all about conversation. A spotlight post may be a little bit more promotional than some of the other types of content listed in this chapter, but the focus of your message should focus on the value added to the consumer, rather than selfishly focusing on the sale.

TIP

When it comes to new media, the easiest way to find success with Millennials is to leverage the soft sell. Focus on the benefit to the consumer. While the soft sell has several layers — from the simple brand exposure to the slightly more aggressive spotlight listed in the preceding section — it is the soft sell that encourages engagement. What's more, highlighting how your brand or product adds value to the customer goes a longer way toward creating a relationship than simply outlining a product's features. Outline the problem and then feature the solution.

Lighthearted weekend

Before ushering in the weekend, you should send a weekly post wishing your followers well. You can even take it a step further and encourage engagement by asking your followers what they're planning. This weekly post drives consistent engagement with a growing group of followers. This post functions much like the audience activation content. It leads to increased organic reach and engagement among your followers. Figure 6-8 shows examples of how the women's blogging network SheSavvy (www.shesavvy.com) shares a weekly post on Friday afternoons using the hashtag #PuppyFriday.

Considering the nature of this type of content, it needs to be shared weekly. Lighthearted weekend content is simply part of a larger umbrella of weekly content types that you can regularly post to Facebook. These types of content include daily themes, where a catchy name is given to each day, or some days, of the week.

You can use something along the lines of Tip Tuesdays to share an industry tip or best practice every Tuesday. Another example is Fun Fridays where a silly industry or brand relevant meme or video is shared to your Facebook channel.

FIGURE 6-8:
Women's
blogging network
SheSavvy shares
a weekly post
every Friday.

REMEMBER

The idea with these themes is consistency. Regularly sharing a familiar piece of content that is rooted in the tastes and preferences of your Millennial audience will drive up engagement.

Tips and tricks

Regularly sharing tips and tricks that are relevant to your Millennial audience is another surefire way to drive up engagement. In keeping with the theme outlined in the Spotlight section, posting weekly on something like Tip Tuesdays provides value to your audience.

REMEMBER

Regardless what industry you're in, You'll almost certainly have an opportunity to share tips and tricks that your followers will find useful.

Tips are excellent for two reasons:

>> **Tips are a content type that is hugely engaging.** Tips are often stumbled upon and watched, or read, or clicked on as a result of an intent-driven search or desire online. Unexpected content can be very engaging.

>> **Tips are an example of a very powerful soft selling technique**. Tips can highlight your expertise without overtly pushing your brand or product. For example, suppose that you sell a variety of computer storage and portable flash drives. Every Tip Tuesday, you can share a brief video or image that showcases how to select the right drive for your computer, how to split a disk, or how to repair damaged storage devices. With this type of useful content, you cement yourself as a leader in your particular field.

The regularity of these weekly posts means that your brand becomes ingrained in the minds of viewers. So, when they're ready to make a purchase, you have a significantly higher chance of being the first company that comes to mind. They consider you first because of the relationship that has formed and the trust that has been built over time.

Time-sensitive offers

Best Buy is, perhaps, the best-known brand example of leveraging new media to push time-sensitive offers. In the early days of Twitter, Best Buy recognized that it could share limited time or quantity offers to an enthusiastic, highly engaged group of users to significantly drive up short-term sales. You can use your editorial calendar on Facebook for the same purpose on new media.

Imagine that you share a weekly special, limited time or quantity offer called Sale Saturday every Saturday on Facebook. This offer is highly attractive to Millennials. Millennials have noted that offers, specials, and promotions are one of the primary reasons why they follow brands or purchase a newspaper. Creating a regularly scheduled offer entices organic engagement from a group that is both price sensitive and looking for offers and specials from the brands they follow. Figure 6-9 shows an example of a simple offer used to entice Millennial engagement on a regular basis.

FIGURE 6-9:
This basic
offer goes a
very long way.

Behind-the-scenes featurette

Behind-the-scenes material has become hugely popular among Millennials, particularly since the launch of Snapchat. When building an editorial calendar, consider sprinkling in a few bits of content that showcase the process leading to the end result. This achieves two objectives with your Millennial audience:

>> It gives the audience members some insight into your work process and expertise, which strengthens a user's familiarity with your brand. It's pretty interesting to see.

>> This kind of exclusive content connects the users to your brand in a significant way. It gives them an insider's look. For example, imagine a restaurant owned by a famous chef.

You may be very familiar with the chef, her restaurant, and signature dish, but that familiarity doesn't necessarily mean you feel any personal connection to the business or the individual. Now, imagine if, once every month, this chef signed on to Facebook Live and walked you through the intricacies of preparing one of her popular dishes. You don't necessarily need to do the recipe yourself, but that type of experience is one that Millennials connect with very closely.

Behind-the-scenes content for any business can be hugely effective in driving up loyalty with Millennials. You should leverage this content as part of a content strategy and include it in any editorial calendar you plan to create.

Seasonal

Your editorial calendar needs to change and evolve. Keep in mind that Millennials don't have a particularly extended attention span. The more often you change up your editorial calendar, the better it will increase your engagement rates. Incorporating planned content for different months and seasons will also be easier.

TIP

Whether you're planning content around a holiday, a particular time of year, such as Back to School season, or a particular cause, such as Breast Cancer Awareness Month in October, planning for seasonal content is a very valuable practice.

Relevance is a high priority for your target audience's News Feed on Facebook. If your message relates to the conversations that Millennials have (often about trending topics or a seasonal event like Halloween), the message has a higher likelihood of organically reaching a larger audience.

Considering thematic content development

Developing thematic content is a useful tactic when building out your Millennial content strategy on Facebook. The frequency and regularity with which Millennials see this content will help build your organic reach and engagement over time. Several types of thematic content are easily tailored and adapted to any brand or industry. Consider the following types of thematic content when developing your content strategy:

>> **Q&A:** Asking your audience a question is a great way to entice engagement and get a feel for how tastes and preferences evolve. Asking a question helps you optimize your content strategy on an ongoing basis because of the real-time insights you receive about your audience.

>> **Opinion Poll:** Much like a Q&A, asking your audience to share its opinions is an excellent way of tapping into the evolving nature of Millennial interests on Facebook. Not only are opinion polls and Facebook survey content great tools to use, the results of these surveys and polls also provide valuable inspiration for new content on editorial calendars.

>> **Tips & Tricks:** Tips and tricks provide a value added to your audience, as well as showcase your expertise as a brand. These two benefits make this type of content extremely worthwhile to include in your themed content. For more on themed content, see the "Tips and tricks" section, earlier in this chapter.

>> **How-To:** Instructional content is always popular and serves a similar purpose as tips. The difference with how-to content, however, is the in-depth nature of this material. A tip may be a brief bit of easily digested information that your audience can absorb very quickly. How-to content provides much more detail, showcasing a process and your expertise. How-to content is also searched for and clicked on with intent. Millennial users watching a how-to video or reading a how-to article can be more motivated to take action.

>> **Sneak Peek/Behind-the-Scenes:** The more sneak-peek material you can provide to your Millennial audience, the closer it will feel to your brand. Whenever you have the option to either create or stream content with this theme, consider it seriously. Behind-the-scenes content is highly engaging, particularly when it is on a platform such as Facebook Live, shown in Figure 6-10.

>> **Inspiration/Motivation:** Positivity goes a long way on Facebook. Inspirational content is a powerful theme. This content can either be in the form of philosophical motivation, such as a positive quote, or inspirational in the form of an idea to help your audience get started on a project.

Most thematic content is universal. You can share it with the general public using some of the more uniform traits of your Millennial audience. The purpose of this content is to encourage ongoing audience engagement and build a broader organic reach. Using narrowly focused content helps you spend your ad dollars on more action–oriented campaigns and content. These campaigns and content make up the most important component of your Millennial content strategy on Facebook.

Developing hypertargeted content

Personalization is key when you attempt to drive action from your Millennial audience. Relationships matter a great deal to Millennials. Sending personalized, hypertargeted content is the best way to build loyalty, higher-than-average engagement, and conversions.

Hypertargeting is the process of taking your content customization a step further. Instead of simply tailoring your content to some of the universal audience traits that you identified in your initial analysis, you're going to dive deep into each of the segmented audience clusters. This deep-diving process will help you identify the most unique traits for each segment. It will also help you tailor your campaign content to focus on the small details that make each of these audience clusters distinctive.

While the overall message in your content may be the same across each of your Millennial audience clusters, the delivery, structure, and creative approach may differ. Those differences can be relatively negligible, such as the use of a particular keyword that regularly leads to a higher click-through rate with one audience. Or those differences may be significant, like the use of a short video with one audience and an image featuring a call-to-action with another. There may also come a time when you identify an audience cluster that suits the target audience criteria for a campaign, while another may not.

REMEMBER

Audience clusters are unique in many ways. Apart from their categorization as Millennials, they're made up of users that significantly differ from one another. You may find yourself launching a campaign that's right for only half of your clusters. Therefore, analyzing the characteristics of each cluster is important to ensure that you don't waste ad dollars on ones that simply don't fit with the objectives, messaging, or structure of a campaign.

To develop hypertargeted content for each campaign, follow these steps:

1. **Identify the audience clusters that fit your campaign.**

   Remember that not every audience cluster will be right for every campaign. You'll do a disservice to yourself by trying to tie every member of your larger audience into every campaign. This approach can cause you to spread your ad dollars too thin. It is better to focus on the most viable audience segments first and then see whether you have an opportunity to incorporate others after you exhaust the potential of your most valuable audience clusters.

2. **Select the defining characteristics of each cluster and let it guide your content development.**

   The small details of these groups are what makes them so valuable. After you identify the audiences that best fit your campaign, review the audience persona outline to see what makes them unique. These unique characteristics will be the guiding force behind your content development.

3. **Prioritize your audience according to value.**

   Based on the objectives that you've outlined, particular audiences will possess traits that make them more valuable than others. It is your job to go through the defining characteristics pulled from Step 2 to determine which ones are the most valuable.

   TIP

   At the beginning of the content development process, you may want to create a numerical scale with brief descriptions, based on a quality score — perhaps 1 through 5. This scale will make the process of determining audience cluster viability much simpler because you'll be able to quickly determine each cluster's viability.

4. **Create universal messaging and content for your campaign.**

   Creating a series of messages that are not tailored to one group or another will make the process of customizing that messaging much simpler. This customization is made easier because the foundation of the message will already be laid out in this step.

5. **Tailor your universal messaging to the idiosyncrasies identified in Step 2 of this process.**

   Finally, take that universal message and tailor the message of your campaign to each one of the Millennial audience segments.

After completing these steps, you'll have the necessary personalized content to use in your campaign. Personalization is a crucial part of building lasting relationships with these users.

Building a Relationship with Your Millennial Audience on Facebook

For Millennials, relationships are the root of loyalty. To build any kind of consistent audience base among this demographic, you need to nurture and form a relationship over time. Despite the common criticism of Millennials, they're fiercely loyal and even willing to pay higher prices for certain products when they feel a personal connection to a brand. The process of finding that connection is difficult for many brands.

Facebook is an ideal starting point to grow and nurture relationships because Millennials spend a significant amount of time on the network. The broad selection of capabilities for both desktop and mobile devices means that engagement can come in many forms on an ongoing basis. This feature is mostly unique to Facebook. You can adopt several engagement strategies to build these relationships, including

» Hypertargeting

» Exclusivity

» Responsiveness

» Consistency

» Value

Hypertargeting

Hypertargeting is one of the most effective ways to build a relationship with your audience. It shows that you care about your fans and followers, which causes them to relate to your brand on a level that extends beyond an appreciation for the product or service. This connection is something that builds a much longer lasting relationship with your followers.

For more on hypertargeting, see the section "Developing hypertargeted content," earlier in this chapter.

Exclusivity

Sharing exclusive offers, content, and information with your fans and followers makes them feel special. It encourages them to pay closer attention to what you're sharing. Building up your audience by providing it with something unique — whether it's an invite to an exclusive event, a special offer that is only available to your fans, or access to content before the general public — creates a very close connection to your brand.

Responsiveness

Don't leave your most loyal audience members hanging. When a fan, follower, or customer reaches out to you on Facebook (whether it's on Messenger, in a post, or in a comment), you should be ready to respond. Small gestures go a very long way in building relationships. Simply liking a comment or answering a question can have a profound effect on a fan or follower.

Obviously, when a crisis strikes, your engagement and responsiveness strategy will significantly change. But under normal circumstances, these examples are considered positive brand experiences and should be practiced on a regular basis.

Consistency

Your editorial calendar won't necessarily contain planned content every single day. If your content strategy doesn't call for daily posts, then it isn't something you should force. What you'll want to do is maintain a consistent stream of content flowing into the News Feeds of your audience members.

Sporadic posts hinder your potential growth rate from two angles:

>> Sharing content randomly doesn't encourage your audience to expect new material. If they know that something like a Tuesday tip is coming, organic engagement will be significantly higher. Without that consistency, organic reach can plateau, and you'll find it particularly difficult to increase it.

>> A lack of uniformity makes it tough for your audience to determine when your content has been shared. Therefore, competitors who regularly share content can overshadow the visibility of your brand.

Consistency also impacts your brand voice. When you develop a recognizable tone of voice on Facebook, your users become accustomed to a particular style of writing or design. This consistency and audience familiarity helps you maintain organic growth and decreases mandatory ad spending.

Value

Millennials highly value experience. When they feel a connection to a brand, they get more out of the engagement than a simple exchange. Therefore, the relationship between the Millennial consumer and the brand deepens. The best way to encourage this trust is to always provide tangible value in the content you share. This value can come in many forms. It can be something as simple as sharing a bit of information that helps make life easier — for example, life hacks, tips, or tricks of the trade. Or, it can be something more detailed and robust, like a complicated process explained in an instructional video.

Several of the content types covered in this chapter are designed to improve the day-to-day life of your audience. Instructional videos or quick tips are excellent ways of strengthening the relationship with Millennials. The content is not overtly self-promotional, but it does highlight your expertise in a given field. It also encourages your audience to continually engage with your brand, particularly when it's clear that you share content that goes beyond the sales pitch.

Advertising to Millennials on Facebook

After you develop your content strategy, brand voice, audience clusters, and editorial calendar, you're ready to begin taking advantage of Facebook's robust ad platform. While network's like Twitter, Pinterest, Snapchat, and others offer advertising options, Facebook is perhaps the most valuable when it comes to reaching Millennials in segmented clusters. Between the targeting mechanisms, the dashboard structure, and the detailed real-time reporting data, there is a lot to like about Facebook advertising.

Launching your campaign

To reach Millennials through the use of Facebook's ad dashboard, there are several steps to follow. Of course, your objectives may change from one campaign to another, but considering you've already created segmented audiences, the process is significantly simpler and results can be far above average.

TECHNICAL STUFF

Much like organic engagement on Facebook, engagement rates in your ad campaigns will generally run anywhere between 1 to 3 percent, depending on the audience, the objectives, and the desired action to be taken from your audience.

To launch a Millennial-focused Facebook advertising campaign, follow these steps:

1. **Access your Facebook Ads Manager dashboard and create a new campaign.**

   In the top right-hand corner of your Ads Manager dashboard, click on the green icon, to create a new ad campaign.

2. **Select the marketing objective that best defines what you're trying to achieve.**

   You have a fairly broad set of objectives to choose from (see Figure 6-11). Not all will be ideally suited for your campaign, and, perhaps more importantly, not all will be ideally suited when it comes to the kinds of actions Millennials take on Facebook. Carefully choose the right objective in Facebook to match your goals.

TIP

Plan how you'll measure the success of your campaign and the performance of your program before launching a campaign. Facebook provides some in-depth insights into your campaign performance that you can tie directly to business performance, but you'll also want to have your own measures laid out. After all, how do you know whether something is successful unless you've clearly identified your success benchmarks?

TECHNICAL STUFF

While most of the outlined objectives in Facebook lead to similarly structured campaigns, the key difference lies in the way Facebook charges your account. Facebook may charge on a per-action basis, a per-click basis, a hybrid between impressions and clicks, or based on conversions. Make sure that you know ahead of time how you'll be charged.

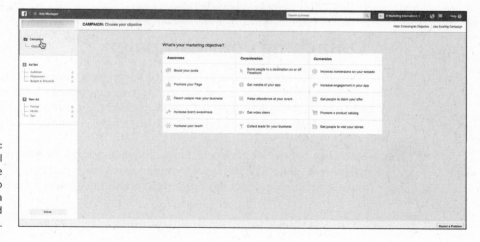

FIGURE 6-11: You have several possible objectives to choose from in a Facebook ad campaign.

3. Choose a Saved Audience from your segmented Millennial clusters.

Instead of building out a new audience, which is often times what you'll do when running a campaign, you're going to choose from among the hypertargeted audience clusters within your Facebook account. When defining an ad set, you can choose a Saved Audience from the pull-down list, shown in Figure 6-12.

FIGURE 6-12:
Choose a Saved Audience in order to build a more targeted campaign.

4. Identify your ad placements manually.

Facebook offers two forms of ad placements, as shown in Figure 6-13:

- Automatically placing your ads on Facebook, Instagram, and within Facebook's Audience Network by the ad server
- Manually choosing where you'd like to place your ad

TIP

While having this process done automatically is easier, I highly recommend that, when trying to reach Millennials, you do this manually. The reason is simple: Millennials engage in unique ways from one platform to another and from one network to another. The way one user engages with Facebook content on a desktop compared to how that user engages with Instagram content on a mobile device will significantly differ. Your content needs to vary to account for that difference. Creating ad sets within a campaign that are structured both for the specific audience selected as well as the placement stand a significantly higher chance of performing above expectations.

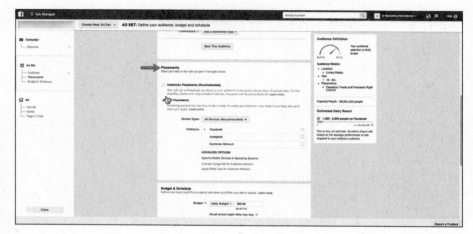

FIGURE 6-13:
Choose separate placements in order to optimize each aspect of the campaign for the location of the ad.

5. **Determine how you would like to structure your bidding process.**

   Much like the ad placements in Step 4, your bids can be automatically or manually adjusted. Automatic Bidding is easy and effective, but can lead to overpaying for clicks. Manual bidding allows you to carefully monitor the cost and rate at which your ads are receiving clicks and make the necessary adjustments. Manual bidding is more time-consuming, but it ensures that clicks at each bid level (whether it's a bid of $0.10 per click or $1.00) is extracted and maximized. Ask yourself, "Why should I pay even a few cents more for clicks that I can get for less?"

6. **Load your audience segment-specific creative design.**

   Your content strategy includes the development of hypertargeted pieces of content based on specific themes. These pieces are pushed to your audience clusters based on some of the more intricate details of their personalities.

Making your campaign more successful

After you create content that fits each audience cluster (see preceding section), you're ready to model similar content with the message of your ad campaign.

You'll want to remember certain tips when making your way through this process that will make it unique:

>> Not every objective is going to be well suited for a Millennial audience

>> Choose specific audiences for each ad set

>> Separate your Facebook and Instagram ad campaigns

>> Think mobile-first when choosing your ad's creative design

Not every objective is going to be well suited for a Millennial audience

When conducting an awareness campaign, you may want to consider selecting the option to reach local users as opposed to focusing only on your Millennial audience. Millennials nearby are on their mobile devices and accessing Facebook. If you're looking for foot traffic to a brick-and-mortar location, reaching local users is an excellent way to go.

REMEMBER

When running a consideration campaign and choosing to send people to your website, you need to select a very specific landing page. One of the worst mistakes a marketer can make in a campaign is to send users to either a convoluted page or one with too much information. An even worse mistake would be to send them to your home page. Select a page that matches the content and creative design of your ad so that your audience knows that it's in the right place when it arrives on your site.

Choose specific audiences for each ad set

There is a reason that you segmented these users. While many of them may share a couple of characteristics in common, the little differences in their personalities are what sets them apart. Many of those little differences can lead to a significantly higher engagement rate.

Separate your Facebook and Instagram ad campaigns

Placement matters more to a campaign's success than you may think. If you decide to group all or most of your Facebook placements together — for example, in the desktop News Feed, Audience Network, and right-hand column — then at the very least, separate your Instagram placement.

While Instagram and Facebook ads are managed within the same dashboard, you should not treat them as the same network. They're used differently, so content should appear differently. User personalities change from one network to another, and your objectives on one may not be the same as on the other. For those reasons, ad sets should not group both networks together.

Think mobile-first when choosing your ad's creative design

Mobile is where Millennials live. When developing a Facebook ad campaign, mobile needs to be top of mind. Your creative design needs to stand out, but it shouldn't be so busy or unclear that it's ignored.

The goal of most campaigns is to drive your targeted audience to take some form of action. On a mobile device, where scrolling through singularly delivered content happens very quickly, your creative design needs to match what appeals to the audience in question. (Developing a mobile-centric marketing strategy is covered in Chapter 10.)

The term *singularly* delivered is used here because a social network like Facebook or Instagram operates in a single-column layout on a mobile device. Content is, therefore, delivered very quickly, on a rolling basis, more or less one item at a time.

Consider a control group of your general audience to test results against the average

There is nothing wrong with using part of your ad budget at the beginning of any campaign to test average engagement with generic content and your total Millennial audience. This approach allows you to see how average, nonparticular audience members are engaging with your content and set benchmarks accordingly. Then run your hypertargeted elements of the campaign with each group and measure their performance against the average. This meticulous process will highlight where your campaigns are succeeding in their mission and where particular campaigns need adjustments or should be discontinued.

Chapter **7**

Communicating with Millennials Using Twitter and Video

When people think of modern, new media communication, one of the characteristics that almost certainly comes to mind is its bite-sized nature. A question often asked by or to marketers is, "What's your 140-character pitch?" (Twitter communications are limited to 140 characters.) Several micromedia examples exist across multiple platforms, but the example that fits most neatly into a Millennial marketing strategy is Twitter.

In this chapter, I look at the ways you can leverage Twitter to reach your Millennial audience. I also look at the types of video content you can create to engage Millennials.

Determining How Millennials Use Twitter

Twitter once served as a medium through which celebrities shared information on their day-to-day lives. Now, 63 percent of users claim to reference it as a primary news source (Pew); 81 percent of Millennial Twitter users check in daily

(Twitter); and 15 percent of Millennial users check in more than ten times per day (Twitter).

Here are a few traits about Millennials using Twitter that you should know:

>> Millennials primarily follow brands on Twitter to both support them and find out about deals and special offers.

>> Twitter is often the first stop for an angry Millennial customer.

>> The primary source Millennials turn to for news is new media — specifically Twitter.

>> One of the top uses of Twitter, according to Millennials, is to cure boredom.

>> Engagement among Millennials is significantly higher around specific events, such as a sporting match or a major news story.

>> The majority of Millennial Twitter users access the network via a mobile device.

Twitter is an important place for Millennials, and the nature of the content is largely unique for a lot of marketers. What you share is extremely brief. Real estate in a user's feed is highly sought after and therefore quickly fleeting. The endless bombardment of content to a user's feed means that he pays little attention to most of what is appearing. To capitalize on some of the Millennial-focused benefits that you can extract from Twitter, you need a precise strategy and a willingness to invest in targeted advertising.

Building a content strategy for Twitter

Twitter is a pseudo-broadcast network, so a certain degree of self-promotion is not only tolerated by users but is expected. That reality doesn't mean that Twitter users want overt, aggressive sales pitches from branded accounts on an ongoing basis. It just means that it's not unexpected for a brand to showcase content or products more regularly and look to drive users off of the network and onto a landing page.

Building a content strategy on Twitter differs from building one on Facebook, however:

>> **Unlike Facebook, Twitter is far more one-dimensional.** The integrated capabilities, such as branded Pages with events, custom add-ons, and other features don't exist on Twitter as they do on Facebook. To compensate, brands need to be a little more aggressive in their push to drive tangible results from the network (emphasis here on the term "a little"). All of these

network traits factor heavily into the structure of your content strategy on Twitter.

>> **Like on Facebook, a content strategy on Twitter involves quite a few components.** However, the depth into which you'll go with each of these steps isn't quite at the same level as on Facebook. Facebook will serve as the backbone of your Millennial strategy, particularly when it comes to your data.

>> **The elements involved with your content strategy on Twitter are localized to the network.** After you've built up a following on Twitter, you'll be able to get to know them a little bit better.

>> **The audience analysis conducted on Twitter will be carried out within your specific audience.** While loading custom audience lists to Twitter — for example, from an email database — is possible, those lists can be used only for advertising. In Facebook, you can complete an analysis on a particular audience cluster, while in Twitter, the analysis will take place on your followers as a whole.

>> **The data you analyze is largely made up of inferences by Twitter.** These inferences are examined critically based on your audience's engagement statistics, accounts followed, and content shared. Just be aware that while some data is self-reported and very accurate, some may not be as accurate as a profile complete with entirely self-reported information.

REMEMBER

All user data on Twitter is analyzed because, unlike Facebook, everything that happens within a user's Twitter account about data collection happens publicly. So when you see certain bits of information about your followers, you know that this information is highly accurate when compared to a network that pulls only from the accounts that have opted to allow for information to be made public.

Analyzing your Twitter audience

With these vital details understood, you can begin the process of analyzing your Twitter audience. Here are the key steps involved:

1. **Access your Twitter Analytics dashboard and select your Audiences tab.**

   You can find the Twitter Analytics dashboard at `http://analytics.twitter.com` where the Audiences access button is featured in the top menu bar of the dashboard. Access that tab to begin your analysis.

   TECHNICAL
   STUFF

   You can execute this process only after you have a Twitter following and your Analytics account has been accessed. It may take up to 48 hours for your insights to become available, but you can access the account for free at any time. The larger your audience, the more detailed and accurate your insights will be.

2. Identify the size of your Millennial audience.

Access the Demographics tab, shown in Figure 7-1, and identify the size of the group of Millennials in your Twitter audience. In most cases, your Millennial audience will make up the majority of the total audience. The data you're analyzing comes from all users, in all demographic clusters. However, the most active and largest group will be Millennials, which allows you to get an accurate breakdown of their traits.

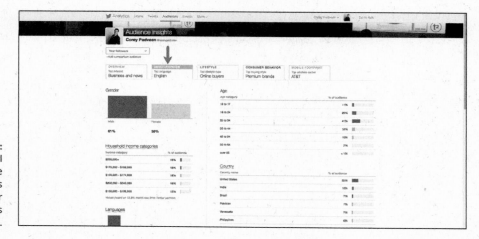

FIGURE 7-1:
The Millennial audience in the Demographics tab of your Audiences dashboard.

TIP

In cases where your Millennial audience is not the largest demographic, you should limit your analysis to only those features that fall onto either all users, at a saturation rate of 100 percent, or at least the vast majority, which in this case would need to be at a saturation rate of 70 percent or higher.

3. Analyze lifestyle categories.

In the Lifestyle and Consumer Behavior tabs, shown in Figure 7-2, start by reviewing the interests associated with your audience, then their buying styles, and finally TV genres that they enjoy watching.

4. Build a brief persona outline.

Unlike the persona you develop on Facebook, which is written in a narrative style, the one for Twitter is going to be much briefer. The details about your audience are more generic, so keep your persona focused on its interests. Also, take into account some of the additional details about household net worth and income pulled from the Demographics tab.

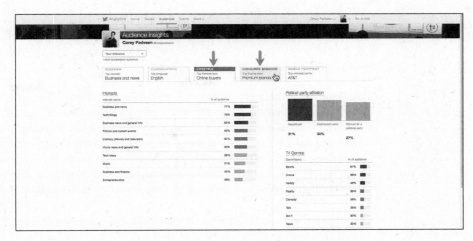

FIGURE 7-2:
The Lifestyle and Consumer Behavior tabs.

After you identify some characteristics that define your audience, you can begin working on the content that drives them to take the actions you desire. Here are a few pointers to keep in mind that make the whole process a lot simpler:

>> **Focus on heavily favored interests.** Look for audience interests that register above 60 percent. The more one-dimensional nature of Twitter should cause you to frame your content in a way that your audience finds intriguing. High rates of interest saturation are a good way to do focus on heavily favored interests.

>> **Don't take your findings too literally.** Because a lot of these findings are based on inferences, there is no guarantee that the information is entirely accurate. Unless a user follows only political accounts and tweets about politics, there is no way to guarantee that politics will be a keen interest of that user. It may just be a coincidence that politics fell into the interest category of a user who, on a whim, followed several political accounts.

REMEMBER

Your voice needs to shine through on Twitter, which may mean sometimes sharing content that is only of partial interest to your audience but demonstrates who you are.

>> **Remember TV genres.** Though TV genre interests may not be crucial to your day-to-day content strategy, they'll be a major factor in your advertising plan. Twitter TV targeting is a powerful tool. You can read more about this topic in Chapter 5.

Planning content strategy segmenting

After you have a better understanding of the users that make up your Twitter audience, you can begin developing the content that will fill your editorial calendar. Remember that Twitter is a real-time platform and the half-life of your content is going to be significantly shorter than it is on Facebook. For that reason, you should use several styles of content, messaging structures, and themes in your content strategy.

To determine the voice you'll use, ask yourself whether the tone and personality you've developed on Facebook will carry over to Twitter. It's likely that it will. You've cultivated a voice on Facebook that is rooted in a significant amount of analyzed data. While your audience persona may shift slightly from one network to the other, maintaining a level of consistency across media is important. So, while you may take a slightly more conversational or professional approach on Twitter, there will definitely be echoes of the voice you've cultivated on Facebook.

To plan out content segments for your editorial calendar, you need to establish the ratio of branded, third-party, and network content you'll use on Twitter:

>> **Branded content** is owned content that you create and control. It's your messaging and your voice. This content will feature links to your website, pseudo-promotional materials, and the messages you've decided to use in your content strategy.

>> **Third-party content** is other people's content shared by you. It's shared simply to provide value to your audience and isn't self-promotional. You may be sharing statistics or figures from another source or linking users to an interesting web article. The focus is on providing some sort of benefit to your audience and highlights a reason to engage with your brand.

>> **Network content** comes in the form of retweets, mentions, and replies. It's far more conversational and is one of the easiest ways to build up the size of your network. While you don't necessarily want to retweet too aggressively and flood your followers' feeds, it's a beneficial form of engagement, particularly for Millennials who weigh small gestures of engagement from brands very heavily.

CALCULATING HALF-LIFE

The *half-life* of your content refers primarily to the amount of engagement your content receives. Essentially, a half-life is defined as the amount of time that it takes for your piece of content to receive half of the engagement it will receive in its lifetime. So, if your content receives 100 engagement points (in the form of likes, shares, comments, and so on), then its half-life will be calculated as the amount of time it takes to reach 50 engagement points. This means that if you receive 50 engagement points in 20 minutes and it takes another six hours to reach 100, your half-life is 20 minutes.

Determining the ratios at which you're going to share these three types of content is an important step. A good approach to the branded, third-party, and network ratio is 40-40-20. Of course, this ratio may change based on how you plan to use Twitter, but it's a good starting point. Follow this ratio with some close analysis of the results and adjust the ratios as you see engagement begin to take shape.

Choosing content for Millennials

The next stage of planning is related to your content segments themselves. After you decide your tone and your ratios, you can apply them to a variety of content types that make up the mix you want to share. Certain types of content will resonate with Millennials much better than others on Twitter. Following are some content types to consider:

>> **Humor:** Millennials love to laugh. That has been made clear with the abundance of new media trends that have made their way into the mainstream. These trends include such things as memes, GIFs, and videos. Thematically, you may want to consider incorporating humor into your content mix where it's appropriate. That isn't to say that you need to shift away from the voice you've created. If humor doesn't mix well with your brand, then don't force it. Twitter, by nature, is ripe for brief, comedic content. If you can add humor to the mix, do it.

>> **Visuals:** If a visual accompaniment like a GIF or an image is available for a tweet, you should consider it. Millennials primarily use Twitter on mobile devices where visual components are displayed more prominently, so your tweet has a much better chance of being seen as a user scrolls through his feed.

>> **Expertise:** Sharing your expertise is an essential part of any successful content strategy and should be included in the mix. Not only is it great content for your audience, but it highlights your industry-leading expertise as well.

>> **Offers:** Millennials are expressly on Twitter to receive specials and discounts ahead of the general public. Share them whenever possible.

>> **Topical information:** Twitter's brief, real-time nature means that if a broad conversation is taking place online, your audience may be a part of it. Jump into conversations using a hashtag trending in your network. You can also determine trending topics from your audience analysis. Simply cross-reference the interest categories with trending topics to find an opportunity to participate in a timely conversation.

>> **Information about causes:** Social issues and causes are themes that are found at the root of many Millennial conversations. Showing your support for an issue can be a powerful means of connecting with your audience.

However, many of these topics can be divisive. Decide whether to participate in these conversations on a case-by-case basis.

>> **Customer service:** Social care or customer service on social media was first popularized using Twitter. Now, of course, social care takes place across all media. However, Twitter is still seen as one of the crucial cornerstones of any successful social care strategy. Offering assistance and providing service over Twitter is well-received by Millennials who prefer new media outreach to traditional forms of customer service.

Developing Your Editorial Calendar

Your editorial calendar on Twitter is going to differ significantly from your editorial calendar on Facebook (see Chapter 6). Your network and topical content are examples of content that you can't plan. Therefore, they can't show up in your editorial calendar. What you can plan, however, is your branded content and, to some extent, your third-party content.

Figure 7-3 shows you an example of an editorial calendar designed for Twitter. The table is broken down to cover any and all aspects of content that will be shared on Twitter. While your editorial calendar doesn't need to be as detailed as the one shown in Figure 7-3, it should feature your branded tweets. You can share, reuse, and repurpose these tweets on an ongoing basis. If you want to promote a particular white paper or blog post over time, you should create a series of tweets that you can share with your network.

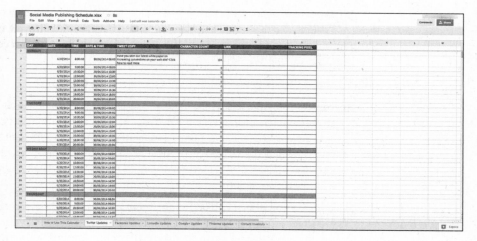

FIGURE 7-3: An example of an editorial calendar designed for Twitter.

Only a small fraction of your audience will see your content when it's posted. Of those users, an even smaller segment will actually pay attention to it. For this reason, you need to regularly schedule the same tweets to show up on your monthly editorial calendar.

Repurposing your content on a rolling basis

There is no reason for previously posted content to disappear from your editorial calendar. Repurpose it as often as possible while it's still relevant. You can easily rework tweets that link your audience to a particular post or landing page. You can use different kinds of media and structures to entice users to click without having to repeat the same message. For example, an audience member may overlook an article with a particular title, but sharing that same article with an image, statistic, or any other media type may capture that member's attention. Just a bit of reworking can make all the difference.

Keeping your schedule flexible

On Twitter, an editorial calendar should function more like a guidebook than a rulebook. Some themes may change, or new content may become available. Some event may arise that causes you to abandon your calendar for a few hours, days, or even weeks.

The purpose of your calendar is to help you develop new content and keep tweets flowing. It should not be treated as a document that is set in stone.

Planning for themed content

Remember to include themed posts and days in your editorial calendar. These themes may repeat over the course of the week or month and can certainly overlap with the ones you created for Facebook.

Leveraging insights

You can determine when you have the highest engagement using the Twitter Analytics dashboard, shown in Figure 7-4. High engagement at certain times doesn't mean that you shouldn't also tweet when there is less activity with your content. It only means that when you start out, you should schedule your most important and objective-oriented tweets during the most active times. Also, test other times on your own to see whether opportunities exist that Twitter hasn't identified.

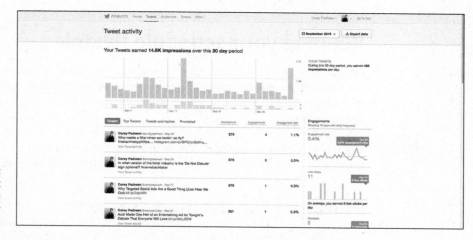

FIGURE 7-4: Analyze the best time to share with your Twitter audience.

Determining your evergreen content

If you have content that will be relevant for the foreseeable future, it's considered to be *evergreen*. You can share your evergreen content at any time, during any cycle, and still lead to clicks and engagement from your audience. Identifying that content will help you drive up your engagement and traffic on Twitter.

Making time for promotional content

You need to pick certain times when you're going to share promotional content. You should share promotional content sparingly, and it should be relatively tame. Gently sprinkle it throughout your editorial calendar and don't let the frequency overtake any other form of content.

Developing Twitter Content

With the rest of your strategy in place, you can develop your Twitter content. Of course, you can't prepare all of your content ahead of time. Third-party and network content will be spontaneous. The content you do want to develop ahead of time for Twitter will include

>> Evergreen

>> Promotional

>> Third-party sourced

Evergreen content

Your evergreen content will be sourced from your own media — primarily your website and blog — and you can continue to put it in rotation. Of course, your tweets will need to differ, and the structure of that messaging may change, but the landing page or content will remain the same.

Evergreen content comes in many forms, such as

>> Questions to your audience

>> Fun facts about your organization's process or history

>> Industry facts and figures, which you may need to simply update as they change

>> Links to branded content, such as white papers, eBooks, or nontopical blog posts

TIP

You can use evergreen content at any point in time, so it can very quickly fill holes in your editorial calendar.

Promotional content

While some evergreen content directs users to your website and branded content, it's not overtly promotional. Millennials reject aggressive sales techniques on social media. They are, however, somewhat more accepting of broadcast content designed to drive traffic to your website or push a particular product or service on Twitter.

TIP

Develop some soft sell content that you can use to promote your brand, but remember that this content is merely tolerated, not enjoyed. In Figure 7-5, you can see an example of a promotional tweet that isn't particularly aggressive. Develop content that fits this mold and use it sparingly.

FIGURE 7-5:
An example of promotional content on Twitter.

Third-party sourced content

The last type of content you need to develop won't be content at all. It will be a Twitter list. This list will contain the primary accounts from which you'll pull content to retweet, reply to, or mention. Of course, you'll add other accounts over time, but developing a preliminary list of accounts that share great content is a great way to simplify the process.

TECHNICAL STUFF

To create a list on Twitter, click on the profile picture icon and choose Lists from the menu. Then select the option to create a new list and name your list something along the lines of Third Party Content Providers. Then, when an account is found that may fit into this list, select the small gear icon on the user's profile and choose to add the user to your new list, as shown in Figure 7-6.

FIGURE 7-6:
Adding a user to
a list on Twitter.

Reaching Millennial Twitter Users

After your content strategy is in place, you should take full advantage of Twitter's advertising platform. Because Twitter data doesn't zero in on Millennials like it does on Facebook, you should access your Twitter advertising dashboard and begin promoting specific tweets. You should also start running targeted campaigns geared toward Millennials.

Targeting Millennials in Twitter ads

Because of ad restrictions, targeting by age group isn't available on Twitter. Therefore, you should focus on targeting the Millennial mindset. You can target Millennials largely through interest and behavioral identification. Simply follow these steps:

1. **Access your Twitter Ads dashboard and create a new free campaign by visiting** `http://ads.twitter.com`.

   The button to create a new campaign appears in the top right-hand corner of the screen, as shown in Figure 7-7.

2. **Select the campaign type you'd like to run.**

   You can run several kinds of campaigns on Twitter. Each one is constructed to either drive engagement or performance.

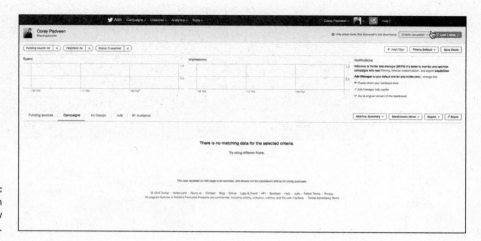

FIGURE 7-7:
Click this button
to create a new
campaign.

3. **Choose the locations where you'd like to reach Millennials.**

   Identify locations where you'd like your ads to be seen.

4. **Begin by selecting a series of interests.**

   Remember that you're building a Millennial mindset audience that isn't rooted in age, so interests and behaviors are the most important considerations. Though the two criteria are largely interchangeable, interests have a slight edge over behaviors because they're more indicative of the levels of engagement your target audience has when faced with certain types of content.

   In Figure 7-8, you can see some examples of the interests list from which you can choose. They can include interests such as automotive, business, gaming, health, movies, technology, and several dozen more.

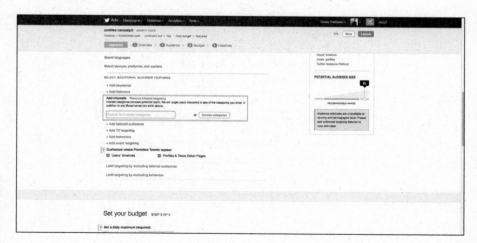

FIGURE 7-8:
Choose the
interests of your
Millennial
audience.

5. **Select audience characteristics.**

Next, focus on behaviors that fit your target user. This step is where you can target the socioeconomic status of Millennials. In Figure 7-9, you can see choices as they relate to home ownership.

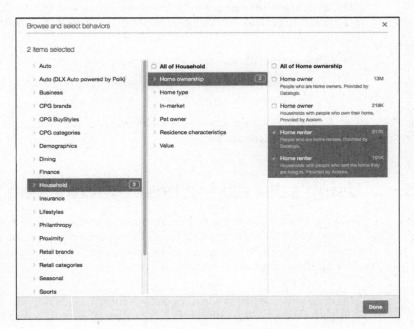

FIGURE 7-9:
Targeting users
that rent as
opposed to
owning a home.

6. **Select accounts that users follow on Twitter and/or choose keywords they've used.**

If you like, you can consider choosing followers and keywords that match your content and voice, which allows you to get specific in your targeting. Being specific ensures that the rhetoric you're using fits with terms they've used in the past.

Running campaigns on Twitter

You can run several different campaigns on Twitter. The following list highlights tactics and objectives for nine types:

>> **Tweet engagements:** Select a series of tweets that have been shared or created for the campaign to promote within your selected users' feeds to drive up engagement.

- » **Video views:** Increase views of a native video with a targeted group of users.

- » **Website visits/conversions:** Drive clicks to or conversions on your website with populated previews of the selected landing page, making your tweet more visible.

- » **App installs/re-engagements:** Drive up installs of your app directly from Twitter or get users to re-engage with your app when they haven't opened it in some time.

- » **Followers:** Build your follower base with a very specific selection of criteria.

- » **Leads on Twitter:** Collect user data from targeted Twitter users interested in finding out more about your product, service, or offer.

- » **Awareness:** Raise awareness of your brand and your message on a cost-per-thousand-impression basis.

Using advertising best practices on Twitter

You need to keep in mind certain best practices when running an ad campaign on Twitter. Millennials engage at a much higher rate with content that fits certain criteria. To drive up your organic engagement and maximize your ad budget, consider implementing the following best practices:

TIP

- » **Keep your messages short.** Tweets are short to begin with, but the shorter your tweet, the higher the likelihood it catches the eye of your audience. It may sound counterintuitive, but the reality is that Millennials tend to skip over longer tweets and messages and read those that are short and to the point. If you can get your message across in fewer than 140 characters, do it.

  Studies have shown that the ideal length for a tweet is roughly 100 characters. You should aim to hit that number without compromising the focus of your message.

- » **Avoid mysterious or ominous tweets.** If there is one thing that Millennials don't have time for, it's guessing games. The click-to-reveal approach to marketing and advertising may have worked with previous generations, but Millennials have plenty of other content and media to get to. The majority of your Millennial audience will completely ignore any tweet or a link that doesn't clearly state what it is.

- » **Address a problem and offer a link to the solution.** Showcase your product or service in your message and clearly indicate why it's of value to your target audience. Highlighting the benefits of clicking on a link or sharing data will lead to a much more intent-driven level of engagement.

>> **Include graphics that help explain your point.** The graphic you choose should help build your message. If your tweet is sending users to an eBook, an image of the cover is ideal. If you're an auto parts dealer and you're promoting a sale on mufflers, showcase a muffler in your image. This advice may seem like common sense, but all too often a generic image or a quirky image that does little to complement the tweet is used. That's a wasted opportunity.

>> **Avoid the overuse of hashtags.** Simply put, one hashtag is more than enough. Unless you have a particular reason for the use of a hashtag, it doesn't have a place in your ads. Hashtags today are much more useful for tagging specific events or topics.

WARNING

If your tweet features the word marketing, don't put a hashtag in front of it. That is a dated practice, and the abundance of hashtags screams spam to any Millennial user.

>> **Tailor your message to your targeted audience.** Take the time to develop content tailored to the characteristics you've identified. Personalization is the name of the game when it comes to Millennials, so get as personal as possible with your content.

Engaging with Your Audience Using Video

By nature, Millennials are a visual bunch. The fastest growing social networks of the last several years — for example, Instagram, Pinterest, and Snapchat — are visual platforms. And who are the users that make up this fast-growing base? Millennials, of course. It's a good idea to accompany most, if not all, of your new media content with a visual. No visual medium is more engaging, attractive, and effective than video.

What makes video so compelling to Millennials? For starters, video is the most easily digestible medium. In a matter of seconds, viewers can make a determination as to whether or not video content appeals to them. If not, they move on to the next piece of content without much of an investment. Video is also the most entertaining and interactive media type. Moving pictures have captivated audiences since the Lumière Brothers first introduced them to audiences in 1895. That interest level has only increased over time. Also, Millennials have grown up at a time when visual technologies have significantly advanced.

A generation ago, video existed at the movies and on television. Today, for even the oldest of Millennials, that reality never existed. Portable video has been available in the form of hand-held gaming devices since 1989. That has expanded over the last few decades to include smartphones and tablets. Millennials have evolved into their consumer selves in a world where video content has been the primary source of knowledge transfer and content delivery. It's the preferred way for Millennials to receive information. Put simply, if you want to attract Millennials, video needs to be a part of your strategy.

Creating video content that resonates with Millennials

While Millennials prefer receiving information in video form, simply creating a video won't guarantee that you attract them to your brand. Millennials possess certain traits that you'll want to consider when creating your video strategy:

>> **Millennials have a short attention span.** A 2015 Canadian study by Microsoft entitled "Attention Spans" found that the average attention span of adults is about eight seconds. With so much content flooding the average consumer's life, attention is pulled in many directions. Millennials are exposed to thousands of branded pieces of content every day, and your video content is competing for some of that time.

REMEMBER

Because of the abundance of content and their notoriously short attention span, Millennials have developed a subconscious process to determine the value of a video. If they quickly determine that the video isn't stimulating enough, then it's on to the next one. Remember that process when you're developing the opening content.

>> **Video needs to provide real value.** If the viewer can't derive utility, it does more harm than good to your brand. You need to provide some benefit to the Millennial viewer if you want to build a lasting relationship. That benefit can be humor, information, or one of the other values covered in this section.

>> **Most viewers won't see the end.** The majority of your Millennial viewers, even those that stick around the longest, won't see the very end of your video. Once the climax of your video closes out, there is a distinct possibility that your audience will move on to something else.

>> **Quality isn't crucial, but it matters.** This generation has grown up collecting hours of video footage on a small, hand-held device. High-end production quality is great to have, so if it's an option, you should choose it. But Millennials watch hours of Snapchat video, Facebook Live video, and other mobile and hand-held video content. If your video content isn't studio quality, it won't necessarily discourage Millennials from engaging with it. That said, professionalism is something that Millennials care about, so keep it as professional as possible. You should use the best quality video that you can afford. Also, native

video is always the preference. Millennials engage much more heavily with video that was loaded to a network than to external links that populate a feed. YouTube videos are watched most on YouTube, Facebook videos on the social network itself, and so on.

A video is considered to be *native* when it's shared directly to the network and not loaded as a link. A video loaded to Facebook and played within the app or on the desktop version of the network is a native video, while a video loaded to YouTube and linked to a post on Facebook isn't considered native.

Looking at content types

After you have a better understanding of how Millennials view video content on new media, you can begin developing your own. Of course, you should aim to develop content that fits your brand and strategy. However, certain types of content resonate very well with Millennials:

>> **Information:** How-to, instructional, lifehack, and other information-filled videos are a great way to drive engagement and are often the most searched for by Millennials. These searches are intent-driven, and video is the most easily digested form of content in this case. Informational videos benefit you by showcasing your expertise and your brand.

>> **Humor:** Humor is always a topic that viewers flock to, but remember that humor is subjective. Satire is another area that can lead to high engagement, but satire can also be a sensitive topic for some viewers, so approach it with caution.

>> **Behind-the-scenes:** One of the best ways to build a relationship with Millennials is to use behind-the-scenes content that showcases your process and the inner workings of your organization. This type of content develops a greater connection between the viewer and your brand and helps build loyalty.

>> **Reviews and opinion:** When conducting prepurchase research, Millennials often turn to online video reviews. They feel that these reviews display a level of honesty that doesn't come across in written reviews. Millennials believe that when a product's actual user is walking them through the pros and cons of the product, they're receiving an unbiased opinion.

>> **Interviews:** Conducting an interview with an industry leader or influencer will certainly get the interest of your Millennial audience. If that interview is broadcast live, with the option to open up the floor for questions, you can probably expect a huge amount of engagement. For this reason, you should identify your industry influencers and leverage that influence to build a large audience of prospects.

Making your content work

After you understand your Millennial audience's affinity for video content and are familiar with the types of content they like, you're almost ready to get started on the development of your video content. You'll want to keep in mind the following pointers to ensure that your video content is successful:

>> **Keep your content short.** Millennials don't like to waste time. Unless they have an absolute need, such as a class assignment or work project, to watch your entire video, they likely will abandon the video if it drags on too long. A two-minute video is ideal. If you create anything longer, your retention rate will likely begin to slip. If you can get your point across in less time, that's even better.

>> **Use a light touch when branding your videos.** You don't want to use overt sales tactics when branding your video content. A small logo or floating bar at the bottom of your video with your website URL should suffice. The branding at the beginning and end of your video can be a little bit more apparent, but while sharing content in the body of the video, subtlety is the name of the game.

>> **Don't place your call-to-action at the end.** If you wait until the very last minute to share a call-to-action, a lot of Millennial viewers who have already left will miss it. Integrating a call-to-action or using an overlay in the middle of your video, as shown in Figure 7-10, can lead to a much higher engagement rate. One reason for this is that it will simply be seen by more prospects.

FIGURE 7-10:
A call-to-action overlay in your YouTube video can lead to a much higher interaction rate.

A *call-to-action* is an instruction to the audience designed to encourage an immediate response. A call-to-action pushes your audience to go beyond the current page or piece of content using actionable phrases such as "Buy Now," "Click Here," or "Find Out More."

>> **Sound matters more than pictures.** Because of a Millennial's focus on visuals, you may think that picture quality matters more than sound quality. However, that's not the case. Millennials have grown up with mobile video primarily shot and viewed through a mobile device's camera, so they pay more attention to the sound quality than the picture quality. So, regarding an investment, you'd be better off investing in higher quality audio recording equipment than video equipment.

>> **Quickly get to the content's value.** In a two-minute video, you shouldn't spend 45 seconds introducing the concept before getting to the value-added content in the body. Your audience can go elsewhere if its members feel like you're taking too long to get to the point. Millennials are looking for utility when they actively engage with a piece of content, so get to that utility quickly!

Soft-selling your brand with video content

It can be challenging to create video content that both promotes your brand and provides value. The key is to balance the two objectives without losing sight of either one. If your focus is too geared toward the value proposition, Millennials will likely overlook your branding and never connect with your business. If you focus too much on branding, Millennials may never stick around to see what you have to offer. The following useful pointers help you create balanced video content:

>> **Bookend your branding.** Your videos should both open and close with an explicit reference to your brand. The opening and closing are essentially the only two places where an overt reference to your company is appropriate. While you may have some subtle branding on a floating bar at the top or bottom of your screen throughout the entire video, clear, full-screen branding will be useful both at the start and end of your content.

>> **Reference your brand, products, or services when appropriate.** When discussing a process in a how-to-video, for example, you should try to work your products or services into the description. Say, for example, you're an exercise equipment manufacturer, and you're sharing the proper technique for a particular exercise in your video. This demonstration provides you with the opportunity to use your own equipment and reference it by name.

» **Close with a verbal call-to-action.** Although you may have a call-to-action overlay in your video or a call-to-action featured at the end of your video, you should include a verbal call-to-action as part of your video's conclusion. Integrated buttons and calls-to-action can be effective, but users are engaged in the video itself. If the call-to-action can be a part of it, then there is an even higher likelihood that Millennials will listen to it and take action.

» **Highlight your successes.** When possible, highlight a unique approach that your company has taken and explain how it has generated success for your clients. This soft-sell technique showcases why your brand may be a better choice than the competition.

Chapter **8**

Using Native Mobile Social Media

I f you expect to captivate a Millennial audience using social media, one primary focus should be mobile. (The steps to developing a comprehensive mobile marketing strategy are covered in Chapter 10.)

In this chapter, you develop a more robust understanding of the social networks that function primarily, if not entirely, on mobile. You find out how you can strategically leverage these applications and networks to effectively engage Millennials.

Delving into Instagram and Snapchat

Two networks with entirely mobile experiences are Instagram and Snapchat. Both of these networks have seen explosive growth. While Instagram is owned by Facebook and shares several marketing and business tools with its parent company, you need to take an entirely different marketing approach on Instagram.

Being aware of the following characteristics can help you develop your strategies for these two networks:

>> **Instagram and Snapchat users can't be bothered to leave the app.** To engage Millennials within either of these networks, you need to do it in a way that allows them to stay in the app. (Instagram does have options that will allow users to click through to a landing page, but the overwhelming preference is to stay put.)

>> **Snapchat is a very personal experience.** It seems only fitting that as the generation of intimate sharers grew, a product would be introduced that offered the most intimate environment of all — just you and your network with close-up pictures. This structure makes Snapchat an ideal network to use when building relationships with your Millennials.

>> **A like on Instagram doesn't necessarily indicate interest.** Millennials may like a post they come across on Instagram, but that doesn't indicate their interest in the product or brand. On Instagram, a like may equate to a "Thanks for sharing" rather than a marker of interest. This characteristic makes measuring user interest and audience viability harder for marketers.

>> **Millennials are attracted to visual storytelling methods.** Instagram and Snapchat are pure visual media. There may be options to add a description on Instagram or a caption on Snapchat, but at their core, they are both all about the visuals. Millennials are visual creatures, and they want to digest a brand narrative in a visual way.

Creating a Strategy to Reach Millennials on Instagram

Before you begin crafting your Instagram strategy, you need to ask yourself, "Does this network make sense for my brand?" This question is important because any organization can easily just dive right in. However, if you're going to force visuals into your content strategy when it doesn't fit, it simply won't benefit you or your Millennial audience. Your efforts will go unnoticed and you'll waste your investment. If, however, you can create a meaningful visual content strategy for your brand, then Instagram is where you'll engage Millennials most effectively.

To develop an effective Instagram marketing strategy, ask yourself the following questions in order. (Each answer will help you move on to the next point.)

>> **Which segments of your Millennial audience would you like to reach on Instagram?** To answer this question, you can look at the audience analysis you conducted on Facebook and choose the Millennial audience pockets that you'd most like to engage on Instagram.

Look at some of the characteristics Millennials possess and identify those that are somewhat more creative. The nature of Instagram suggests that these audience clusters will be far more receptive to your content.

>> **What are the driving characteristics that engage these audience segments?** Look for commonalities among your selected audience pockets. Finding common ground will make the development of your Instagram content significantly easier.

>> **What creative spin can you put on these driving characteristics?** After you identify some common ground and define criteria in your audience clusters, determine how to creatively exploit those details. Remember that Instagram offers options for both photo and short video content, so your content strategy can leverage either or both of them to attract the selected audience.

>> **How often do you want to share Instagram content?** Just as you've created editorial calendars for your other social media platforms, you'll want to develop a calendar for Instagram as well. Put together a preliminary idea of how frequently you'll share content to Instagram based on

- The type of content you're sharing

- The audience you're targeting

- The amount of Instagram advertising you're planning

>> **What advertising investment would you like to make on Instagram?** Advertising on Instagram is a little bit more expensive than it is on Facebook, but your audience is highly engaged. While you don't need to decide on an exact budget figure right away, you should determine what ratio of your ad dollars will be allocated to Instagram once you're ready to start a campaign.

Although Instagram is crucial to use when reaching Millennials, it isn't going to have as robust an impact as Facebook. Much of your Instagram efforts will fall into the brand awareness and relationship development categories because, like Snapchat, Millennial users don't want to be pulled away from the application. However, running ad campaigns on the network does have benefits, and you can leverage the network itself to take your brand awareness and Millennial relationships even further.

Leveraging influencer marketing on Instagram

Instagram is a particularly effective platform to use to leverage influencers. Several influencers on the network have large, fiercely loyal Millennial followings. To reach these influencers, some universal steps will apply to virtually every influencer outreach campaign on which you embark:

1. **Compile a list of your industry's top influencers on Instagram.**

   This step is going to take some research on your part. Of course, there are Instagram influencer outreach tools like Ninja Outreach (`https://ninjaoutreach.com`), shown in Figure 8-1. These types of tools can make your life simpler, but some manual work will be needed to pinpoint the exact selection of influencers that matter to your audience.

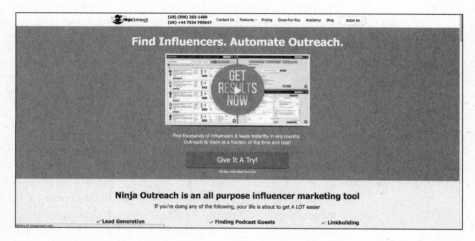

FIGURE 8-1:
Ninja Outreach finds Instagram influencers.

2. **Narrow your list to include those influencers that connect with your target Millennial audience**

   After you've built your list of influencers, you need to start digging a little deeper. Review the types of audience members and engagement these influencers have with their followers. Are these the right Millennials to reach with your message? Will your brand make sense to this audience?

3. **Prioritize your list of influencers according to the impact they can have on your target audience**

   After you've identified the influencers that are both in your industry and reaching your target prospects, it's time to prioritize these accounts according to audience value. This step is where the hard work comes in. You need to determine the kind of engagement each influencer receives and prioritize those that have the highest, actionable engagement with your targeted group.

TIP

When evaluating influencer engagement, look for active keywords or phrases that suggest that the audience enjoys the content and plans to take the specified action. For example, a user may tag a friend and add a comment like "This is awesome!" suggesting an action be taken. Or it may take the form of a statement of intent, like "I'm getting this." Be on the lookout for this specific kind of engagement when prioritizing your influencers.

4. **Identify the influencers that would most logically pair with your brand**

While an influencer may have plenty of followers on Instagram, it doesn't mean that they're ideally suited to pair with your product. Review the content and messaging shared by each of your selected influencers and determine the best fit. Those highest on the prioritized follower list should be the first influencers you contact.

5. **Develop an outreach strategy tailored to each of your selected influencers**

Influencers are contacted on a regular basis. If you want a chance of connecting with them, you should personalize your outreach. Take some time to get to know the influencer beyond simple stats and tailor your outreach to a unique trait or feature. The way to customize your message to each influencer is the same as the way you hypertarget messaging to individual audience clusters.

6. **Begin the outreach process**

After you have customized messaging and a prioritized list of influencers, it's time to start reaching out to them.

7. **Create campaigns that fit with each influencer's unique style**

Be prepared to change up your campaign for each individual influencer. Remember that many of these users have followers in common. You don't want their followers to get the exact same content on several of their accounts.

8. **Stagger your outreach campaigns**

On the same note, stagger your campaigns over time. You don't want to blunt the impact of your brand awareness campaigns by sending them all at the same time. If six influencers share your content at the same time, the campaign will be less effective. All the content will flood users' feeds right away and then simply disappear. Even if Instagram's algorithm causes the content to show up several times in an individual user's feed, it's not worth the risk.

Advertising best practices on Instagram

Your content strategy on Instagram will be geared largely toward engaging Millennials' creative sides. This organic process takes time and greatly benefits your brand's awareness. When you want these users to start taking action, it's time to make the investment in an Instagram advertising campaign.

While Instagram ad campaigns are managed in the same ad dashboard as Facebook, it's a mistake to equate the two platforms. You'd be hard pressed to find an example of an advertising campaign that is precisely the same on both. The platforms are different, the media is different, and the user base is different. Perhaps most important is the fact that the value and objectives of each network are different. Figure 8-2 shows how to choose an Instagram campaign on Facebook Ads Manager.

FIGURE 8-2: Run an Instagram campaign as a stand-alone option on Facebook.

When you run an Instagram campaign, you want to stick to certain industry best practices. The following list highlights the most important ones:

>> **Convey as much information in your image or video as possible.** When choosing your creative design, be sure to select something that really highlights what you're trying to say. You have several design options, such as video or a slideshow (see Figure 8-3). You could complete your Instagram ad with just a description, but because Instagram is an entirely visual network, the majority of Millennial users are going to take a moment to digest your visuals and then move on. If you can't get your message across using visual media, then your concept may not be right for an Instagram ad campaign.

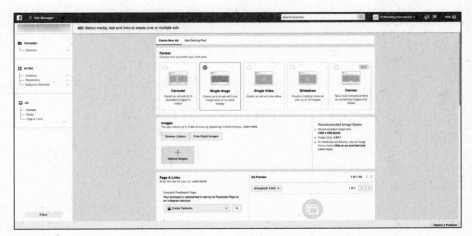

FIGURE 8-3:
Visual choices for
an Instagram ad.

>> **Choose an objective that leads to instant action.** When running an Instagram campaign, you can choose from several objectives, such as sending clicks to your website, getting conversions on your website, encouraging app installs, getting video views, and driving reach, awareness, or page post engagement. Most users want to stay within the app, which is why so many of these objectives allow users to remain on Instagram. To derive real benefits from Instagram, focus your efforts on an actionable campaign that goes beyond awareness or post engagement.

>> **Leverage the power of short videos.** Considering that your creative content needs to convey as much information as possible, a short video may be the most valuable type of content for you to share. If you're in the business of selling cookware, you may want to consider a video that showcases your products in action with a call-to-action to drive viewers to a checkout page.

>> **Tailor the ad to the selected audience cluster.** Just as you've done with your content and ad campaigns on all the other networks, you want to ensure that your Instagram ad content and target audience matches up closely. Instagram is a particularly personal experience, so your ads need to be personalized as well. You'll waste valuable ad dollars sending a generic campaign to a general Millennial audience.

Navigating Snapchat

Snapchat is a network that is not for everyone. In fact, most brands haven't figured out the best way to use it. While advertising options do exist, some are cost-prohibitive. Those that are accessible are mainly geared toward brand awareness.

To ensure that a presence on Snapchat is right for your brand, ask yourself the following checklist of questions:

>> Are you a particularly visual brand?

>> Do you have an interesting process or team?

>> Can you devote time to developing and sharing content?

>> Are brand awareness and audience engagement high on your list of priorities?

>> Do you have enough content to maintain a steady flow?

If you answered yes to all these questions, then your brand is right for Snapchat.

Encouraging engagement

To effectively use Snapchat, you must be willing to devote time to regularly sharing content without being able to measure it. Unlike Facebook, Twitter, and other major social networks, Snapchat doesn't currently have an insights dashboard from which to evaluate your successes or failures. The app is really made to encourage engagement, which you can do in three way:

>> Snaps

>> Stories

>> Advertising

Snaps

At the root of Snapchat's functionality is the individual snap itself. This one-to-one or one-to-few process is the core functionality of the ephemeral photo-sharing application. Your brand can engage in image or text-based conversations with individual users in the chat section of the app and leverage the capability to create a more personal connection to your brand.

TECHNICAL STUFF

References to one-to-one, one-to-few, or one-to-many have to do with the scale of reach of a particular content initiative. A *one-to-one interaction* is one between one user (in this case, you) and one individual. *One-to-few interactions* take place between one user and a select few that are handpicked. *One-to-many interactions* occur when content is shared to the public or an audience outside the control of the sharer — for example, a public Facebook post, a tweet, or, in the case of Snapchat, a Story (see the next section).

While individual chat services exist between consumers and brands, such as Face-book Messenger and Twitter Direct Messages, the nature of Snapchat lends itself to a much more human experience. You may not engage in direct snap conversations as regularly as you might leverage other aspects of the product, such as Stories, but it's a valuable feature that can help build your brand's persona and create loyalty among your Millennial fans and followers.

Stories

Stories fall into the one-to-many category of marketing. When sharing a snap to your story, you're creating a linear narrative made up of a series of publicly shared snaps. By default, your Stories are shared to all your followers. On Snapchat, your followers are made up of users you've added to your network and those who have added you. As a brand, however, you want to reach even more people so that you can quickly make your Stories public by accessing your Snapchat settings, shown in Figure 8-4. Stories allow you to humanize your brand and share content directly to mobile devices, which translates into a much more personal interaction than traditional media.

FIGURE 8-4:
Reach more Snapchat users by switching your Story share settings to public.

Advertising

Individuals and brands can leverage the popularity of what Snapchat calls Filters. You can create custom Geofilters for both personal and business use. When a snap is taken, users can scroll through a series of Filters — ranging from location markers to temperature stamps — and apply one to the image. You can create Geofilters under the labels of Community and On-Demand.

Artists and designers can create Community Geofilters for free to showcase a city, university, landmark, or public location. In these cases, brand logos or personal markers can't be featured. Once approved by Snapchat, these Geofilters can be applied to the users' snaps. In the case of On-Demand Geofilters, users and brands can pay to create personalized artwork for events, businesses, locations, and more. In this case, a logo can be used, and a specific area can be selected and targeted with the filter.

Filters aren't particularly expensive. They're similarly priced for both personal and business use and can be targeted to a particular location. An example of the On-Demand Geofilter dashboard is shown in Figure 8-5.

FIGURE 8-5: On-Demand Geofilters are a great way to feature your branding.

Measurement criteria on Snapchat are limited, so you need to be comfortable not receiving detailed reporting if you decide to leverage these tactics. For most brands, additional forms of advertising are cost-prohibitive. Custom Lenses and advertising in Discover are really available only to the largest of media companies. In January 2015, Snapchat advertising started at about $750,000 per day. While that number has gone down significantly, it's still much higher than any other form of social advertising.

Using content best practices on Snapchat

To engage Millennials on Snapchat, certain best practices can help you build a following:

>> **Choose a discoverable name.** In order for users to find you on Snapchat, they need to type the exact handle you've selected. For that reason, you should choose a username that is easy to recognize and, if necessary, easy to guess. If your brand name is John's Store, don't choose the username johnniestopshop because users will start their search by using your brand's name. If your brand name isn't an option, try something universal, like thebeststore or something along those lines. This name would be easy enough to find and may lead to audience development from parties simply searching for that term.

>> **Make your stories public.** After you've set up your brand account, configure your Snapchat profile so that it's as discoverable as possible. In your Settings, which you can access by clicking on the small widget in the right corner of your Snapchat screens, scroll down to the section titled Who Can. There, you'll want to make sure that both options are set to Everyone as opposed to the default My Friends.

>> **Keep it clean.** This tip may sound like a given, and yet it's surprising how often brands find themselves on the wrong end of a PR nightmare. Typically, something that should have been reviewed was shared without a second thought.

Follow this simple rule when it comes to sharing content on Snapchat: If you need to ask yourself whether or not what you're sharing is appropriate, you'd be better off not sharing it. You can apply that rule, by the way, across all social media. Cultivate a voice and stick with that while sharing content in the app.

>> **Pick your moments.** It can be tempting to share every little thing to your story, but users get bored quickly. If you aren't grabbing their attention with short, digestible content that fits your voice and content strategy, they simply

won't watch what you share. Take time to refine your content and choose the moments you share based on that refined strategy. If it's casual Friday in the office, for example, and you're sharing a snap or two of the workforce, that's fine. But don't get too carried away and share every single outfit the staff is wearing. On Snapchat, repetitive content is much more apparent, and an overzealous sharing strategy can quickly turn off your audience.

» **Avoid self-promotion.** A branded Geofilter or a logo somewhere in the shot is fine, but unlike Twitter or even Facebook, Snapchat is far from a broadcast network. One of the easiest ways to chase away your audience is to consistently share blatantly promotional materials.

REMEMBER

A cold, stoic branded snap with no personality or attempt to connect with your audience beyond self-promotion is a surefire way to lose followers and views. A brand connection has already been established through the act of following. Now it is up to you to build their loyalty through content.

Chapter 9

Creating a Multichannel Media Strategy

The goal to finding success with Millennial audience members is to embrace their differences without abandoning your brand's individuality. This blending can, at times, be difficult. You need a strategy that you can adjust to fit both the specifics of the network as well as the idiosyncrasies of your target audience. All the while, you want to maintain the brand persona you've worked so hard to cultivate. (The differentiating characteristics that define traditional and new media are covered in Chapters 5 and 6.)

In this chapter, the theme is unity. An important key to acquiring and retaining a Millennial audience is creating a brand presence that is identifiable, relatable, and consistent. To reach a point where your brand presence possesses these qualities, you need to unify your brand's persona on every one of the networks, platforms, and applications on which you have a presence.

Grasping the Unity of Media Types

Every action you take, whether through print, TV targeting, social, or mobile, will either help or hinder the growth of your brand persona and reputation.

Consider how active Millennials are on various media types. The American Press Institute (www.americanpressinstitute.org) has found that Millennials are, on average, active on 2.9 to 3.7 of the major seven social networks(Facebook, Twitter, YouTube, Instagram, Pinterest, Reddit, and Tumblr), which helps explain why every media type is closely connected. If you're engaging on various media and attempting to reach Millennials, they're going to find you and follow you from one platform to the next. To facilitate this discovery of your brand across platforms, you need to understand the ecosystem and the value of its parts. Then you need to develop a strategy that takes that interconnectedness into account.

Media has a few defining characteristics that you'll want to familiarize yourself with as you plan your strategy:

>> **Everything is connected.** When a proper strategy is developed, you'll quickly notice that every one of the networks you are on is connected to one another. Millennials operate across the entire platform ecosystem.

>> **Each platform should have a narrow strategy in relation to the ecosystem.** Your individual media strategies, covered in Chapters 5 and 6, include several objectives and micro-strategies. You'll find that when you use an omni-channel strategy, each active media target is significantly narrowed. Instead of leveraging each media type for similar goals, you should focus on its particular strengths in relation to the larger ecosystem.

An *omni-channel experience* creates a seamless user experience on a variety of media, as opposed to each medium acting independently,

>> **Traditional and new media work together.** There is no reason to think that online and offline media can't work together. There are methods of connecting these two worlds, many of which are covered in this chapter, and they should be explored heavily in order to capitalize on the opportunities presented in cross-channel marketing.

Millennials may not use traditional media in the same way preceding generations did. That doesn't mean that traditional media can't fit into a comprehensive, multi-channel marketing strategy. For more on the power of traditional media, see Chapter 5.

Everything can and should be tracked. Regardless of your objectives, selected media, target audience clusters, or content strategies, you'll notice that there is a way to track everything that you're doing. As media has evolved, the demand for precision and measurability has grown as well. As that trend has taken hold, tracking capabilities have become the focal point of all media types.

Developing a Unified Omni-Channel Communications Strategy

Your marketing goal is to reach Millennials where they are. You want to get to know them on an intimate level and build lasting relationships with them. That goal can't happen if you focus entirely on a single channel or media type. Ignoring the Millennial's buying and loyalty process across platforms is a fatal mistake.

An example of this media touchpoint ecosystem created by me is shown in Figure 9-1. To build a Millennial's loyalty, you need to tie together several of the platforms that Millennial consumers use on a regular basis. To link these channels together effectively, you need to develop a carefully laid-out communications strategy.

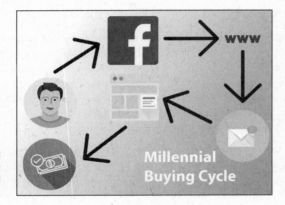

FIGURE 9-1:
Touchpoints in the Millennial buying cycle.

Identifying opportunities by media type

Pinpointing opportunities will play a key role in developing your marketing objectives. If you create an umbrella strategy that applies to all your channels, you're going to be duplicating work and will get only a fraction of the potential results. Each platform where Millennials are active, the majority of which are covered in Chapters 5 and 6, serves a purpose in the buying journey. Here are three stages in the buying process where you'll want to find opportunities:

>> **Awareness:** The awareness stage of the buying process for Millennials is all about exposure. You want to identify opportunities to reach a large Millennial audience that is easy, inexpensive, or free. This opportunity may be in the form of advertising, content sharing, or direct communication in public

forums. In the early stages of your brand's existence, you to need to be prepared to invest in some form of advertising.

Reaching a mass audience organically has become increasingly difficult because social networks have moved toward a pay-to-play model, whereby extensive reach can really only be achieved if you're willing to invest in advertising. This is not to say that you can't do it. But particularly with a Millennial audience that may not have engaged with your brand, advertising will be your path of least resistance.

>> **Consideration:** At this stage, you want to drive Millennials to consider your brand over a competitor's. This is done primarily through the identification of audience tastes and preferences. This practice is covered in Chapter 3. Essentially, by segmenting and analyzing Millennial audience pockets on Facebook, you can identify some of the characteristics that drive Millennials to act. After you've gone through this process, you can observe content, groups, and conversations on different media types to identify opportunities to connect with Millennials at this crucial stage in the buying cycle.

>> **Action:** It's time to leverage the opportunities in the action stage of the buying process. This stage is where you want to consider taking a more aggressive approach. It may even focus on overt marketing or sales techniques. Of course, with regard to Millennials, the definition of overt is not what it used to be. Millennials don't want to be pushed into making a purchase of any kind. But, with a strong relationship developed in the previous buying stages, you have a much better chance of being listened to when sharing a more targeted, sales-oriented message.

It is helpful to review conversations and identify key terms or phrases across all media that suggest a Millennial consumer is ready to make a decision or purchase.

Choosing the right media for your objectives

The media that you choose to leverage will largely depend on the marketing objectives you've outlined for yourself. Your objectives will fall into one of the three buying stages described in the previous section: awareness, consideration, or action.

In the case of awareness, your goal is to get your brand out there and in front of Millennials. Of course, driving these users to take some sort of action is ideal, but the goal is to make your name known among your target audience.

In the consideration stage, you want to highlight the advantages of your brand over your competitor's brand. Highlight the added value that you offer and demonstrate where your competitors are lacking. The goal here is to build a relationship and showcase your value. Encourage your audience to take another step beyond a basic engagement with your brand.

Choosing the right media to encourage brand engagement is crucial for two reasons:

>> You don't want your work to overlap and cause redundancies.

>> You don't want to invest time, effort, and resources in mining for opportunities on a channel that doesn't fit the audience.

Therefore, understanding which media fit different objectives is an important step in the process of building your omni-channel strategy.

Awareness: Getting to know your brand

During the awareness stage of the buying process, the ad platforms on Facebook and Instagram help you find your audience. The ability to filter your target audience by familiarity with your brand Page on Facebook, shown in Figure 9-2, makes it an ideal tool for building awareness. To justify an ad spend, you can attach a call-to-action. Just be sure that you don't produce a sales-oriented ad, which won't be well-received by Millennials at this stage.

FIGURE 9-2:
Filtering your target audience by new users.

At the awareness stage, you want to reach new users as opposed to those who already like or follow your brand. So, rather than choosing your existing Custom Audiences in Facebook (made up of users that have already shared their information with you), create Lookalike Audiences. This allows you to reach a unique set of Facebook users that fit the criteria of your existing Custom Audiences. For more information on creating a Custom Audience in Facebook, visit Chapter 3.

Consideration: Showcasing your value

After you establish an initial connection with your audience in the awareness phase, you want to drive users to your website or blog to further build that relationship. To accomplish this goal, your content needs to cater to the tastes and preferences expressed by targeted Millennials.

The consideration stage of the process is a good time to leverage traditional media. One of the strategies covered in Chapter 5 is the use of TV targeting on Twitter. You want to establish common ground. Connecting with these users on a personal level is crucial if you want to build loyalty in the long-run. Sharing content on Twitter while they're engaged on both the platform and an event on television allows you to become a part of an ongoing conversation.

Action: Driving action

To reach your objectives, it's key that you use media that provides you with measurable data. Gathering and accessing this data is easiest when you have complete control over the process, like on your website. New media, such as Facebook, also offers copious amounts of data that can help ensure that every action you take leads to a positive sum end result.

A *positive sum end result* refers to the benefits derived from each step of the conversion process. It's important to ensure that every one of your investments is working toward achieving a goal related to your ultimate objectives.

Establishing engagement goals by media

Engagement is a term that is often thrown around by marketers without a proper definition. Engagement can mean many things. If you don't clearly define what you're referring to, determining the value of a particular action taken by an audience member is difficult. A Like on one of your posts probably doesn't have the same value as a user completing a form and downloading an eBook, but often-times marketers lump these two actions together.

TIP

Define what engagement means at each of the three phases of the Millennial buying cycle. Then prioritize Millennials' abilities to achieve the objectives you've outlined for each of your selected media.

At each of the three stages of the Millennial buying journey, you can follow a specific six-step process to establish effective goals:

1. **Establish your definition for a successful conversion.**

   What does it take for you to consider a new prospect an acquired customer? Does it need to be a purchase or a form completion? This definition is something that you need to establish and keep top of mind as you build out the objectives related to each one of the selected channels.

2. **Outline the various paths to final conversion.**

   After you know what it is you're trying to achieve, you'll need to determine the path that a Millennial prospect can take in order to get there. Of course, the structure of an omni-channel campaign means that they can take a virtually endless series of touchpoint paths. Your job in this step is to outline the most likely and/or your preferred sets of conversion paths that Millennials can take to achieve your global objectives.

3. **Pinpoint your ideal path to action.**

   This path is essentially your path of least resistance, where the conversion takes place with the least amount of effort or investment on your part. It will almost certainly be the first path you outline in Step 2.

4. **Identify the greatest strength of each medium in those paths.**

   Every one of the media that you leverage in your overall strategy will have strengths and weaknesses. In this step, you need to look at your universal objectives and determine what role each of your selected media will play in getting your prospects to convert.

5. **Determine the positive sum action that prospects should take at each step of the process.**

   After you know the strengths of each of your selected media, clearly define the action you want your prospects to take at each turn. This step helps you build out the content you need for each step of the way.

6. **Define micro-objectives that you can count toward your prospect's progression at each step of the path.**

   With a clear understanding of the path and media you're going to use in the consumer cycle for your Millennial audience, you can now outline what you define as a *micro-conversion* (a small, campaign-specific conversion that isn't necessarily related to your long-term goals) at each step of the way.

TIP

Micro-conversions don't necessarily mean that you've acquired a lifelong Millennial customer. It simply means that the prospect in question has taken the desired action at the designated step. Getting to this point, however, means that each medium is operating independently and functions as part of a cohesive unit. To ensure that this cohesiveness happens, establishing engagement and conversion metrics at each step of the way is crucial.

Creating content that appeals to Millennials on each channel

To get a detailed understanding of how to create content that appeals to Millennials on each of your active channels, refer to Chapters 5 and 6. However, you'll want to keep in mind some universal tips when developing content on various media:

>> **Get to know your audience on each channel.** Millennials are going to engage with brands and content differently on every channel. Take what you learn in your audience analysis (see Chapter 3) and use it as a universal model for your Millennial audiences. Make sure to note subtle differences in data from one media type to another.

>> **Create content that is unique to each of your selected channels.** Create content that is unique to each channel's specific characteristics as well as each of the micro-objectives for each of your selected media.

>> **Focus your content on the intended action you want to drive on each channel.** As you create this unique content, you want to ensure that each channel's content connects to the objective you hope to achieve. Whether it relates to awareness, consideration, or action, everything you create should direct your Millennial audience to engage in the way that your conversion path dictates.

>> **Quickly showcase the purpose of your content.** Why are you sharing what you're sharing? Millennials have a short attention span and a lot of content options. Keep your content short and to the point and highlight why Millennials should engage with it. What does your audience gain by engaging with your content?

>> **Be visual wherever it is possible.** If there's an option to be visual, take it. A visual piece of content is easier to digest and is more noticeable in a news feed on both the desktop and mobile devices.

>> **Think mobile-first in every case.** Millennials are generally engaging on most media platforms with mobile devices. You want to be as visual as possible and think about how your content looks on these devices.

Determining KPIs

Just as you set objectives for each of your selected media, you need to determine the KPIs you'll use to measure the results. After all, how can you know if your efforts are paying off if you haven't indicated what constitutes success?

KPIs come in all shapes and sizes. There are two types:

>> **Tangible KPIs:** These are easy to define. They represent distinct measures — like growth or engagement rates on a selected medium.

>> **Intangible KPIs:** These can be a little harder to define. While you probably won't have many intangible KPIs to monitor, those you choose are likely to be important in measuring the success of a campaign. Think about brand awareness or recognition. These are conceptual ideas, but they have a significant impact on the success of your efforts.

Following are some of the most common KPIs used to measure the growth and success of a particular medium that you've chosen to leverage in a campaign or long-term communications strategy:

Audience growth rate

Your audience growth rate is indicative of two important things:

>> It tells you whether you've reached a plateau with regard the virality of your content on a particular medium, suggesting that it may be time for a change.

>> It alerts you to a drastic change in your audience growth rate from one measurement period to another. This can indicate a major pitfall or huge opportunity in terms of content, a new audience, or other factor.

Virality is a measurement term that relates to how much your content is shared to secondary and tertiary audiences. It's the shareable quality of your content.

Key audience segment growth rate

In addition to monitoring the growth of your audience on each of your chosen media, you'll want to pay close attention to the growth rate of specific, high-value audience segments.

Marketing qualified lead (MQL) generation ratio

When a prospect has expressed some form of interest in your product or service by taking a certain action, this individual is considered a *marketing qualified lead.* These prospects are of a particularly high value. Paying attention to how many of these hard leads are generated as a proportion of your total lead generation efforts will be a useful indicator to track.

Cost per lead (CPL)

How much does it cost for you to acquire a lead? *Cost per lead* is a metric that you can apply to any medium where you collect user data. Ultimately, your goal is to see this number decrease over time, which would suggest improved targeting and content strategies.

Cost per acquisition (CPA)

Going one step further than your cost per lead, pay close attention to your cost per acquisition. It may be great if you're collecting plenty of leads at a lower cost, but if you can't convert those leads and your cost per acquisition is increasing over time, you'll have to identify where the issues lies — between interest and action.

Cost per click (CPC)

When you're running an ad campaign, whether it's on AdWords, Facebook, Twitter, or some other ad platform — traditional or new media — the cost per click, or cost per call with certain campaigns, is an important indicator.

Cost per thousand impressions (CPM)

A lot of ad campaigns have moved away from the cost per thousand impressions model. However, you can still monitor it despite the fact that you likely won't run a campaign using this cost model. Tracking your cost per thousand impressions can be indicative of the accuracy of your targeting. You may find that the alignment between your ad content and your target audience is a good match.

New website visitor volume

Are your traffic generation campaigns working? You can determine your success by looking at your website visitor ratios. As your brand's exposure goes up, you should start to see more new visits to your site. With regard to new visitors, pay more attention to volume.

Return website visitor ratio

While volume matters more with new website visits, ratio matters when it comes to return visits. This indicator tells you how well you're targeting audience segments with your content. If you're trying to reach Millennials, but you haven't put together the right content, offer, or landing page, monitoring this KPI will help you realize that.

Website goal conversion rate

Website goal conversion rate is a pretty straightforward KPI. The higher your goal conversion rate, the greater your performance. The important thing to remember when it comes to your goals, however, is that they don't necessarily need to be a purchase or a monetary conversion. If you're using Google Analytics, then your goals can be something as simple as a visitor following a specific path before taking an action on your website. But keeping that rate up and rising above your benchmarks is most important, regardless of the goal you're monitoring.

Onsite interaction rate

In Google Analytics, your interaction rates are made up of your average session duration, pages per session, and bounce rate data points, as shown in Figure 9-3. These interaction rates are indicative of the degree of interest your audience has in your content and the viability of the strategies that drive audience members to your website. If your total sessions or unique sessions on Google Analytics are up but your interaction rates are down, then you may have mismatched content and target audiences.

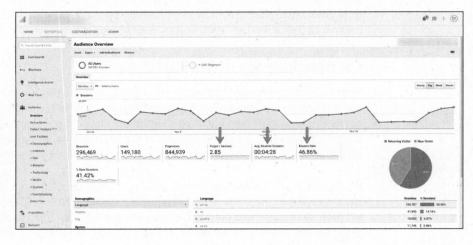

FIGURE 9-3: Average session duration, pages per session, and bounce rate highlighted on the Google Analytics Audience dashboard.

TECHNICAL STUFF

Several measurement criteria within your Google Analytics dashboard are indicative of visitor engagement. *Average session duration* refers to the amount of time the average visitor spends on your website. *Pages per session* relates to the number of pages the average visitor views in any given session. Lastly, your *bounce rate* is the ratio of visitors that leave your website after having viewed only one page — the page on which they arrived. While you want to drive average session duration and pages per session up over time, your goal with your bounce rate should be to push it down. This decrease will happen as your pages per session data increases, as this metric has a negatively correlated relationship with bounce rates.

Effectively, as one of these points goes up, it stands to reason that the other will go down.

Organic click-through rate

When you share content on one of your external new media platforms, such as your Facebook Page, you want to pay close attention to the rate at which your originally reached audience clicks through to a landing page on your website. Organic reach on all major social networks has decreased, especially on networks like Twitter and Instagram that have been updated to use algorithmic feeds as opposed to chronological ones. The ability to drive traffic to your website without the need to spend has become a more valuable strength than ever before. Keeping your organic click-through rate up by understanding your audience on each platform and sharing content specifically for those users is an important practice.

Paid click-through rate

Regardless of how well your content is performing organically, you're almost certainly going to have to invest in your brand on most, if not all, third-party platforms. Click-through rates for paid campaigns are just as important, if not more important, than they are for organic content because a low click-through rate may mean a higher cost-per-click and a poor targeting strategy.

Content engagement half-life

Your *content engagement half-life* is the amount of time it takes for your content to receive half of the engagement it will ever get. The half-life of your audience's engagement is an extremely important metric. It indicates how much value can be extracted from each piece of content. It also tells you how frequently you need to invest in the creation of new content and the growth of your editorial calendar.

For example, if, on average, your audience engages with each piece of content 100 times, then your content half-life is the amount of time it takes for your content to reach 50 engagement points. Engagement can take the form of clicks, comments, likes, or any other interaction as defined by you. If it takes a week to reach 100 engagement points and 1 hour to reach 50, then your content half-life is one hour.

Search engine ranking

Free options on the market allow you to monitor your search engine ranking for specific keywords, but if you're serious about monitoring this KPI and using what you've learned to improve your standings, then you may want to consider investing in an SEO tool like Moz, shown in Figure 9-4. These paid tools provide more detail about your search optimization progress, and the detail in the data significantly surpasses the detail offered by free tools.

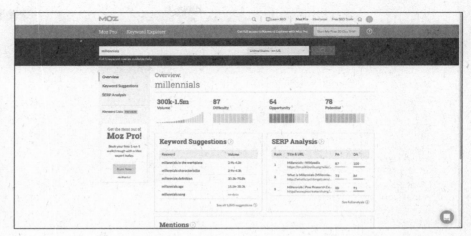

FIGURE 9-4:
Moz SEO
software offers
insights into
specific keywords
and several other
tools to help with
your search
engine optimiza-
tion efforts.

Email engagement rate

Email is still a viable tool that serves several purposes during the consumer buy-ing cycle. It's personal, meaning a user has no distractions when engaging with it. You can't say the same about content on a social network. Because of its personal nature, email is ideal for targeting Millennials on mobile devices.

Engagement rates in an email campaign are your email open rates, click-through rates, and if you're measurement continues beyond the email, then conversion rates as well.

Net Promoter Score

Your brand's *Net Promoter Score* (NPS) is an index that ranges from 1 to 100. It cal-culates the willingness of your customers and those who have interacted with your brand to recommend it to others in their circles. Your NPS is essentially a combination of customer satisfaction and loyalty and is a good indicator of poten-tial growth.

The numbers relate to detractors, which are shown in negative numbers, and advocates, expressed with positive numbers. If you have more detractors than promoters, then your NPS will be negative. If you have more advocates than detractors, your NPS will be positive.

Ultimately, your goal should be to reach 100, which indicates complete market satisfaction. You can use the free tool NPS Calculator at `www.npscalculator.com` (see Figure 9-5) to determine your Net Promoter Score.

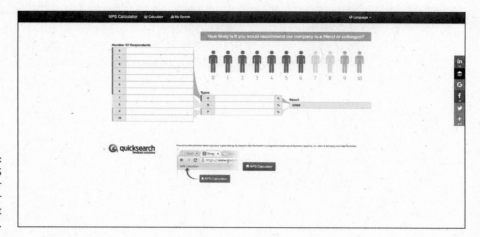

FIGURE 9-5:
The NPS Calculator determines your brand's Net Promoter Score.

Brand awareness

Brand awareness is worth much more than simple recognition. While brand awareness isn't a tangible indicator per se, it's an observable KPI based on elements such as share of voice and audience sentiment. If you can control the majority of the conversation or if you find your brand is mentioned in a positive light more frequently than your competitors, then the benefits can be great.

This indicator transcends media type because conversations can take place anywhere. Ultimately, increased brand awareness can mean a quicker path to conversion. It shortens the process needed to introduce prospects to your brand and results in a decreased cost-per-acquisition thanks to audience familiarity.

TECHNICAL STUFF

Share of voice is a metric that showcases how much of the social conversation is about your brand. For example, if 100 discussions mention you or your competitors and you are mentioned in 40 of them, then your share of voice is 40 percent. The higher your share of voice (positive or negative), the higher your brand awareness. Of course, your goal should be to keep all conversations and mentions about your brand positive.

Brand advocacy ratio

When calculating your Net Promoter Score, you analyze the ratio of customers and engaged users that are talking positively about your brand. When looking at your brand advocacy ratio, you take that analysis a step further. You look not only at those speaking positively about your brand, but also at those advocating for your brand over competitors. This includes those that are actively defending your brand against detractors. The higher this ratio, the greater the loyalty your audience has to your brand.

Greater loyalty means a greater customer lifetime value (CLTV), lower cost-per-retention to keep customers coming back, and a potentially lowered cost-per-acquisition. This is, in part, thanks to the advocacy work of your brand loyalists who promote your product willingly and without incentive. It may be worth investing in a loyalty program or incentive structure to show your advocates and defenders that you notice their efforts and appreciate everything they do for you.

Marketing brand value

Calculating brand equity can be a pretty tough task, especially when you consider the fact that so much of a brand's value is intangible and can come from a variety of sources. But while it may not be the easiest task in the world, you can certainly follow a process to determine your brand equity. This process takes into account the costs of building your brand on all media, your pricing, and some characteristics of your audience. To find out more about the process of determining your brand value, follow the steps in *Branding For Dummies* (Wiley) by Bill Chiaravalle and Barbara Findlay Schenck or visit www.dummies.com/business/marketing/branding/how-to-calculate-your-brands-equity.

Return on marketing investment

If there's one topic that finds its way into any marketing meeting, it's return on investment. Any business owner, executive, or marketer wants to know whether the resources that are being invested into a campaign or strategy are producing the desired results. That is why your most important KPI is likely going to be the measurement of your return on marketing investment.

The generally accepted method used for calculating ROI is as follows:

[(Revenues-Costs)/Costs] x100

This equation will produce a percentage. The higher the percentage, the greater your return.

WARNING

If the number produced is negative, your costs have exceeded your returns, and you're losing money on an initiative. In this case, you either need to make changes right away, or your campaign needs to end.

In terms of tracking this KPI, you want to see your returns consistently on the rise. Over time, you should focus on either increasing revenues while maintaining a fixed cost or, alternatively, decreasing marginal cost for a given campaign or strategic implementation, both of which lead to a higher return on marketing investment.

Opportunity identification rate

When running a data or audience segment analysis, one of the focuses of the process is the identification of new opportunities. This identification can be in the form of a new audience pocket, content variations, or one of several other potentially lucrative data points.

As you refine your data analysis processes, the identification of new opportunities is something that should become more frequent. When you know what to look for, it becomes obvious.

Aim to keep this metric rising with each strategy audit, which is covered in Chapter 11.

Investment-to-return ratio change

At each stage of your audit and analysis, you're going to calculate your return on marketing investment. This means that at every interval after your first audit, you'll be able to see the change in your ROI ratios.

Over time, you want this ratio to increase. If it does, it shows that your investments are generating greater returns. This increase means that everything you put in to your campaigns and strategies will perform at a greater rate.

Goodwill brand value growth rate

When you partner with a cause or donate a portion of your proceeds from a sale to a specific charity, you generate goodwill. Goodwill and this kind of cause alignment adds value to your brand. While you don't regularly track this metric, you want to analyze it every time you engage in some sort of cause-oriented initiative. Determining the impact it has on positive sentiment and brand advocacy chatter will give you an idea of the value added to your brand's equity.

Targeting Your Strategy to Millennials

Creating an omni-channel communications strategy isn't a practice unique to Millennial marketing. The media landscape requires that all marketers think in terms of multiple channels rather than focusing on each medium in a vacuum. An omni-channel communications strategy is the only way a long-term program can succeed.

When it comes to Millennial marketing, certain components are unique. The unique aspects of Millennial marketing strategies are a result of the new norms that buyers expect to encounter in the buying journey.

Creating a seamless content experience

You need to identify your brand's persona target at every touchpoint in the customer journey. A clearly identifiable piece of content that highlights your brand will increase the likelihood that your Millennial audience will notice you.

Here are a few important points to remember when trying to create your seamless content experience:

>> **Standardize your message.** Your audience should be able to instantly recognize your content. You can help this recognition along in quite a few ways. One of the most important ways is through the consistency of your message. Though the message you share may change from one platform to the next, the way in which it's expressed should remain largely uniform. Normalizing your message ensures that your Millennial audience is more likely to recall the content from one platform to the next. Repetition and a mid to high message frequency is necessary before your audience responds to your call-to-action.

>> **Maintain a standardized color scheme.** Just as your message should be standardized, the colors you use in your creative design should match from one medium to the next. This standardized color scheme will help your audience recognize your content as they move across platforms.

>> **Highlight your call-to-action.** Your call-to-action should be front and center and differentiate itself from the rest of your content. In every place that your message is being shown, your call-to-action must stand out. Calling it out may mean highlighting it with a sticker or starburst, using a button available in one of your ad campaigns, or using a different color, font, and size to make it clear that you're asking your audience to take some sort of action.

WARNING

One of the worst mistakes you can make is blending your call-to-action into the creative design or post. In the few brief moments that Millennials give to your content, you want the request you're making to pop out from everything else.

Personalizing the content experience for Millennials

In addition to creating content that flows and clearly matches your brand, you want to focus on personalization whenever possible. In general, most of the campaigns that focus on the same message or call-to-action allow for limited hypertargeted personalization. However, email or targeted advertising allows you to more closely tailor the elements of your campaign to the targeted audience's characteristics.

Tailoring a campaign means that you can adjust your content or messaging to appeal to the interests and behaviors identified within certain segments of your audience. In some cases, personalization can go as far as tailoring a message to an individual. Following are some cases that allow for greater personalization:

>> **Social advertising:** One of the greatest benefits of social advertising is the ability to tailor your content to specific, targeted groups in your advertising dashboards. This ability is particularly true when it comes to Facebook and Twitter. Their tools have the capability to build audiences, analyze them, and then create ad content specifically designed to target the identified characteristics. While your personalization techniques are limited to tailoring your message to the qualities of certain pockets, the ability to analyze those segments is unparalleled. After you develop an understanding of your audience (see Chapter 3), you can create several sets of content that are designed to capture the attention of a specific segment.

>> **Email:** You can customize your email both individually and at the segment level. Modern email clients, such as Constant Contact or MailChimp, offer the ability to tailor your subject line and parts of your message to the individual. Of course, you'll also want to create emails that are designed to engage users based on the list they have subscribed to or the platform on which they subscribed. Going a step further and personalizing the message with a subscriber's name and perhaps some information that is unique to them (something you can't do automatically using email client features) will impress your Millennial audience.

>> **Search remarketing:** Search engine marketing and paid advertising on display networks is a great way to drive both action and brand recognition. Remarketing uniquely personalizes the ad experience by pushing the content that users have already viewed on your website back to them as they peruse third-party websites.

For example, if a visitor landed on a particular product page on your website, a remarketing campaign can prompt a customized ad with tailored messaging and the product in question to follow the user around the web. This remarketing campaign keeps your brand top of mind, even if the user doesn't click-through on the ad. Brand recognition is an important factor to consider in the buying process, and remarketing is a great way to ensure that your brand stays in front of a prospect throughout his or her buying journey.

Chapter **10**

Creating a Mobile Strategy Tailored to Millennials

Millennials live their lives on the go and online, which means that in order to generate results from your marketing efforts, you need to closely focus on mobile. Mobile has experienced an explosive rise in both penetration and usage as smartphones have become commonplace.

In this chapter, you discover the full set of components that make up a mobile marketing strategy designed to reach Millennials.

The very nature of mobile is that it is, well, mobile! With other platforms, connecting the digital side of marketing to action requires a lot more steps between the initial engagement and physical, on-site interaction. Mobile helps limit those steps. This chapter shows you how to put together a strategy to reach Millennials through this valuable channel.

Establishing Mobile-Specific Goals

Unlike other media, where your audience members can easily become distracted, content on mobile devices is largely served up in a *singular* fashion. This means that you have more of an opportunity to engage with a Millennial on a mobile device because your content is the only thing he or she is seeing.

TECHNICAL STUFF

When the term *singular* is used to describe user engagement, it refers to the nature in which content is digested. On a desktop, for example, content is shown in a number of areas of the screen, and multiple pieces of content can often be seen on the same Facebook feed, for example. On a mobile device, content is delivered singularly, meaning that everything that comes across the user's eyes is the only piece of content that this person is seeing for at least a moment or two.

Because mobile offers opportunities that aren't available on other media, you can achieve objectives that would otherwise be difficult to plan for or cost-prohibitive. Some of the goal themes that are much more easily attainable on mobile fall into the following categories:

>> Data collection

>> Online-to-offline conversion

>> Customer service

>> Behavioral segmentation and targeting

>> Experience personalization

The following sections take a closer look at each of these categories and some detailed objectives that you can establish within your mobile strategy.

Data collection

Data sits at the core of your entire strategy. Data collected on mobile devices is extremely valuable because of the level of engagement involved on the part of the user. A study from the Pew Research Center found that 86 percent of Millennials own a smartphone, and additional research by Nielsen found that Millennials in the United States are spending 4.7 hours a day on their devices. Both of those statistics beat out the next most engaging medium significantly, so the question is, "What kind of goals can you establish with regards to data collection?" Here are just a few:

>> Increasing form submissions from contact forms or content downloads

>> Simplifying the path to conversion on mobile devices based on observable habits of Millennial visitors

>> Improving the design of your retail location by triangulating in-store hot spots through the use of beacon technology.

Setting these goals early means you can collect data on an ongoing basis and use it to improve the overall customer journey both on and offline.

If you need more information on data, see Chapter 4.

Online-to-offline conversion

Once again, because mobile devices move with your customers, you should establish goals that link the online experience to the physical one, assuming, of course, your business exists both on and offline. Your goal is to increase retail referrals from Millennial visitors to your mobile website with mobile-specific promotions and offers.

Customer service

Millennials want to engage with your brand on the platforms with which they are most familiar. Research from Desk.com, a Salesforce company, shows that 25 percent of Millennials want a response within ten minutes of reaching out to your brand on social media. A response within 10 minutes should be the goal you set when offering some form of social care. *Social care* is the term used in the marketing industry to refer to customer service on social media.

You should also set a goal that strives to increase the volume of help desk tickets that your customer service team can resolve per hour.

Behavioral segmentation and targeting

Considering how much time Millennials spend on their mobile devices, the little things that you can learn about them allow you to create targeted campaigns that cater to the tastes and preferences of your audience (see Chapter 3). Your goals revole primarily around improving the way in which you understand your Millennial audience. Here are two examples of these goals:

- » Shortening the path to conversion based on engagement rates on tested content and messaging
- » Increasing engagement rates with content campaigns targeted to smaller, more robustly understood segments of your Millennial audience

Experience personalization

Millennials love a personalized experience. Anything that you can do to make personalization a reality leads to a significant increase in engagement, conversion, and, perhaps most importantly, loyalty. These goals dictate that you've been successful in your efforts to personalize the online and offline experiences for your Millennial audience:

- » Increasing your Millennial audience social media engagement rates
- » Increasing on-site engagement with your Millennial audience by measuring time on-site, bounce rate, pages per session, and average session duration, which are all Google Analytics measurements
- » Increasing positive sentiment mentions of your brand or organization across social platforms

Creating Mobile-Specific Content for Your Website

In a perfect world, every organization would have a native mobile application in order to engage with Millennials, as mobile is their preferred means of engaging with a brand. Because having a native mobile application isn't a reality for most companies, mobile-specific content is a safe and useful alternative.

Creating a fully responsive site or mobile version of your website

If you have the ability to create a fully responsive site or a mobile version of your website — which you can do inexpensively now with tools and services like Duda (www.dudamobile.com), shown in Figure 10-1 — you need to keep a few things in mind:

FIGURE 10-1: Duda offers the ability to create simple, native websites.

>> Keep your paragraphs short and to the point because Millennials have short attention spans and won't want to scroll through unnecessary text.

>> Shrink your images — both in terms of their actual size and the file size — and avoid using video, unless it's necessary or embedded from YouTube, for improved performance.

>> Ensure that your forms are mobile ready.

>> Review your downloadable content in order to ensure that they're mobile-friendly, particularly in the case of PDFs.

>> Integrate social login capabilities in order to collect more robust data from your Millennial audience, which largely prefers social login to traditional account setups.

>> Create offers that are unique to the mobile experience in order to differentiate your mobile and desktop campaigns even further.

>> Pay close attention to your site load time using a tool like Google's Test My Site (https://testmysite.thinkwithgoogle.com/), shown in Figure 10-2.

>> Consider offering mobile-specific outreach methods that Millennials prefer, such as Twitter, SMS text messages, or a native chat option like Facebook Messenger or WhatsApp.

FIGURE 10-2:
Use Test My Site
to monitor the
load time of your
mobile website.

Adapting your existing webpages to mobile

If, alternatively, you are working on a mobile-friendly website that simply adapts your existing webpages to the mobile device in question, review your content in order to ensure that it meets the following criteria:

>> Pages should not be overly wordy or filled with more content than they need to have.

>> Compress existing images on your website, which you can do with a free tool like Compress JPEG (http://CompressJPEG.com), shown in Figure 10-3.

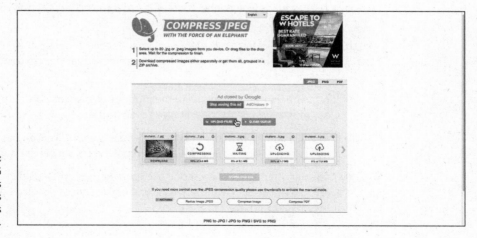

FIGURE 10-3:
Compress JPEG
allows users
to compress
large image files
for free.

>> Use Google's free Mobile-Friendly Test tool (see Figure 10-4) to review your website's pages and inform you of issues that your mobile site visitors may be experiencing.

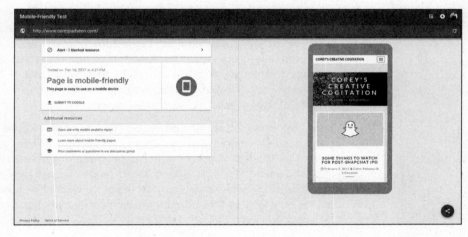

FIGURE 10-4:
Google's Mobile-Friendly Test will grade your mobile website and highlight areas that need improvement.

>> Test all integrations that might not format correctly on a mobile device, which holds especially true for third-party website add-ins like forms and WordPress plugins.

>> Avoid having any Flash on your website because it slows your load time, renders poorly on mobile devices, and can actually be damaging to your search rankings on mobile.

>> If you have videos, embedding them from a third-party website like YouTube or Vimeo is a good way to ensure that your site speed isn't impacted.

Using Social at the Core of Your Mobile Strategy

Social media is at the root of the everyday lives of Millennials. Research from Mobile Advertising Watch shows that, on average, Millennials check their social accounts 17 times per day, and the majority of those checks take place on a smartphone. The reality is that social is going to play an enormous role in your mobile strategy.

The ability to integrate some form of social sign-in for your members holds great potential for your data collection. But what other uses does social have in terms of mobile? Those exist both on and off of social networks like Facebook and Twitter. Here are a few of the benefits of working with social and mobile together:

» **Work with native apps.** Millennials want to spend more time engaging on social networks on their mobile phones rather than on your website, so whenever a campaign can leverage native apps, it should. Create events and offers and collect data within Facebook itself. Keep in mind that you can't leverage third-party software as a Facebook Page tab on mobile, but anything you create within Facebook that is part of the network's built-in services, such as Events, will appear on mobile devices as well.

» **Keep your photos clean and on brand.** This approach is a good one to adopt in general for social media, but it's particularly true when you're trying to think mobile-first. Your audience members are flying through their news feed on a device. The busier your content appears at quick glance, the less attractive it looks when it scrolls by. What's more, without a clear maintenance of your branding, it will be a largely wasted post for a predominantly Millennial audience.

TIP

I'm not saying that every one of your posts needs to be branded. A healthy mix of branded, promotional, and eclectic content is always encouraged. That said, the voice that you've cultivated for yourself should be almost instantly recognizable because Millennials will move quickly past a piece of content if it's not.

» **Make sure that your content is concise and to the point, particularly on Facebook.** The last thing your Millennial audience is going to do is click on a See More button in a news feed description. Millennials want to digest their content fast, and they want to receive all necessary information upfront without the need to keep reading. That way, they can make their split-second decision about whether or not to click on your content before moving on to the next item on their news feed.

» **Create mobile-specific content on a per network basis in order to ensure that it's digested as it's intended to be on each medium.** Millennials have unique personalities from one network to another. The way they interact on Facebook is very different from the way they engage on Twitter. If you want to drive them to take action, you need to adapt your mobile messaging to the idiosyncrasies of the network in terms of best practices (see Chapter 6), as well as the idiosyncrasies of the users.

Targeting Millennials with Mobile Advertising

These days, advertising comes in many shapes and sizes, can be overt or subtle, and can be found on more or less any outlet imaginable. Where advertising is perhaps most crucial for Millennials is on mobile. On a mobile device, advertising is available in several forms, and when executed correctly with best practices kept top of mind, it means a lot of potential for your brand.

While several umbrella categories of mobile advertising cover most consumers, a few are particularly attractive when trying to appeal to Millennials:

>> Search advertising on Google

>> Display advertising

>> Facebook Audience Network advertising

>> Twitter advertising

>> Instagram creative campaigns

>> Snapchat's ad options

Search advertising on Google

Why specify a focus on Google here as opposed to a competitor like Bing (www.bing.com)? While Bing may have made a lot of great strides in the last few years with regards to capturing market share, those users are largely older and are predominantly using Internet Explorer, so Bing is their default search engine. Millennials are by and large using Google, so that's where you will want to spend your mobile ad dollars if you're trying to capture them.

A 2016 Google AdWords update opened up the opportunity to allow advertisers to segment their ads, bids, campaigns, and strategies by medium, as shown in Figure 10-5. So, if you're running campaigns targeting desktop, mobile, and tablet users, you can focus on each one of these media in a silo. If your goal is to reach Millennials on mobile devices in search, focusing on each of these platforms individually and making separate adjustments is what you'll want to do.

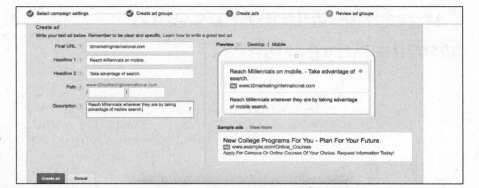

FIGURE 10-5:
An example of the mobile layout for a search ad in Google AdWords.

In order to maximize clicks using Google AdWords on mobile, remember these important pointers:

>> **Don't send users to your home page because they're most likely engaged in an active search.** These searches are intent-driven because of some immediate need, and your home page almost certainly doesn't have that information on it. Send them to a landing page that is more relevant to the search query.

>> **Use long-tail search terms for mobile searches.** This technique ensures that the clicks you receive from the target audience are highly relevant to both you and the user clicking on your ad.

TECHNICAL STUFF

Long-tail search terms use three or more words in order to target users who are searching for very specific results, rather than those searching for more general terms. For example, a general search may be for the term "power drill," while a long-tail search would be more along the lines of "8-volt right angle cordless power drill."

>> **Be specific with your ad content.** Ensure that the users clicking on an ad know exactly where they're going and what they'll be getting after they land on your page. The alternative — whereby you're vague or too broad in your ad content — results in a lose-lose scenario where your audience member doesn't find the content he or she was looking for, and you spend money on a click that doesn't generate the results you were hoping for.

>> **Avoid using generic terms for your mobile campaigns.** While these general industry terms may be useful in desktop searches, Millennials use mobile search with intent. They want easily digestible content that answers a question or concern they have.

Display advertising

In the case of display advertising, networks like Google, Bing, and Yahoo! are equally viable ways to reach Millennials. All three of these search engines have networks that extend far beyond the search properties themselves, such as Google or Bing. In fact, these three networks reach virtually every available display property available across the web by placing ads in the designated spaces showcased in Figure 10-6.

FIGURE 10-6: A look at the spots where Display Network ads may appear within Google's network.

In order to maximize the results from your display campaigns, here are some valuable tips:

» **Keep your content clean.** Remember that on a mobile device, the busier your ad, the less likely it is for a Millennial to pay any attention to it. Ensure that your ad is clean and focuses on a single message in order to capture the attention of your target audience members.

» **Consider focusing on brand awareness.** Leverage the power of display for volume and impressions as opposed to focusing only on clicks. Millennials will register your brand and see its presence while they surf web pages within the Google Display Network or other search engine networks, but they won't necessarily click on an ad from a brand with which they haven't already engaged.

» **Drive up clicks through display campaigns by remarketing to Millennials who have visited your website.** Building a remarketing list involves sending at least a thousand visitors to the pages in question, but once that happens, the remarketing pixel that has been dropped on these pages goes live, and you can begin pushing out your display ads to an audience that is already familiar with your content. This is a great way to drive second visits from your target audience.

TECHNICAL STUFF

Remarketing is the practice of placing targeted display ads in front of an audience that has already visited your website. You can customize these ads to the individual (based on his or her interaction with your content) and use them to drive additional visits.

Facebook Audience Network advertising

Leveraging the Facebook Audience Network, which focuses on placing your Facebook ads on the mobile devices of Facebook users, is an excellent way to reach Millennials — Facebook's largest user demographic. While advertisers are prompted by Facebook itself to create Facebook ad campaigns that incorporate all placement options when a new campaign is launched, you'd be better suited to create your Facebook Audience Network ads as a stand-alone campaign, as shown in Figure 10-7.

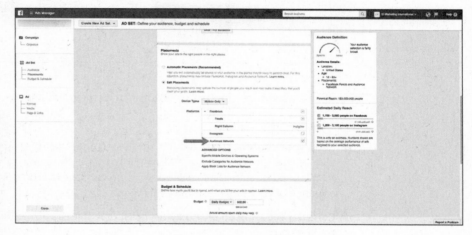

FIGURE 10-7: Create a campaign that focuses entirely on the Audience Network in order to maximize the potential of mobile.

The Audience Network is essentially third-party ad placements by Facebook on websites within its partner sphere. Millennials aren't engaging with Facebook directly, but rather with other media. In this case, Millennials are reading articles, watching videos, and using apps that fall within the Facebook Audience Network. They'll be engaging with your ad content the same way they'd engage with display ads on the Google Display Network, for example. Of course, remarketing is done a little differently on Facebook, but the idiosyncrasies of structuring your Audience Network campaign will remain largely the same.

Twitter advertising

More than 80 percent of Twitter users are accessing the social network on a mobile device, and roughly 35 percent of all Twitter users are Millennials. These statistics mean that when you strategize for reaching Millennials on mobile devices, Twitter advertising factors into the success of your plan considerably.

Twitter has a broad selection of campaign types that work very well for different objectives and circumstances:

>> Twitter cards, of which there are four kinds

>> Promoted tweets

>> Promoted account campaigns

>> App installs

>> Lead generation and data collection campaigns

>> Website visits and conversions

These ad types all offer something unique. They serve a variety of purposes that are ideally suited to help you achieve a number of objectives. Choosing the right ad type on Twitter can make all the difference.

Twitter cards

Twitter cards are larger than the average ad or tweet, which is particularly useful on mobile devices because a large card stands out to your audience. Remember, Millennials scroll through content quickly, so any item that takes up the majority of a mobile device's screen has a greater chance of grabbing the attention of your audience.

Twitter cards vary quite a bit, and they each offer something unique:

>> **Summary card:** This card is used to highlight an article or piece of content that you'd like to share, as shown in Figure 10-8.

>> **Summary card with a large image:** The concept is the same as the regular summary card, but with a larger, more prominently featured image, as shown in Figure 10-9.

TIP

Because you want to fill up as much of the screen as possible on a mobile device, you'd likely choose a summary card with a large image. But keep in mind that your image must be clean and the message clear in order to drive the results you want.

FIGURE 10-8:
Summary card.

FIGURE 10-9:
Summary card
with a large
image.

>> **App card:** If you're trying to drive downloads of a mobile application, this card allows you to link users to a direct download, as shown in Figure 10-10.

>> **Player card:** This card is designed to let you play rich media (for example, audio or video) automatically within the Twitter feed of the users you target. This technique is ideally suited if you're running a campaign designed to educate Millennials on a specific subject and choose to do so through video. Figure 10-11 shows an example.

FIGURE 10-10:
App card.

FIGURE 10-11:
Player card.

Promoted tweets

When you're trying to get a particular message in front of the eyes of Millennials, opt for a promoted tweet campaign. Promoting your tweets to a specific audience, particularly when the message is tailored to Millennials, drives up engagement considerably. Figure 10-12 shows how a promoted tweet campaign might appear on a mobile device.

FIGURE 10-12:
A promoted
tweet appears in
a user's feed.

Promoted account campaign

If you're trying to build your Millennial audience base on Twitter, consider running a promoted account campaign. A *sponsored account campaign* is a straightforward audience development campaign whereby your account appears in front of targeted users as an account that Twitter suggests they follow, as shown in Figure 10-13.

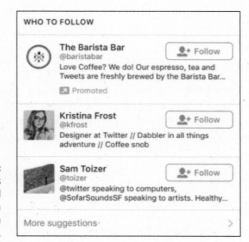

FIGURE 10-13:
The various ways
a sponsored
account can
appear on a
mobile device.

App installs

If your goal is to drive up app installs for your branded app or game, then you'll leverage a Twitter app install campaign, which you can see in Figure 10-14. Remarketing to a Millennial audience that has visited your website using a pixel available within the Twitter ad platform can help drive up actions for this kind of campaign.

TIP

If you plan to run an app install campaign to a new audience that hasn't yet visited your site, make sure that the content you use in the ad is detailed enough to showcase the value of the product to a virgin audience. They don't know what you're proposing to them, so your job is to make that clear right away.

Lead generation and data collection

A *lead generation campaign* (see Figure 10-15), which is a campaign designed to gather user information from prospects interested in your product or service, is one of the simplest and most effective ways to gather user data on Twitter, and among the more effective ways to do so across most social media ad platforms. Lead generation is an ideal campaign to use when your objective is to drive opt-ins from Millennials.

Again, remarketing with an offer or a download will lead to significantly higher engagement, but a well-described first offer, particularly one with some value added for the user, leads to very positive results. Millennials want some sort of benefit to come from sharing their information. A lead generation campaign should offer some sort of benefit to them as a result.

FIGURE 10-15:
Collecting individual user data with Twitter can be highly effective.

Website visits and conversions

When the goal is to get Millennials to take action on a particular page or element on your website, a website visits campaign is the kind of campaign that you'll run. You can see one in Figure 10-16.

Keep in mind, however, that just like search ads, sending users to your home page generates nothing. Twitter is an even more linear environment than search. If users — fast-moving Millennials in particular — click on a piece of content, they want to see the message, digest it, and decide whether or not to take action right away. Use this type of campaign only if your landing page has been designed specifically with the single-objective, fast-decision mentality in mind.

Corey Padveen
@coreypadveen

The card for your Promoted Tweet will
look something like this!

10:10 PM - 5 May 2013

Card image

Visit my website!

FIGURE 10-16:
Website visits
campaign.

Instagram creative campaigns

Millennials and Instagram go hand in hand. And Instagram ads exist within the
Facebook advertising ecosystem, which means it's fairly easy to run an Instagram
ad campaign when you're already familiar with Facebook's backend.

Millennials check Instagram throughout the day — starting when they wake up
and ending before they go to bed — and engage with content at a significantly
high rate.

With all of this in mind, Instagram seems like an obvious choice for any mobile
campaign that targets Millennials. To effectively leverage Instagram in your Millennial mobile marketing strategy, a more robust understanding of the medium is
needed:

>> **Instagram is hugely engaging, but it functions primarily in a vacuum.**
Users won't necessarily be willing to click on a link that takes them outside the
app unless some sort of value is added to do so. When building your
Instagram ad campaign, focus on how a click will benefit the user and make
that incentive clear with your creative.

>> **Develop your Instagram strategy as a stand-alone campaign.** Much like
the Audience Network campaigns, you'll want to create Instagram campaigns
without any other channels selected, the configuration of which is shown in
Figure 10-17. Instagram users, though they might be the same people, have
different personalities and will engage with content in a different way than
Facebook users.

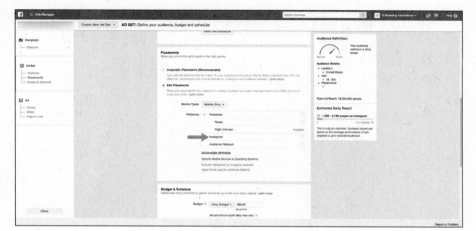

FIGURE 10-17:
Select the option
to show your
content only on
Instagram, as
opposed to all
options on
Facebook.

>> **Consider using Instagram for brand awareness.** If you do want to use Instagram in a more robust Facebook ad campaign, you can easily use it as a brand recognition and building tool within your Facebook ad campaigns. Keep in mind, however, that it may not lead to many clicks with Millennials if no value is added, but seeing your brand on Instagram can certainly offer an assist in your Facebook campaign.

>> **Your content must be clean and eye-catching.** Remember that you're competing for the attention of Millennials who are not all that willing to give you more than a few seconds. Unlike Facebook and Twitter, the written content and call-to-action fall below the image, which means that if your image isn't captivating, it will be completely ignored. You can avoid this pitfall by creating an ad with text in the image, as shown in Figure 10-18.

TIP

Instagram allows you to place as much text as you want on an image, unlike Facebook where the image may not be approved or may not show if you have too much text. Try testing samples of images that are calls-to-action themselves and see how your audience responds. But remember that this method won't always work, and your call-to-action must highlight a value-added if a targeted user clicks on it.

Snapchat's ad options

Snapchat is another Millennial haven. Though many of the ad options, such as a Sponsored Lens, which can run upwards of tens of thousands of dollars per day, are cost-prohibitive at this point, options exist where your brand can take advantage of the platform and its highly engaged audience.

Instagram

Corey Padveen   Sponsored ⌄

buy now
pay later

Shop Now   ›

♡   ◯   ↪

Buy the product today and pay later!

FIGURE 10-18:
An Instagram ad
with text in
the image.

REMEMBER

Snapchat is an entirely native experience, and the ad options that are available are designed to help your brand build and maintain a relationship with your audience. That means that if your goal is to directly drive traffic to your website or drive conversions, it won't be possible. Still, you can take advantage of trends like flash sales offering users a special code for short-term discounts that your followers can claim.

If your brand has a physical presence or you'd like to drive up awareness of your brand at an event like a trade show or conference, then a Custom Geofilter is an affordable way to do so. You can brand these filters, which Snapchat users can apply to their snaps, with your logo and place them in a specific location for a determined period of time. This is a brand awareness campaign but one that certainly ties in to the mobile habits of Millennials.

If you work for an organization that has big ad budgets and is looking to work within Snapchat's more robust advertising network, the way to get started is to contact them directly.

Running a Cohesive Mobile Campaign That Targets Millennials

While every campaign is going to have a unique set of parameters and elements, a few universal aspects apply to all marketers in virtually any industry. The following is a step-by-step guide to developing and executing a mobile campaign that reaches and converts Millennials:

1. **Establish your objectives.**

   Objectives range from the very simple, such as simple data collection, to the more complex, like audience segmentation and improved content targeting. Whatever your objectives are when it comes to reaching Millennials on mobile, you need to establish them right away.

2. **Set independent mobile measurement criteria.**

   One of the most common mistakes marketers make when it comes to working with various media types is forgetting to establish measurement criteria for each one. How you measure and determine success on a desktop campaign won't necessarily be how you measure the success of a mobile campaign. After you establish your objectives, set benchmarks and key performance indicators for each as they relate to mobile. Have a look at Chapter 9 for more detailed information on your key performance indicators, or KPIs.

3. **Clearly define your audience.**

   Not all Millennials are alike, and not all Millennials will engage with your mobile campaign. Take some time after you've set your objectives and benchmarks to create the audience that your campaign will target. This upfront planning makes the next step significantly easier.

4. **Develop the mobile-specific content you'll use in each aspect of the campaign.**

   Once again, remember that despite the fact that all of this is taking place on mobile, Millennials will engage with content differently from one medium to the next. Plan accordingly and create content that follows best practices on each one of these media.

Chapter **11**

Conducting a Millennial Marketing Strategy Audit

The identification of new opportunities is the cornerstone of every successful marketing strategy. To guide your decisions, you need to conduct frequent, planned audits. You also need to consider unplanned audits when key elements change on short notice.

In this chapter, you focus on analyzing and modifying the strategies you've implemented to build your audience.

Cornerstones of a Strategy Audit

Not every audit will consist of the same elements, and not every audit will be comprehensive, but certain key elements are regularly going to play a part in your audits, both large and small:

» Analyzing the foundation of your program

» Reviewing the progress you've made towards your objectives

>> Measuring against your established key performance indicators, or KPIs

>> Identifying new opportunities rooted in your data

Reviewing the Foundation of Your Strategy

You should consider several foundational elements when you begin to formulate your Millennial marketing strategy. The elements described in the following sections will guide the creation of your campaigns and dictate media choices.

Objectives

You can't develop an effective strategy without carefully considering each of your goals. Every step you take and everything you plan will help you achieve short- and long-term goals. When conducting an audit of your Millennial marketing strategy, you need to focus on two things:

>> You need to look at existing goals to determine how far along you are in achieving them. Are all your goals still realistic? Does something need to change? Do your established objectives still make sense?

>> You need to determine whether new data has uncovered previously unseen growth opportunities. At each interval of an audit, you want to analyze whether new opportunities create objectives you can incorporate into your current strategy.

Key Performance Indicators (KPIs)

Have you selected the right indicators associated with each of your objectives? You'll know the answer to this question if you conduct your first audit close to the implementation of your strategy. By doing this, you ensure that the success measurement criteria you've selected is correct and that you've made the right call choosing one KPI over another. (Chapter 9 covers the subject of KPIs in detail.)

TECHNICAL STUFF

Some generic KPIs are associated with growth. These KPIs can include the size of your audience on a particular medium or the engagement half-life of your content on another medium (see Chapter 9). Accurate measurement can become tricky when you analyze elements, such as brand awareness or brand marketing value. It can take some clever maneuvering to measure these aspects accurately, so it's best to catch a misstep early in your analysis technique.

Benchmarks

If there is one mistake that marketers often make, it's setting their sights too high, too early. This mistake is why an early analysis of your benchmarks will be crucial. Even if you set fairly modest benchmarks at the start, there is still a chance that they're either too high or too low. Following your first audit, review your benchmarks to analyze your performance and establish new goals.

You set your benchmarks to measure how well you're progressing toward your objectives. Some of these benchmarks are short-term and relate primarily to a specific campaign. Others are ongoing and measure performance of the campaign over its lifetime. In some cases, its performance will underwhelm you. In this case, either your benchmark was set too high, or you've made a few missteps toward achieving your goal. If so, re-establish your benchmark at a lower level.

Another reason to review your benchmarks is to establish new ones based on your program's performance.

TIP

The only time that you want to lower your benchmark (as opposed to changing elements of your campaign) is when you find that your benchmark was set for an outlying period of performance. Lower the benchmark for the next audit so that you re-align it with the normalized growth path you're witnessing over time.

Data

Auditing your data is perhaps the most important component of any review. It provides the foundation of your complete strategy and affects every decision you make. Every time you conduct an audit, your data should be the first consideration. In fact, you should analyze it more thoroughly than any other aspect of your analysis.

The important point to keep in mind regarding your data is that unlike objectives, benchmarks, KPIs, or any other itemized element of your audit, your data exists everywhere. It's up to you to identify the sources of your unstructured or semi-structured data. Then you need to gather and analyze it in depth. Analyzing your data can take many forms, several of which are discussed in more detail later in this chapter in the section entitled "Identifying New Opportunities with Data."

Audience segments

At every audit interval, you want to ask yourself whether you've ideally structured the segments of Millennials you've targeted. Frequently revising your audience targets can lead to the optimization of your targeting mechanisms. It can actually help you develop new content that better fits the changing needs of your audience.

Keep in mind that audiences on new media in particular are evolving and often exhibit new traits and characteristics from one audit period to the next. There is no guarantee that what works today will work in a year, or even a month. Examine your audience segments using the tactics outlined in Chapter 3. It will help you determine the direction in which your Millennial audience is headed and help you stay relevant. You don't want to lose the relationships you've worked so hard to build.

Selected media

One quick way to achieve your objectives is to focus on executing your strategy in the leanest way possible. What exactly does that mean? It means that any time your audit indicates that you can remove a particular media component, you should trim it.

Staying lean saves you both time and money. The media you select in one period may not be ideally suited for continued use. This is not to say that you should completely wipe out a medium. You may simply want to scale back your invest-ment in an underperforming area and reallocate those resources to one that is generating significantly better results.

Evaluating Your Objectives

Objectives are always the starting point for a Millennial marketing strategy audit. Analysis of these objectives can take several forms. To analyze your data, you want to determine

>> **Overall progress:** Your audit should review your overall progress. This standard progress report evaluates both your short- and long-term goals in an effort to determine whether you're moving in the right direction.

>> **Restructuring of specific short-term objectives:** The second form of analysis tells you whether to eliminate or re-align your objectives based on current data. If your data suggests that an objective is unrealistic or no longer pertinent to the success of your brand, eliminate it.

>> **Creation of new objectives:** Lastly, your data can find new objectives. These new objectives may be short-term objectives related to time of year or a particularly hot issue, or they may be long-term objectives that reshape some of your universal strategy. Either way, your data can present new opportuni-ties to exploit.

Progress

Progress toward your goals isn't necessarily going to be linear. In a standard Point A to Point B model, you measure your progress based on how far you've come along your designated path. The more abstract objective of building lasting relationships isn't quite as easy to measure.

For intangible objectives, like brand awareness and affinity, you want to look closely at your KPIs (see the next section). You can measure the tangible objectives, however, such as conversions and growth, using traditional methods. In Figure 11-1, you can see an example of audience growth on Facebook. This is a straightforward example of an upwardly moving trend line.

FIGURE 11-1:
The growth of your audience over a designated period.

Restructuring

Are all your objectives on target? Do you need to remove any of them? You might remove an objective from a strategy during an audit for three reasons:

>> **You're overwhelmed.** When you create your strategy, you may identify several opportunities and plan to tackle each one right away. However, after a short time, you feel overwhelmed by the amount of work it takes to effectively execute every aspect of your strategy. In this case, keep the most relevant and best performing ones and eliminate extraneous objectives that are more about vanity than quality.

>> **You have unrealistic goals.** When creating your objectives both for the short and long-term, you may plan something that ultimately proves to be

unrealistic. This mistake doesn't always mean eliminating an objective from your mix. You can restructure or realign your benchmarks. However, on some occasions, a stated objective may actually be an incorrect one. For example, a market you hoped to capture simply doesn't exist in the numbers you thought it did. This error can occur because of a miscalculation or a *statistical anomaly* (data that lies outside the norm). In either case, remove this goal from your strategy.

>> **You can use your resources better elsewhere.** Of course, resources are finite. You can allocate only so much of your marketing budget to acquire and retain Millennials. This means that on occasion, you're going to have to make tough decisions about where to cut funding. If you have objectives that lead to conversion and increased retention, place your bets on those objectives and eliminate the losers.

Creation

Conducting an audit can help you identify data that leads to the creation of new objectives. These newly created objectives are often short term and can be achieved by running a highly targeted campaign. The key is to identify areas of sustained growth or performance that indicate an opportunity may exist related to

>> A particular form of engagement

>> An action taken by a particular audience segment

>> Some action related to a specific topic or time of year

Whatever the case may be, these behaviors and data points present a chance to create new goals related to your overall strategy.

Examining Your KPIs

You can do an analysis of your KPIs in conjunction with the analysis of your objectives. Over the course of your audit, you may note that an element you were hoping to analyze isn't available, which can indicate that you're missing a KPI. In fact, missing indicators or information is something that you want to pay attention to over the course of the entire audit. Sometimes the data that is missing is as valuable to your audit as the data that you can find.

When data is missing, you're alerted to the fact that you need to do one of the following:

>> Find a way to collect it

>> Establish a new KPI

>> Measure data that is being collected but not analyzed

You should pay close attention to a few factors when auditing your KPIs. Perhaps the easiest way to complete this phase of your audit is to ask yourself a series of questions:

>> **Are you tracking every one of your objectives?** It seems like common sense to track your performance in terms of your objectives, but the reality is that when you establish your KPIs at the outset, you may overlook potentially useful data. In addition, you may identify an intangible KPI that you can't measure with the data you currently have. Don't lose sight of it. You may find data you can use at a later date. (You can find a comprehensive list of both tangible and intangible KPIs in Chapter 9.)

>> **Is there anything in your audit that you can't explain?** If you find data pointing to a huge success or major issue but can't determine what it's related to, you may need to create a new indicator to measure it. This need will be clear when you note outliers or influence points that you can't attach to a particular objective or measurement, as shown in Figure 11-2.

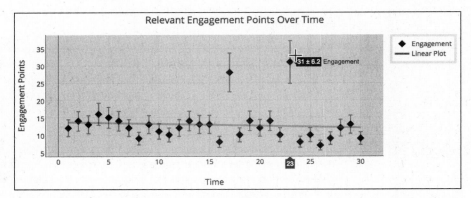

FIGURE 11-2:
An example of outliers found within a data set.

>> **How well can you measure your progress?** Sloppy or incomplete measurement is the enemy of success. You must back up your decisions using real data. If you have trouble measuring the success of a medium, campaign, or particular strategic component, incorporate new KPIs and wait for the next audit period to make a decision.

>> **Have new criteria become relevant?** A criteria or concept may gain in importance between audits. In this case, create a new KPI and then measure it at each subsequent audit. Don't worry that you missed something at the beginning of your audit because you know that things are constantly changing.

Pacing Your Audit

Only you can determine the best intervals at which to conduct your audits. However, certain rules will hold true regardless of the pacing you choose:

>> **You should conduct your first audit soon after implementation.** Your first audit is the most important one you conduct because your strategy is live for the first time. Rather than relying on historical data, the data you collect and analyze relates to the campaign you've just implemented. While you may be comfortable running a comprehensive audit every month or two, your first audit should take place within a few weeks of the campaign launch.

WARNING

Be careful not to run your first analysis too soon. You want to give your program some time to level out and start collecting relevant data. In addition, this data will serve as a basis for more realistic benchmarks for your next audit. You'll also be able to alter some program components based on your initial findings.

>> **You can audit campaigns individually and at shorter intervals.** When you're running a long-term campaign, you can also run small, campaign-based audits. You don't need to take all the other elements of your long-term program into account. Some campaigns possess crucial elements like ad budgets. They should be individually analyzed and optimized so that you don't spend more money than you need to.

>> **You must put audits on your schedule.** With so much going on and so many tasks to complete on a regular basis, you can easily forget to audit your Millennial marketing campaigns. Put a notation in your calendar every month at a specific date to remind you to run a basic audit along with a comprehensive one every few months. These audits serve a valuable purpose, and conducting them regularly can ensure that you achieve your goals in the shortest possible time.

>> **You should time your reviews to coincide with other business-relevant projects.** A good way to pace your audits is to align them with other corporate reviews, like budget analyses or sales reviews. If you regularly conduct a

particular audit at your organization, make your life easier by timing it to coincide with your Millennial marketing campaign audits.

>> **You don't need to standardize audit intervals.** While it may be easy to begin by standardizing the rate at which you conduct an audit, you certainly don't need to stick to a rigid schedule. One point to remember when it comes to Millennials is that the ecosystem in which they exist is alive and ever-changing. That means that you may notice a strange data set or statistical anomaly that requires you to dig a little deeper. Even if your most recent audit was a few weeks ago and you weren't planning another one for a month, you can still feel free to conduct an audit and make the necessary changes to a component or even the program as a whole.

>> **You don't have to change benchmarks.** Just because you're conducting an audit, it doesn't mean that everything about your program needs to change. That's something to keep in mind with regard to benchmarks. If you set a growth rate benchmark at 1 percent and find that you have narrowly hit it at the time of an audit, don't feel compelled to increase it. If the established benchmark makes sense moving forward and aligns with your efforts, you should keep it at the same level.

>> **Your audits don't need to follow the same structure each time.** Different aspects of your strategy are highlighted from one audit to the next. If you want to focus on one particular issue or audience segment, you can. Comprehensive audits may cover all aspects of your strategy, but again, they don't need to conform to a rigid structure. One of the good things about analyzing and optimizing a strategy is that the data guides you through the structure of the audit, not the other way around.

Considering the fact that audits can be loosely timed and structured, it can be difficult to decide when an appropriate time to conduct an audit might be. The following points are worth noting when deciding on the pacing of your Millennial marketing strategy audits:

>> **Pay attention to linear dips in engagement rates.** When you notice these dips, you might want to consider analyzing your strategy to determine why you're seeing the rate of change decrease. You may have completely exploited the opportunity you identified or it might indicate a more serious issue. That's something you'll want to catch early. You can see an example of one of these in Figure 11-3.

>> **Allow at least two weeks of data collection.** While data begins to collect right away, you want to give your changes at least two weeks to normalize before conducting another audit. Too many factors are at play to make any judgment calls any sooner. Two weeks allows the data you analyze to be much more accurate and will lead to smarter decisions.

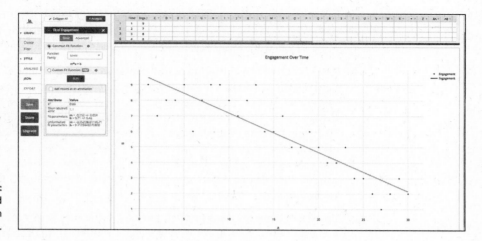

FIGURE 11-3:
A downward
trend in
engagement.

» **Audit paid campaign budgets more frequently.** Any time you're making a monetary investment, your primary goal is obviously a return. The best way to maximize that return is to implement optimization processes, and those are derived from effective audits.

» **Don't be afraid to run an audit if you notice an issue.** This does not even have to be a complete audit; you can run a mini-analysis to determine what may be causing the issue. When an anomaly is apparent, you're better off conducting an immediate audit rather than allowing the issue to snowball.

Identifying New Opportunities with Data

One of the most valuable takeaways from a data analysis is the identification of new opportunities. (For a complete overview of how to analyze your data in detail, refer to Chapter 4.)

The following sections walk you through some of the elements you want to be on the lookout for when identifying these opportunities within your data.

Outliers and influence points

When analyzing a data set, keep an eye out for statistical outliers or influence points that either fall out of the realm of standard deviation or manipulate the curve of the best of fit line that you've applied to your data set. (For more on the best of fit curve, see the nearby sidebar.)

BEST OF FIT CURVE

The *best of fit* curve is the linear curve that best fits the data sample collected. The easiest way to run this analysis is by determining a linear best of fit curve that fits the function $y = a * x + b$, where a is your slope. When you analyze the data set for a margin of error, or standard deviation, you will note certain points that are far above or below the curve and don't fit the margin of error. In this case, you're interested in the points above the curve, as those will hold information about potential opportunities to exploit new media, content, or audiences. For more on this topic, see Chapter 4.

Dramatic rates of change

Another data point you'll want to carefully review are your rates of change. Generally, over time, you'll see that your audience, engagement, and traffic grow at steady rates. You may see some fluctuations, but for the most part, that rate will remain constant.

If, however, you note that a sudden jump in the rate at which a particular aspect of your program is growing, you'll want to find out why. You'll want to identify what the source is in order to work with it and maintain the rate change for the long run. You can see an example of a significant spike in the rate of change in Figure 11-4.

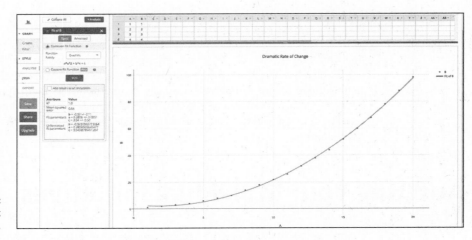

FIGURE 11-4:
A dramatic
change rate.

Sustained highs

Outliers and influence points are one thing, but if you see a major jump in a particular data set that leads to a new normal, you'll need to figure out what happened and how you can keep this new normal going. The difference between this sustained high and a variation in the rate of change is that in this case, an initial spike in rate of change simply adjusts averages without much variation in the rate of change, as shown in Figure 11-5. With the rate of change, growth is exponential as opposed to linear.

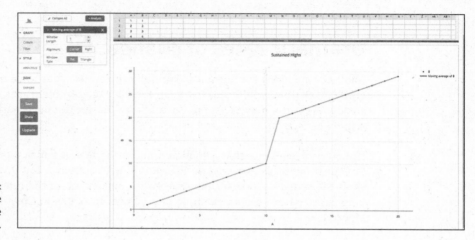

FIGURE 11-5:
Focus on the point where change occurred.

High-value correlations

Keep an eye out for correlations among your data when analyzing certain key points that led to action from your Millennial audience. Millennials within a particular cluster tend to operate similarly to one another. Identifying correlations between both audience and content characteristics can help you improve your content development process and aid in hypertargeting of content to certain audience clusters.

Auditing Your Individual Initiatives

Campaign audits have some characteristics that differentiate them from your overall strategy audits. They're smaller and take into account certain elements that are unique to campaigns. For example, they focus on a singular objective and have measurements that you can analyze individually.

Measuring against established benchmarks

Typically, you hope to hit or exceed your benchmarks. However, *budgetary benchmarks* are ceilings you want to avoid. A budgetary benchmark is a benchmark that you've established as a maximum you're willing to spend to achieve a certain goal. This benchmark can be campaign costs, costs for certain audience actions, or any other budget-involved aspect of a campaign.

So, an example of a budgetary benchmark may be a cost-per-acquisition benchmark. If you've set your maximum cost per new acquisition at $100, then anything under that number is a win. If you see that you're acquiring customers at a cost that is higher than this benchmark, then you need to make some changes in order to drop your costs below your threshold.

In the case of campaigns, specifically campaigns that relate to these strategy-affiliated financial benchmarks, you want to beat these numbers by a significant margin. The reason is that you have full control of your budget in a campaign. By applying certain budgetary maneuvers, such as incremental bidding, you can increase the chances that you outperform your benchmarks in every campaign.

TECHNICAL STUFF

Incremental bidding is the process of manually bidding on actions that range from clicks to downloads to purchases at incremental levels. While the number of actions taken at each level of your bid may not be at the same volume as a standard average bid (and it may take longer to exhaust your budget), you'll be extracting the potential from every bid level. You'll also avoid overpaying for certain bids. After all, why should you pay $10 for an action that you can obtain for $1?

Re-evaluating your target Millennial audience segment

If there's one thing that becomes clear in the early stages of a campaign, it's whether you've targeted the right audience with the right content. When auditing a campaign, particularly at the first audit, you want to pay close attention to the engagement rates of your selected audience and measure those against projections and established benchmarks. If they're falling short, it may be worth considering a different audience, offer, or content.

In the case of audience selection, running campaigns for a number of audiences, with varying content types for each, is wise. While you may design a campaign or an offer with a specific audience segment in mind, you always have the chance that it appeals to additional segments. This appeal will become apparent only through a series of early stage tests.

Recognizing the reasons
to end an initiative

Because Millennials are an unpredictable base of consumers, it's sometimes wise to cut your losses and call a campaign a failure. While Millennials provide a tremendous amount of data, you can't always account for the sudden changes in tastes and preferences. You need to act quickly on your data because you have no guarantee that it will hold true for very long. You may have only a small window to take advantage of an identified opportunity, which is why audits and optimization are so important.

In some cases, you simply need to recognize that a campaign is no longer worth your investment. In order to make that call, you want to be on the lookout for some of the following telltale signs that a campaign isn't worth saving:

>> Engagement rates sustained at 40 percent or more below your average between your first and second audit

>> Cost-per-action at 25 percent or more higher than your average between your first and second audit

>> Cost-per-conversion at 40 percent or more higher than your average between your first and second audit

>> A viscerally negative reaction from 40 percent or more of your audience at the point of your first audit

3

Analyzing Millennial-Specific Engagement Opportunities

Take an in-depth look at the rise and power of the share economy and how your brand can use it.

Create a brand experience that engages your audience and builds close, lasting relationships with its members.

Leverage the desire by Millennials for on-demand products and services in your outreach and branding strategies.

Pivot your brand's efforts in order to cater to the unique consumption habits of Millennials.

Integrate a cause into your marketing efforts in order to connect with Millennials on a deeper level.

Chapter **12**

Utilizing the Share Economy

Millennials are patient. That statement may seem ironic to anyone who sees the on-demand nature of the web as proof that Millennials embrace immediacy. But, the truth is that while immediacy and short-term gain are favored by Millennials, the share economy highlights the patience that Millennials possess. For example, the explosive growth of services like Airbnb and Uber demonstrate that sharing has trumped the importance of ownership. Millennials would rather share a car than buy one they can't afford.

In this chapter, I highlight the importance of the share economy and present strategies you can use to participate in the sharing of goods, services, or even content. Leveraging the share economy is a great way to drive up familiarity with your brand and build lasting relationships with these new consumers.

Positioning Your Brand Around Sharing

Leveraging the share economy isn't going to be a strategy that suits every brand. For some, there simply isn't going to be a way to organically integrate a sharing component into a product or marketing strategy. To effectively leverage the share economy, you can run through a checklist that will help you determine whether your brand is capable of utilizing the strategy. See how many of the following items you can check off:

>> You have an active community forum.

>> You have a peer-to-peer opportunity.

>> You can afford short-term opportunity costs.

>> Your product or service has an online component.

The following sections look at each item in turn.

You have an active community forum

You need to have a community focus if you want to participate in the share economy. If your customer experience doesn't include engaging with a larger community about your brand, product, or even your industry, then taking full advantage of the share economy may be difficult.

A community forum can take different shapes. It can be owned by your brand, where the majority of participants are either customers or hot prospects, or it can be industry-based. If you manufacture power tools, for example, the community forum may include a topic like home improvement with an audience made up of general contractors or builders. The key is to have an online discussion that engages your specific audience.

You have a peer-to-peer opportunity

The ability to share content has been a pain point for many industries that rely on individual consumption, as opposed to community use of a limitless, digital product, such as software accessed via a cloud service online. As brands have recognized that fighting market demand has no value, they have made adjustments. Instead of adjusting to this demand, your aim should be to create supply for it. Your digital content should be shareable and possess certain qualities that actually encourage users to share your information with one another.

You can afford short-term opportunity costs

Being able to afford short-term opportunity costs is likely going to be the hardest point to check off on your share economy campaign checklist. Service-based organizations that provide a platform for sharing, such as Uber or Airbnb, don't have the same opportunity cost as other brands because they own their platform.

Leveraging the share economy may mean providing your product for free or for a single fee to several users. In the past, you may have individually charged each user. The benefit of this kind of sharing with Millennials produces short-term brand exposure and long-term loyalty.

The question most marketers or business owners need to ask themselves is whether these benefits outweigh the opportunity costs involved in this strategy.

Your product or service has an online component

The online component serves two purposes. For brands that have online content or logins, an online component makes sharing simpler and can lead to a rapid rise in adoption. For all brands, both those with an online product or service and those that operate offline, the online discussion serves to heighten awareness of the campaign and mitigate the short-term opportunity cost.

If you find that your brand, product, or service meets these criteria, then you're in a great position to take advantage of the share economy by capitalizing on the Millennial's desire for access over ownership.

Establishing a Voice

Your involvement in the share economy doesn't mean you need to change the way your business operates. The share economy, like any strategic tool, is something that you apply to a particular segment of your audience. Creating a voice for these users is an important part of your strategy.

Creating your brand's voice specifically for the share economy means focusing on two priorities:

>> **Mapping out your target audience:** Target a very specific segment of your audience with the content you create.

>> **Creating a content strategy:** Focus on the sharing element of your business.

Mapping out your target audience

The first step to launching a campaign that leverages the sharing economy is the identification of a viable audience. This audience may consist of existing customers, or it may be an audience affiliated with your industry. Regardless of where the audience comes from, you need to identify certain traits to ensure that the audience you target with your offers is a viable one.

As you put together a targeted campaign, you'll find that the majority of the audience identification process will take place on your new media ad platforms. The most valuable of these platforms related to narrowing down the audience will undoubtedly be Facebook. The following steps help you narrow down your audience:

1. **Select a general audience of Millennials that is either saved or segmented based on a particular age range.**

   Start with a broad focus and narrow down. In this particular case, you should either begin with your general Millennial audience (see Chapter 3), or just select an age range, as shown in Figure 12-1.

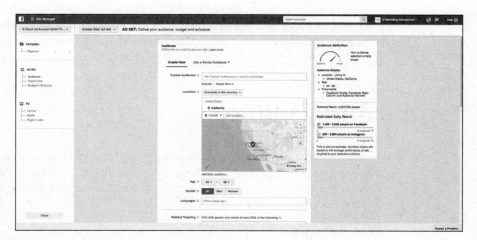

FIGURE 12-1: Begin by choosing a broad audience of Millennial users on Facebook.

2. **Start targeting a specific set of share-based interests.**

   In Figure 12-2, you can see a few examples of share-based interests, but you should expand on these interests so that they include any share economy-associated interests.

FIGURE 12-2:
Initially narrow
your user
selection by
targeting general
share economy-
associated
interests.

3. **Target interests and behaviors affiliated with your brand or industry.**

   After you complete the general share economy targeting, you should include interest categories associated with your brand or industry.

4. **Select specific placements to develop segmented content strategies.**

   REMEMBER

   Content will vary from one medium to the next. Segment your efforts to reach users with your share economy campaign on all current media (see Chapters 6, 7, and 8).

Creating a content strategy

At this point in the development of your share economy campaign, you hopefully have accomplished three crucial tasks:

» You identified your brand as having the right characteristics and the potential to leverage the popularity and value of the share economy.

» You developed a target audience that is likely to engage with your brand in this share-focused campaign.

» You developed content specifically geared toward the traits that define the share economy.

REMEMBER

Several standardized elements of your share economy-focused initiative includes your objectives, target audience, and KPIs. The content is going to be particularly important because its structure, layout, and calls-to-action are the driving force behind the framing of a share-based campaign.

Consider the following to help you communicate that the focal point of your content is sharing:

>> **Create stand-alone landing pages.** Your landing pages should remain separate from your other campaigns. One of the fastest ways to lose your audience's interest is to bait them with content that highlights some information and then sends them to a landing page that doesn't feature anything matching that content.

>> **Highlight the share aspect.** Use keywords like "share," "participate," or "join" to encourage users you sent to your landing page to take part in the share-oriented environment you created for them.

>> **Integrate a community conversation or activity feature.** Your audience may be reluctant to join your community if they don't have enough information to make a decision. To avoid this issue, highlight topics that are popular right on your landing page. Also, offer prospective participants a glimpse into the community to allow them to see what's being discussed.

>> **Provide detailed instructions.** Millennials are intuitive, but you shouldn't take their tech-savvy abilities for granted. If you provide a platform where people upload information about how to do something better, walk them through the process to display it. The upload or communication process may be straightforward and familiar, but don't assume that they can figure everything out on their own.

REMEMBER

Your share economy campaign relies on user-generated information and content. You want your audience to participate as much and as frequently as possible. So, if detailed instructions are one way of encouraging participation, make them as detailed as possible, even if you consider it overkill.

>> **Highlight the benefits of sharing.** You need to demonstrate to your target audience that sharing provides value. Chapters 6, 7, and 8 cover this concept, which is something to keep in mind when you're creating content for your campaigns. You also have to highlight the value of your target audience's specific participation. Audience members are going to ask why they should spend their time sharing about brand. You have to answer that question before they'll take the time and effort to engage.

>> **Consider an incentive-based initiative.** One of the fastest ways to drive up participation in any campaign, including a share economy-focused initiative, is to provide your Millennial audience with some sort of incentive or acknowledgment. It doesn't have to be anything grand, but it should be something that highlights the individual user, like a leaderboard or a Contributor of the Month program.

>> **Communicate with your audience as a peer.** You want your community to establish a real relationship with your brand. To build up the community as quickly as possible, communicate with participants on a peer level. If you hide behind a corporate persona, you can't encourage real relationships.

Running a Niche Campaign for the Share Economy

Your share economy campaigns leverage unique segments of your Millennial audience, which means that the objectives you create will relate to a particular audience construct (niche) and may not necessarily focus on long-term goals. Your goals can relate to universal objectives, such as driving up brand awareness, engagement, or conversions, but they must target a particular segment. If the campaign has the share economy as its focus and your goals relate to the audience that you cultivated for the share economy, then your objectives will work.

Ask yourself the following series of questions to simplify the process of developing your niche goals. They can help you construct readily achievable objectives.

>> **What are you going to measure?** To create your objectives, you need to determine what you want to measure. For example, if you're providing a learning exchange where participants are sharing knowledge with one another, are you going to measure the amount of data collected or the size of your growing user base of experts? These are two separate objectives, and while you can aim to achieve both, you need to have a different objective plan for each one.

>> **Does the share economy campaign operate in a vacuum?** You need to decide just how connected your share economy initiatives will be to your overall objectives. The share economy has some unique aspects to it that may not fit in with the rest of your program, but this isn't to say that it will be different from your brand online. Branding attributes and your brand persona will be consistent wherever you have a presence, so ask yourself this question: How much of your brand and the brand experience (see Chapter 13) will you incorporate into your share economy campaign?

>> **What universal elements of your marketing strategy tie into the share economy campaign?** You shouldn't run the risk of conducting an effective share economy campaign only to find that several members of the community aren't familiar with your brand outside of your share economy platform. For this reason, you need to identify those elements and ensure that they're present and represent your brand well.

>> **Does the campaign end with the share economy, or are secondary actions important?** You're targeting a unique segment of your Millennial audience that is particularly attracted to the concept of sharing. However, you should also include incentives that push your audience to take another step beyond the share economy. It can be a download or an incentive-based signup, such as a discount code that encourages share economy participants to become customers.

REMEMBER

Millennials want access over ownership, at least at first. Providing them with an option to participate in the share economy aspect of your business can mean giving them the desired access until a fraction is eventually ready to buy.

Encouraging Audience Participation

After you establish the objectives of your share economy campaign, you're ready to provide your audience with incentives to participate. For example, you can create a place for your community to share access to online subscription services, such as creative software, instead of requiring them to buy access to each individual product. This incentive can be a very powerful way of pulling users to your brand over a competitor.

However, it's important to create barriers to prevent this kind of service from being abused. Some ways to prevent abuse include

>> Making sure that shared passwords work only with a certain level of subscription

>> Putting a limit on how many documents third parties can save

These methods allow users to access the product until the desire for ownership comes into play, and they move away from simply needing access.

The following sections look at some marketing tactics you can employ to encourage adoption of your newly launched share economy platform.

Reach out to your existing database

Current customers are the easiest ones to get on the share bandwagon. Your existing database of Millennial customers is sure to include some users that fall into the share economy group.

Go through the same audience development process outlined earlier in this chapter, in the section "Mapping out your target audience," but focus on existing customers and fans. Encourage them to participate and push them to check out the new offer.

Leverage native video ads

Mobile is where Millennials spend their time, and the success of share economy mobile applications like Uber and Lyft show that this audience is partial to the mobile platform.

Develop your ads and push them to your selected media on mobile devices. Highlight the benefits of the share concept for your product or industry and provide some incentive to get Millennials to try it.

Target ads to the share economy audience

After you segment the audience that fits into the share economy, create content that focuses exclusively on the sharing aspect. Touch on the fact that your audience may have a pain point that this feature addresses — for example, not needing the full service or product or not being able to afford the full option.

TIP

The model you should use in the case of these ads and pieces of content is the *problem-solution model.* This model involves presenting your target audience with a problem they may or may not know they have and then offering them the solution to that problem all within the ad itself.

Develop incentivized adoption schemes

Incentivizing adoption is your best bet to get the ball rolling. Every one of the models you implement should include some sort of incentive. Incentives will generate the fastest adoption by users in all categories.

The incentive can be something simple like a free sample, gift card, or offer redemption. It can also be something more complicated, like a tiered offer based on subscription level, subscription length, or frequency the product is used.

Measuring Results

When you set out to measure the success of your share economy campaign, what you measure depends to a large extent on your objectives. If your goal is to drive brand awareness, then your focus is going to be on the increase of your reach, share of voice, and other brand-affiliated key performance indicators (KPIs). If your goal is to get new customers then the KPIs you analyze will relate to acquisition.

You'll want to watch for some telltale signs when you determine how to measure your share economy campaign success. Those signs will be evident when you ask yourself a few questions related to measurement:

>> Is the goal to build a new community?

>> Are there secondary goals that extend beyond the share economy?

>> Should you place a timeline on secondary goals, or should you measure those actions in perpetuity?

Is the goal to build a new community?

A simple, one-dimensional goal may be to build a new community of share economy–oriented Millennials. You can analyze this community for insights and opportunities and leverage it for growth. Ultimately, however, if your primary goal is to build out a new audience, your measurement criteria will relate to the size and engagement of your new audience.

Are there secondary goals that extend beyond the share economy?

If your goal goes beyond simply building a new community, then you need to identify how those goals are measured. You may want to include secondary goals, such as conversions that result from an initial introduction to the customer by way of the share economy. You can measure community participation through either touchpoint attribution measurement, or you can directly link conversions or specific actions to the share economy in their entirety. Whatever the case may be, you need to clearly outline how the share economy will factor into these secondary conversions.

TECHNICAL STUFF

A *touchpoint attribution measurement* model looks at a specific touchpoint, or point of contact between the brand and customer, in the buying journey and allocates a specific weighted ratio to that touchpoint. For example, if, over the course of the buying process, a customer engages with your brand five times, then a touchpoint attribution measurement model would assign each of those five touchpoints a specific weight regarding its contribution to the final conversion.

Attribution models can vary significantly in terms of the value given to different touchpoints in the buying journey. In some cases, touchpoints are given equal ratios, and in others, some touchpoints can be weighted more heavily. There are also attribution models where attributed contribution ratios can decay over time, whereby a touchpoint that had a high value when it first occurred becomes less and less relevant as time goes by and other touchpoints come into play. In the case of the share economy conversion that might arise, you may want to consider focusing entirely on the engagement within the share economy and then attributing any subsequent engagement to the activity that has taken place within the share economy. This focus ensures that you'll be able to closely monitor activity within the share economy and with your share economy audience.

Figure 12-3 shows you an example of a touchpoint attribution model whereby each touchpoint along the buying journey is given equal weight, as well as one where touchpoints are given variable weights. In these two examples of Google Analytics models, touchpoints are given a value regarding how much they have contributed to the conversion.

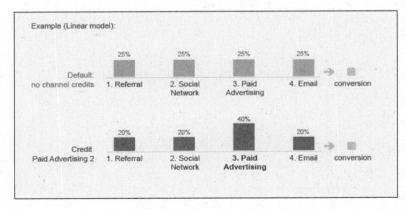

FIGURE 12-3: Attribution models can weigh each touchpoint In Google Analytics.

To find more detailed information on the use and customization of attribution models in Google Analytics, visit `https://support.google.com/analytics/topic/3205717`.

Should you place a timeline on secondary goals?

If you plan to measure secondary objectives that extend beyond simply building a new community and watching it grow, placing a cap on the amount of time that you measure these secondary conversions is worthwhile.

For example, if you measure the number of ebooks downloaded during a campaign, you want to know that the activity took place during the campaign and not a year later. Setting a time limit, perhaps no more than about 30 to 90 days, is a good approach.

Chapter **13**

Leveraging the Desire for Experience

illennials are price sensitive and willing to delay purchases. But when they are ready to spend, a priority for those expenditures will be on experience-oriented purchases. Their desire for brand experiences ties in closely with their pursuit of brand relationships. A brand experience doesn't necessarily need to be some grandiose gesture. It can be subtle. Millennials are observers who appreciate subtleties and look for relationships with companies that don't blast them with overt corporate messages.

This chapter focuses on the creation of a brand experience that extends beyond the simple transaction. You concentrate on integrating the experience into every campaign and look at the tools you need to integrate the brand experience into your larger marketing strategy.

Creating a Brand Experience Strategy

One of the most important things to remember is that during any customer interaction, on any media type, your brand should be instantly recognizable. Instantly recognizable means that everything from your voice to your branding to elements as basic as your color scheme should be consistent.

When developing your brand experience strategy, begin by outlining how you'd like your Millennial prospect to interact with your brand at each point of engagement throughout the customer journey.

The *customer journey* is the path your prospects take when they interact with your brand across web channels. For example, a customer journey can begin with an initial introduction to the brand on social media. That exposure may be followed by an educational interaction with your website, blog, or other social network. Then it may end with a conversion in your online store, completing the initial customer journey. This journey continues after the conversion is made, strengthening the brand relationship and encouraging ongoing business.

To craft the customer journey effectively, start by answering a few important questions:

>> What is the ideal medium for a first interaction?

>> Where will your efforts to educate switch to efforts to sell?

>> Will you invest in establishing multiple entry points?

>> How does the experience differ from prospects to customers?

What is the ideal medium for a first interaction?

Millennials move from one medium to another very easily, so predicting where their first interaction will take place is hard. But you can make an educated guess as to where new prospects will have their first interaction based on two criteria:

>> **Media platform:** When you run an audience analysis (see Chapter 3), you can identify the place where your largest audience exists. Then you can put content of interest to new prospects there.

>> **Industry conversations:** You can look at data analyses (see Chapter 4) to see where the conversation in your industry is taking place. Then you can start there.

These two points will help you determine where you'll meet your new prospects. This location is where you want to establish the brand experience and introduce the audience to your voice.

Where will your efforts to educate switch to efforts to sell?

The first goal of any brand experience is education. To begin developing a relationship, you need to tell prospects

>> Who you are (so that you familiarize your target audience with your brand personality)

>> What products and services you offer

>> Why you're the best option on the market compared to your competitors

After you educate your users, the second goal is to develop a relationship to drive conversions. More often than not, this relationship-building will take place on owned media where you have complete control of the content and the process. This owned media can be your website, your mobile app, your blog, or any other medium that you own.

TECHNICAL STUFF

There are three kinds of media:

>> *Owned media* are all the channels that you control completely. An example can be your website or your branded Facebook Page. On these media, you control the content, the engagement, and the brand representation.

>> *Paid media* are media where your brand's presence is a result of an investment. For example, Google AdWords ad space is an example of paid media, where the media representing your brand is found as a result of your paid efforts.

>> *Earned media* are your most valuable types of content. Third parties that reference your brand have created these pieces of content. While you may not have control of what is being said in some cases, earned media are the most trusted sources of material about your brand because Millennials trust their peers more than they do brands themselves.

Will you invest in establishing multiple entry points?

The more robust you make the brand experience, the more likely it is that your target Millennial audience will first encounter your brand in one of several different places. For this reason, you need to carefully plan where these entry points will occur.

TIP

Any potential entry point that a customer may come across should be designed to funnel users to your most active and valuable assets, such as your website or landing pages.

How does the experience differ from prospects to customers?

After a prospect becomes a customer, the brand experience changes. There are significant differences in the type of engagement a prospect will have with your brand compared to the experiences of an existing customer. These differences can include, for example, the media on which you most commonly engage with a user. While social media may have been the driving force in the brand experience with your prospects, it may change to email or a messaging platform such as Facebook Messenger after that individual becomes a customer. You'll need to establish separate strategies for each of these user types.

An example road map

After you select a starting point for the brand experience, develop a sales strategy, and identify the differences between initial contact and nurturing existing customers, you can get into the process of designing the brand experience. It can be difficult to envision what your brand experience road map may look like when you've never encountered one before. The following steps highlight an example of a brand experience with a consumer product. You can use this example as a guideline when creating your own brand experience road map:

1. You make an initial connection when a prospect sees your Facebook ad.

2. The prospect visits your blog to read an article relevant to your industry.

3. The prospect makes contact with your company and a conversation takes place.

4. The prospect buys something based on a special or promotion offered via email.

5. You re-engage with the customer shortly after the initial purchase to build loyalty.

6. You demonstrate your thanks by delivering private offers or gifts for the existing customer base.

While every customer journey is going to be different, this example shows you the brand experience in action. It demonstrates a process that you can use to establish a connection and build a relationship with prospects.

Identifying Touchpoints for Your Audience

Before you choose touchpoints, you need to keep in mind two things:

>> You don't need to have a robust presence on every network you choose.

>> Every network where you have a touchpoint doesn't need to heavily factor into your brand experience strategy.

Your branding and personality should be evident wherever you have a presence. But with regard to the customer experience, you are the one who should determine which media and touchpoints should be emphasized.

You should consider using the following touchpoints for your brand experience strategy.

>> **Social networks:** Social networks should be the driving force in your brand experience strategy. Social media have become the unstoppable juggernauts they are thanks to Millennials. Therefore, most interactions that take place with your brand occur on some social network. These networks are ideally suited for first encounters and for relationship and loyalty development.

>> **Your website/blog:** When you have complete control over every aspect of a medium, like your website or a blog, it becomes a very powerful tool. These platforms provide an effective way to build on an initial contact. Millennials may not stumble on your website as a first contact, but when they do click-through to your site, you know that you can provide more detailed information because you have their full attention.

>> **Your mobile application:** If you've invested in developing a mobile application, then it's a perfect place to build a relationship and extend the brand engagement experience after you've converted a prospect into a customer.

>> **Mobile messaging applications:** Millennials engage on mobile, which is where they spend the majority of their time. You can further the brand experience on a very personal level by creating an engagement strategy for mobile messaging platforms like Facebook Messenger, WhatsApp, and, of course, text messaging. Chapter 10 covers mobile in detail.

>> **Email:** You may think that email is a forgotten platform by Millennials. But after a consumer has been converted into a client, it can be a valuable asset. You can cultivate the relationship and deepen the brand experience. Millennials may ignore cold emails, but when information from a trusted brand comes into their inbox, they're receptive to what's being offered.

Cold emails are emails that have come from a sender with which the receiver doesn't have a previous relationship. Sending emails to *rented lists*, for example, where you buy addresses for an email campaign, will be ignored by Millennials who will consider it to be spam. Email is widely regarded as one of the last personal spaces where a user has complete control over the content he or she sees and ignores. An email from an unknown sender will either be automatically placed in the Junk folder, or the recipient will ignore it and throw it in the Trash.

Checking Off Elements for Each Touchpoint

Every touchpoint where your audience encounters your brand should add value to both the consumer and to your organization and push the customer toward conversion. To get the most from your brand experience touchpoints, you'll want to include certain elements at each one. These elements help move the journey along and make it a more cohesive experience. A consistent experience encourages the prospect to stay the course and increases your chances of successfully converting your prospect to a customer.

In the initial stages of the brand experience when the consumer is just beginning to become acquainted with your brand, you may want to consider incorporating the following elements:

>> **Clear branding:** You need clear branding that is visible throughout your creative design and copy. In this early stage of the experience, you're introducing the user to your brand, so it's crucial that it's clearly marked — perhaps even overstated, such as a logo or company name that takes up the majority or entirety of an image you share.

>> **Rich media:** Rich media like images and videos immediately attract the attention of users. When used in an ad campaign on a social network like Facebook, a video automatically begins playing in the user's feed. Millennials are visual consumers, so if you can use rich media to capture their attention, take advantage of it.

>> **Solutions:** It's a good idea to include the solution to a problem faced by your prospects right in your copy. In fact, one of the most effective forms of communicating your message to Millennials is to present your product or service as a solution to a problem they may or may not know they have. Think about the classic infomercial structure, where a voiceover begins by asking, "Has this ever happened to you?" You present a problem and then offer a brand solution. In your first interaction with your target audience, you need to clearly spell out the problem to engage the user.

> » **A call-to-action:** In this first step, you're trying to educate the user, not necessarily sell your product. A call-to-action should simply offer the prospect the opportunity to learn more about you. Your call-to-action shouldn't be an aggressive sales pitch, but rather an invitation to learn a little bit more about your brand or solution.

Developing a Customer Relationship

After you make the initial introduction of your brand to your target Millennial audience, you can begin to develop the brand relationship. In this stage of the experience, you can use some sales-oriented content to encourage users to take the next step.

The following sections describe some of the most useful techniques for building a relationship.

Engaging users with conversational content

At the relationship-building stage, it's important not to solely focus on selling to your Millennial prospects. One of the qualities that Millennials seek is value in the content brands share. They're looking for content that gives them a reason to engage. This content can be in the form of a conversation. Ask questions or conduct pools, surveys, or ongoing industry discussions. (I cover the topic of conversational content in Chapter 6.)

REMEMBER

When something relevant to your industry is being discussed, it's appropriate for your brand to participate in the conversation. For example, suppose that you sell a particular tech gadget, and Apple announces a shift in the way some aspect of their devices work. This announcement gives you an opportunity to share your opinion either on your owned channels or on a public forum where a conversation is already taking place.

Sharing useful information that highlights your expertise

By sharing tips and insights that demonstrate your expertise in the industry, you're providing value. You're also highlighting why you're the best of all the options on the market.

Chapter 6 covers the topic of developing value-added content.

Offering first-time customers specials, freebies, or deals

You want to ease the potentially awkward scenario of overtly selling a product or service on a medium like a social network, which is intended to be conversational. One strategy you can apply in the hopes of avoiding that awkward situation is to offer users a special discount or a deal to first-time customers.

TIP

Special deals create an incentive for the customer to convert and help you decrease the conversion time.

Building trust by sharing third-party content that mentions your brand

When you find that third parties, like influential bloggers, discuss your product, you want to make sure that your audience sees it. This content will further cement your status as an industry leader and keep your brand top of mind when your prospect is ready to make a purchase.

After a user becomes a customer, the brand content should shift from pursuit to relationship growth. This stage is where ongoing, personalized communication becomes your most valuable asset for long-run expansion and survival in the market.

To get the most from the touchpoints in this stage of the consumer cycle, you should consider using one-on-one communication, either in real-time in a messaging application or via email.

You also should consider incorporating the following elements into these communications.

>> **Personalization:** It may seem like a small detail, but personalization goes a long way with Millennials. When you can add their name to correspondence — for example, in an email subject or body text — you increase the likelihood that they'll engage with the content.

>> **Appreciation:** Little things go a long way. That is particularly true when it comes to showing your appreciation for your customers and your audience. Sharing content that communicates your gratitude helps solidify the relationship you're building with Millennials. It also enhances the brand experience after a conversion and increases the chances of repeat business. An example is when Cadbury, a UK-based candy maker, shared a video thanking its fans on Facebook after it hit one million fans (see Figure 13-1).

» **Community:** Making your content more about the community, the industry, and, most importantly, the audience after they've converted goes a long way toward solidifying the relationship. It also enhances the brand experience and adds value to your content.

» **Regular communications:** It's hard to build a relationship with a brand that has gone dark after a conversion. Keep up regular contact with your audience, both new and old.

Segmenting Your Content

Of course, you'll regularly share general content designed to appeal to your broad audience. But to optimize the effectiveness of your campaigns and extract the greatest benefit from each target audience, you need to develop content that tells a story. (Chapter 3 covers storytelling.)

You need to craft your brand content in such a way that it guides your target audience through the journey from prospect to customer. You want to gently move them from one step to the next. Be careful, though; you don't want to come across as insistent. You want to ease your audience down a conversion path so that when a prospect is ready, the next step is perfectly clear and easy to make.

Creating experience-specific content

In the sections earlier in this chapter, I cover several rules and guidelines that relate to the more general brand experience strategy.

However, when you create experience-specific campaigns, you want to create a narrative that helps prospects move from prospect to customer. As you develop this experience, you can do a few things to help your audience progress in the right order:

>> Maintain a structured narrative

>> Ensure the fluid connection of your channels

>> Establish a timeline that you can easily follow

>> Connect each stage of the process

>> Gradually blend the experience with standard content

Maintain a structured narrative

When running a brand experience campaign, you need to think of each initiative as having a complete narrative — with a beginning, middle, and end.

You may create a story with the long-term goal of building an ongoing relationship or a short-term goal like getting your audience to participate in a new initiative.

Regardless of whether you're focusing on the brand experience or trying to generate interest in a new product launch, a narrative needs to exist.

Ensure the fluid connection of your channels

When you're building your campaign, it's crucial that you link all your media channels. It should be entirely clear to your prospects that they're engaging with the same brand and the same campaign. This fluid connection requires you to pay close attention to the consistency of your message, rhetoric, branding, and creative elements of the campaign.

You should also build a cross-channel referral component into your content. A *cross-channel referral* means that you refer your audience from one channel to another from within your content. This strategy helps you create a more robust presence for your brand and highlights the versatility of your communication.

Establish a timeline that you can easily follow

Consistency and timing are two keys to success when conducting a brand experience campaign. You need to create a strategic timeline that outlines when you'll share particular types of content and at what rate you'd like your audience to move through the various stages of the experience.

Connect each stage of the process

It should be clear at every touchpoint where your customer should be going next. Remember that the campaign is structured as a narrative. At no point in this process should your audience be confused about where to go or what to do.

Leverage a call-to-action whenever you can to move users from one step to the next. Also, consider presenting complete instructions when appropriate, like during the conversion stage when your audience is highly engaged and willing to follow instructions.

WARNING

Don't give your audience outlined instructions in the early, education stage of the process. In the case of the initial phases, a simple "Learn More" call-to-action should suffice. The pushy approach may be a little bit too much for new prospects to handle and could turn off those Millennial users who dislike aggressive sales tactics.

Gradually blend the experience with standard content

As you build a relationship with your customers, you should gradually blend the brand experience narrative into your day-to-day content. This slow, calculated transition will allow you to maintain a relationship with users and possibly transition them into brand loyalists. Initially, you want to continue sharing segmented content that relates to the brand experience initiative. Then you can slowly work your way toward integrating these users into the general audience and sharing more generalized content with them.

A great way to go about gradually blending is through the strategic use of your Audiences on Facebook, which is a subject covered in Chapter 3. As you engage your new, experience-oriented audience with campaigns, note the level of engagement users exhibit. As this engagement rate increases, you can see that these users are engaged in what you have to say as a brand. This advice is particularly true as time passes after the end of a campaign.

At this point, you can begin integrating this audience with your general audience in ad campaigns by selecting the audience when choosing the targets for a given initiative. This easy integration will help maintain engagement with your new audience and allow you to build up your general audience of engaged users.

Unifying your content across every channel

Unifying your content across all current media is an important part of the brand experience initiative. Your audience will differ from one channel to the next, and — perhaps more importantly — the personalities of these users won't necessarily be the same on one medium as they are on another.

In spite of this difference, you can use the following tactics to connect your content and maintain a degree of consistency across all channels in a brand experience campaign:

>> Create a unique message

>> Deploy remarketing

>> Develop unique assets

Create a unique message

Your audience can easily get lost across various media, even if you've carefully planned each stage of the brand experience campaign. The reality is that so much content is out there that you can easily lose sight of the next step when following a buyer's journey.

Try to create a standout, segmented message and maintain consistency in your branding across all media. This consistency will help your content clearly stand out from your other content and from other brands online.

Deploy remarketing

Remarketing displays ads to users who have arrived at a particular product or page on your website. Essentially, it sends a reminder about a product or page the user has previously shown interest in by clicking on it, giving them a second opportunity to visit the page or buy the product.

The strategic use of remarketing can make it easier to unify your content efforts. Remarketing allows you to place targeted, customized, and, in some cases, even personalized ads in front of select users on a variety of media. These ads can push users to return to a website and complete a purchase, remind them of an item or piece of content that they were viewing at one time or another, or present offers and deals from the website in question. Ultimately, the goal is to use the ads to keep the brand top of mind for prospects and offer reminders or even incentives to the user to return to the brand's website or store.

Develop unique assets

A great way to connect all your brand experience assets and ensure a degree of continuity from one asset to another is by creating stand-alone landing pages, either on mobile or the web.

These landing pages allow your audience to easily identify the brand conducting the campaign. It also makes it easier for you to track the data directly from these pages to gauge audience interest.

Integrating the Experience for an Omni-Channel Strategy

After you create your narrative and develop some of the content you plan to use for your brand experience initiative, you should start thinking about how the brand experience will fit into your overall multichannel strategy. We cover using a multichannel strategy in Chapter 9.

One of the key features of a multichannel strategy is the fluidity with which all aspects of your communications operate across channels. This feature is important to focus on to capture and retain the attention of Millennials. The same holds true for your brand experience. You run the risk of losing your audience along the way because your messages or instructions across the channels were unclear. You can use several methods to avoid audience attrition, including the following:

» Creating an identifiable theme

» Using a tracking mechanism

» Repeating the campaign title or slogan on all media

» Facilitating movement in any direction

» Ensuring that all assets are easily discoverable

Creating an identifiable theme

A theme is a powerful tool that helps your audience follow the campaign experience from one channel to the next. While your branding always needs to be consistent, a particular theme or stylistic identifier can be exactly what your audience needs to ensure that it follows the campaign content from one channel to the next without encountering any hurdles. An example of one such theme or identifier may be a campaign-specific mascot or the use of unique imagery in all creative assets associated with a campaign.

Using a tracking mechanism

Another useful option may be the creation and use of a hashtag on all active media to track a particular campaign.

Hashtags may be more common and useful on networks like Twitter or Tumblr, but when it comes to tracking your audience and your audience tracking your campaign, a hashtag is a simple identifier that any Millennial will understand and be able to follow.

Repeating the campaign title or slogan on all media

Simple branding is all you need to display in your day-to-day content to let your audience know that the content belongs to you. But when it comes to cultivating an experience, reminding your audience of the existence of the campaign becomes more important. For example, showcasing the title or highlighting a particular initiative using a hashtag is an effective way to retain your audience along the entire campaign path.

Facilitating movement in any direction

Your audience doesn't move through your content in a linear fashion. While you may have designed a narrative path that you want your audience to follow, you need to prepare for its divergence from this route.

You need to create links and buttons in your content that allow users to move in any direction they choose to throughout the journey. If they opt to go back to an original touchpoint or visit another touchpoint in the educational stage despite having already visited it, they should be able to do so.

Ensuring that all assets are easily discoverable

When it comes to reactivating dormant prospects, discoverability is key. The brand experience campaign is one that won't necessarily occur in one sitting or on one medium. These kinds of campaigns take time. For this reason, you need to ensure that the content on all channels is easily discoverable.

REMEMBER

Sending frequent reminders about a campaign or content related to an offer to prospects will keep even the most passive of prospects somewhat engaged. Then, when they're ready, it will be easier for them to pick up where they left off.

Tracking the Brand Experience Across Different Media

Tracking your data across all your channels enables you to learn from every action you take. It improves your efforts to optimize your budget and increase your conversion rate. Because brand experience-specific campaigns take place on multiple media, tracking that data requires a little bit of know-how and the occasional assistance of technology. It may also mean that you need to get a little creative about how you track your campaigns and which conversions you measure.

You can use several strategies to track your brand experience campaigns. These strategies may differ from one objective to the next based on the key performance indicators (KPIs) you choose. (I cover KPIs in more detail in Chapter 9.)

You can use the following common tracking methods to track the impact your brand experience campaigns have on things like conversion and retention of new customers and the cultivation of brand advocates:

>> A tag management system

>> Trackable links

>> Segmentation of data

A tag management system

A tag management system allows marketers to place a small piece of code on the pages of a website to track data. A *tag management system* lets you track data from each of your active sources to help you effectively tie together all your campaign efforts. If you use Google Analytics, the most logical choice of a tag management system is Google Tag Manager. Figure 13-2 shows the dashboard for Google Tag Manager.

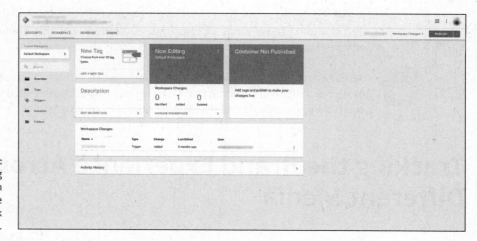

FIGURE 13-2:
Google Tag
Manager can
help you more
precisely track
data.

Trackable links

Whether or not you're using a tag management system, you need to create track-able links. If you're using Google Analytics, you can use Google's URL building service available at `https://ga-dev-tools.appspot.com/campaign-url-builder`, shown in Figure 13-3, to create these links, or you can use an online tracking service like Bitly (`http://bit.ly`), shown in Figure 13-4.

**TECHNICAL
STUFF**

Link tracking allows you to both segment data in your site tracking dashboard and monitor the effectiveness of different media and content individually.

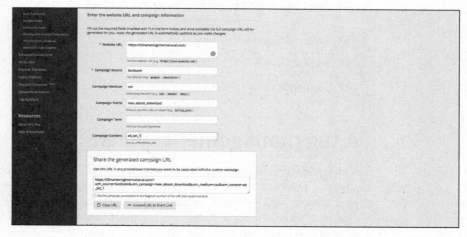

FIGURE 13-3:
Google offers a
free service
where you can
add customized
parameters to an
existing URL to
track more data.

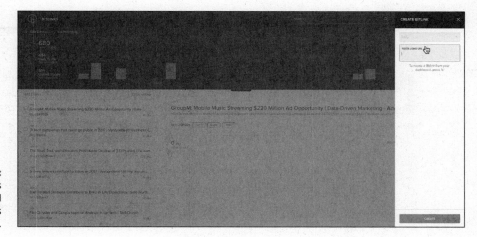

Segmentation of data

As with any campaign, you should be segmenting your brand experience campaign data in your tracking dashboards to get a full, unadulterated picture of how the campaign is working. Using link-shortening tools like Bitly or Google, you can segment your data in an analytics dashboard, such as Google Analytics. Then, from within this dashboard, you can look only at campaign data and analyze how it is performing on its own. You can then compare the solo performance of a campaign with the performance of other initiatives and the benchmarks you've set for your campaigns in terms of key performance indicators. Keeping your data segmented is an important practice that will help you get an isolated picture of the campaign you are running.

Running Brand Experience Campaigns

One of the fundamental differences between a traditional objective-oriented campaign and a brand experience campaign is the seamlessness with which a brand experience campaign is executed. Users can move from one piece of content to another and from one channel to the next without becoming confused about the path designed for the process.

While elements of your brand experience strategy may factor into your standard objective campaigns, the focus of the brand experience campaign is on the immersion of the audience in the story you're telling across various media. As with any campaign, you need to start by developing either a single or a series of objectives that you'd like to achieve by building out a brand experience for your Millennial prospects.

REMEMBER

Objectives, such as your KPIs (see Chapter 9), can be both tangible and intangible. You can collect tangible customer data, which is concrete and measurable, by having customers fill out a form or submit their information. Alternatively, you can try to build loyalty, which can often be an intangible objective as it's not necessarily measured by a concrete statistic but rather a concept that relies much more on observation.

When it comes to the brand experience, some of the most common objectives you should consider when building your campaigns include

>> Increasing brand engagement

>> Driving up brand awareness

>> Building a new segmented audience

>> Selling more product

>> Garnering customer loyalty

>> Fostering relationships

>> Launching a well-rounded campaign

Increasing brand engagement

Continuous engagement helps build your brand awareness. A brand experience campaign is about building that engagement across multiple media. By creating an experience in which your prospects and target Millennial audience can participate, you're driving increased interactions with a broad variety of users on several digital channels. Considering that this increased engagement is going to be an essential component of any brand experience initiative, you need to decide whether engagement is a primary or secondary objective of your campaign.

REMEMBER

Your *primary objective* is the one that you're most interested in achieving. All the work you do and everything you include in your strategy is going to aim to achieve this primary goal. A *secondary objective* is one that may be less of a focus or even just a byproduct of your primary objective. While you may track this objective and even implement a few components that work toward its success, it won't be your primary focus during the campaign.

Driving up brand awareness

Although brand awareness isn't a tangible objective in the traditional sense. it's an objective that you can work toward through the strategic use of a brand experience campaign. As you drive up engagement with your target audience, the conversation around your brand will increase. As that conversation increases, the discoverability of your brand by your target prospects and by new prospects who come across this public discussion will rise.

While there may not be a concrete way to determine brand awareness, one measurement that may be helpful is share of voice. *Share of voice* measures how much industry conversation pertains to your brand as compared to your competitors. As share of voice — a topic covered in Chapter 9 — increases, so does your brand awareness.

TIP

Creating a brand experience that focuses on intrigue can help you garner the attention of new audiences and users. An intrigue-focused campaign may have something to do with a series of clues or references that participants need to follow in order to reach the incentive-fueled end — perhaps a discount or special offer. This kind of campaign is a useful way to drive up brand awareness.

Building a new, segmented audience

One of the benefits of brand experience campaigns is that they can entice new fans. These viewers make it clear that they're willing to engage with brands that provide them with valuable content. (Chapter 6 covers creating useful content on different platforms.)

Selling more product

Of course, one of the goals that you'll work toward is increasing sales. Just remember that when it comes to brand experience, the sales cycle may be a bit longer than what you're used to because the timeline isn't necessarily fixed and the majority of the audience will be focused on getting the most from the experience presented.

You most likely will want to consider increased sales as a secondary objective in your brand experience campaigns. Unlike some of your more sales-oriented objectives, such as an ad campaign with a clear goal at its core, the brand experience is primarily about building relationships.

You may find that over time, these relationships lead to conversions, but the concept of building your brand experience means that you want to encourage the organic growth of a relationship with your prospects. A conversion may take place at any point in the process after the prospect in question feels comfortable enough to buy. Increasing sales, however, is still a viable objective worth monitoring.

Garnering customer loyalty

One of the most valuable byproducts of an experience-oriented campaign is the garnering of audience loyalty. Creating a noteworthy experience for your audience shows that you care about them.

This attention goes a long way in building loyalty among your existing or newly converted audiences.

Fostering relationships

Brand experience campaigns are reliable tools to use when you're trying to deepen the relationships you created with your audience. Though the growth of relationships isn't necessarily the easiest thing to measure, it's a worthwhile objective to monitor.

Launching a well-rounded campaign

To get the most from your campaign, you should follow a series of steps leading up to your launch. The following steps can help ensure that your narrative is clear, your tracking is established, and that you're working toward achieving exactly what you set out to do:

1. **Build out a slightly generalized Millennial audience.**

   With a brand experience campaign, you'll find some Millennial audience members that you wouldn't have necessarily thought to consider. Often, current campaigns drive up engagement from previously dormant users. To encourage the discovery of new audiences, keep your target audience a little bit more general than usual to expose the brand experience campaign to new prospects.

2. **Establish your objectives.**

   Determine exactly what it is you're trying to achieve by creating a brand experience initiative for your audience and selecting objectives that measure their interest.

3. **Construct a narrative.**

   The narrative is the driving force behind the entire brand experience, so it's a critical stage. Spend time outlining the ideal path you'd like users to take and then consider all the variations that you might present. You need to integrate your brand experience, so spend time thinking about all the ways your narrative's pieces are linked.

4. **Determine tracking methods and KPIs.**

   Before launching, identify exactly how you plan to track your progress and pick the key indicators you'll use to measure your success.

5. **Set initial benchmarks.**

   Your benchmarks may change after your brand experience program gets underway, but start with a few benchmarks that you'd like to improve.

6. **Develop your content.**

   This step connects closely to the narrative you structured for your brand experience. Create content that helps your audience move from one stage of the story to the next. Also, consider how the content will help you build a closer ongoing relationship with your audience.

7. **Launch your campaign.**

   Measure your results to see whether your audience is following the linear path that you created for them. You may need to make some changes to guide them along the path you constructed. You also may need to incorporate a new narrative that your audience is organically following.

8. **Make some changes.**

   Be proactive and make necessary changes right away.

Chapter **14**

Mastering the Market of Demand

The expanding capability of technology combined with the rise in popularity of mobile connectivity has fostered the emergence of the demand economy. Brands offering on-demand products and services have a serious edge over the competition. For example, in 2016, a mobile service like Uber, the on-demand car service, had a private market valuation north of $65 billion.

The shockingly rapid growth of Uber resulted from two things. First, Uber presented a solution to the common problem of, "You-can-never-get-a-cab-when-you-need-one." Second, Millennial consumers don't want to wait for anything. Put those together, and you have a multibillion dollar business that is changing an entire global market. This chapter focuses on the rise of that demand market.

Evolving Your Organization to Cater to Demand

Not every business caters to the demand economy. If you'd like to be more responsive to demand, you need to revise the structure of your offerings to cater to this market. Several characteristics need to hold true for your brand to cater to the demand economy:

>> Offering immediate digital access to your product/service

>> Functioning in real time

>> Focusing on mobile as a stand-alone platform

If some of the these characteristics apply to your organization, then you are in an excellent position to cater to Millennials looking for on-demand products and services. If some aren't applicable, don't worry. I present several other strategies throughout this chapter that can help you cater to the demand economy but won't require you to make a significant shift in the way your organization operates.

Offering digital access to your product/service

One of the defining characteristics of the demand economy is immediacy. That real-time, instant accessibility is usually accomplished via a web connection. To take advantage of the demand economy, you need to be able to offer digital access to your product from the cloud or have the ability to download the complete product to a user's computer.

Adobe is an example of a company that has shifted its organizational structure to cater to the demand economy. Previously, Adobe offered a physical product that would require users to purchase a new version when updates were made. Today, Adobe has shifted the configuration of its product offering to focus on cloud-based subscriptions with a monthly fee (see Figure 14-1).

FIGURE 14-1:
Adobe now offers subscription-based software.

REMEMBER

The demand economy isn't all about the Ubers of the world. Most companies need to make operational adjustments to their product to cater to a Millennial generation that wants immediate access to a product when they're ready to buy.

Functioning in real time

The demand economy doesn't only focus on the accessibility of a product or service itself. It also focuses on accessibility to the organization. Millennials want to able to communicate with your company after they buy your product. They want to be assured that after a transaction is complete, they won't be left on their own. It's critical to offer top-notch customer service to nurture the relationships you're building with your Millennial audience.

Focusing on mobile as a stand-alone platform

Mobile is where Millennials spend the majority of their time, so that's where a lot of transactions and interactions are going to take place. You need to have a mobile strategy that presents mobile as a stand-alone platform if you want to succeed at leveraging the demand economy. (See Chapter 10 for details on mobile.)

Creating On-Demand Services

After you evaluate your organization and determine that it has opportunities to leverage the demand economy, you can start developing services and features that fit the on-demand market.

Specifically, you should focus on two things:

>> Services that relate directly to the product or service that your organization offers

>> Communications that you can tailor to address demand whether or not your products can be developed for demand

Tailoring your product to the demand economy

If your product or service can, in fact, be tailored to the demand economy (see preceding section), you can take the following steps to accurately present the product:

1. **Identify the criteria that make your product suitable for the demand economy.**

   You should look for a few essential items when determining which product can function as part of an on-demand service. The most important of these criteria is the immediate availability of your product or service. You should highlight this feature on all your platforms.

2. **Create stand-alone marketing assets with on-demand features as the focal point.**

   You need to cater to the on-demand audience differently than the other audiences you've catered to thus far. While the new audience may consist of some of the same individuals, the appeal will vary. For this group, you want to create marketing assets framed around the fact that your product or service is available on-demand. These assets will include landing pages, social content, and ad content.

3. **Develop a specific audience that you can effectively market the on-demand product to.**

   Chapter 3 describes the process to accomplish this step. The next section also details an approach to handling the demand market.

4. **Launch social ad campaigns geared toward attracting the demand market.**

   Targeted social advertising is the fastest way to promote your on-demand services and drive up conversions in your new audience. You can send ad campaigns with a more sales-oriented tone to users who are already familiar with your brand, but may not have purchased yet.

TIP

If you find these users who have followed your brand, are engaged with your content, and have a penchant for on-demand products, you can likely generate a conversion with an ad campaign.

REMEMBER

The demand market is made up of users that want access above ownership. While they may not be ready to buy and own a physical version of your product, they may be willing to pay for a short-term subscription.

Building your on-demand audience

The audience you want to target for on-demand services may already exist in your larger audience of Millennials. These Millennials want to have access and are willing to pay for that access. This audience characteristic has become apparent in recent years with the rise of the software-as-a-service (SaaS) industry.

The *SaaS* industry is made up of software providers who license access to software on a subscription basis. This model differs from the traditional software sales model where customers purchase new versions of the software with each updated release. The SaaS subscription model allows customers to access the software for a nominal fee whenever they need it, without having to make a large purchase. SaaS products are generally accessed online and can be thought of as on-demand software services.

REMEMBER

Millennials don't typically want to pay a high cost for a product, wait for it to arrive, or have to plan around going to purchase it and then take the time to set up the product before using it. They simply want access to a product or service for a nominal fee when they need it. They don't want to feel obligated to continue with it after they've accomplished what they set out to do. Taking a product of yours and creating an on-demand or subscription-based version of it means catering to an audience of Millennials who may love what you have to offer, but are hesitant to buy it.

To serve these noncommittal buyers, you need to shape your audience. Shaping your audience means taking a new approach to the standard audience development process that is covered in Chapter 3. The steps you can take are as follows:

1. On Facebook, begin by selecting your general Millennial audience.

Your Saved Audiences on Facebook should include a general Millennial audience, which you've compiled over time. To create your on-demand market audience, select this audience at the outset of your campaign.

2. Narrow the audience by selecting users that have liked your Page.

You should segment this Saved Audience by users who have already liked your Page, as shown in Figure 14-2. The reasoning behind this step is to focus more sales-oriented content toward users that are already familiar with your content and don't need to see educational content. I cover educational content in Chapter 13.

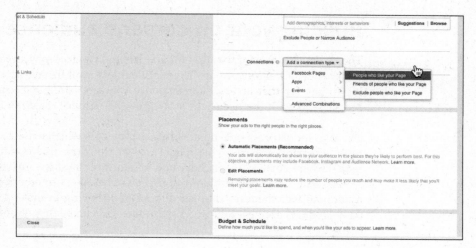

FIGURE 14-2:
Narrow your audience by selecting users that are already connected to your Page.

3. Identify interests related to the demand economy.

Further segment by selecting users who show an interest in the demand economy. Some of these interests, which are presented in Figure 14-3, include Netflix, Uber, video on demand, streaming media, digital television, Apple TV, and live streaming online. Also, include any other on-demand interests you can think of.

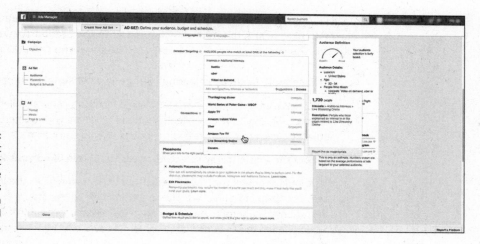

FIGURE 14-3:
Select the interest categories that suggest the audience is interested in on-demand services.

TIP

You don't need to further segment your audience by selecting interests and behaviors related to your industry because these users are already connected to your Page. In other cases, when you don't focus only on existing Page fans, take the extra step and select the interests and behaviors that indicate that your audience is interested in your industry.

4. **Focus on mobile placements.**

The demand economy has been accelerated in part because of the rise of the mobile usage of Millennials. Your demand services should be mobile-friendly, if not mobile-first. Pay particular attention to your ad campaign's mobile activity and placements. This area is where you're bound to see the majority of your demand activity, so segment and favor the mobile side of your ad campaigns.

Mobile-friendly content or campaigns are those that function well on mobile devices and adapt to the screens on which they're being viewed. *Mobile-first* relates to content or campaigns that have been created specifically for mobile devices.

Identifying communications opportunities

If you review your products and services and find that they're not appropriate for the on-demand market, you still have opportunities to connect with this segment of Millennials. These opportunities lay in demand for instantaneous communication with brands. Millennials want answers to their questions right away. The traditional way of conducting customer service, such as through emails, is too slow for Millennials.

While the process of building a real-time communications strategy is detailed in the next section of this chapter, you should look for the following traits to determine whether you can leverage this on-demand strategy:

>> You are in an industry with a vibrant, active audience on social media.

>> You have found mentions of your brand or competitors on various social media in the past.

>> You can find complaints about either your brand or competitors online in public forums within the previous 12 months.

>> You have an individual on your customer service team whose time can be allocated to focus on social media.

If you see these traits in your organization, then you're in a great position to offer real-time customer service and communications. It's an excellent way to appeal to Millennials and separates you from the competition.

Building a Real-Time Response Strategy

When it comes to new media, a lot can happen in the blink of an eye. You need to have a proper strategy in place to tackle any difficult situation when it comes up. Real-time engagement is one of the key elements of the on-demand economy. Millennials want answers to their questions and responses to their concerns right away.

Communicating with your audience in real time

Real-time communications are wildly different from planned, strategic, targeted content and communication. When you're communicating in real time, you need to plan for virtually every scenario. An example that demonstrates the value of good planning is Oreo's Super Bowl "Dunk in the Dark" tweet, shown in Figure 14-4. Oreo took immediate advantage of the Super Bowl power failure in 2013 and produced one of the most successful examples of real-time engagement ever.

FIGURE 14-4: Oreo showed an excellent example of real-time communications during the 2013 Super Bowl.

Alternately, you can find stories of brands that completely missed great opportunities or flubbed their attempt at real-time engagement, such as TGI Friday's 2014 attempt to chime in on the Oscars, shown in Figure 14-5. In this case, TGI Friday's simply wanted to insert itself into the conversation. But, it didn't have a plan or content strategy, so it completely missed the mark. Its attempt drove vir-tually no engagement and confused both consumers and marketers who couldn't figure out why or how TGI Friday's fit into the conversation.

FIGURE 14-5:
TGI Friday's attempt at real-time engagement about the Oscars was misguided.

To effectively leverage the power of communicating with your audience in real-time, you should engage with them socially and handle customer service queries on social media. Make sure that you're paying close attention to these important factors:

>> **A clear and familiar tone of voice:** The voice you've created for your brand is the one that helped you build strong relationships with your Millennial audience. This voice, first introduced in your regular content, needs to be consistent with your real-time communications. Millennial audience acquisi-tion relies on relationships, and a big part of those relationships stem from the creation of your brand voice. If your voice is clear, you're in good shape to move forward with your real-time engagement strategy.

>> **A team that can handle a large influx of communications:** Real-time communications can be tricky because you can't postpone a response. You need to be equipped to deal with situations as they arise and get your content out there at a moment's notice. The need for preparedness doesn't necessarily mean that you need to have an entire team devoted to customer service, though that is always desirable. But, it does mean that you should have someone paying close attention to social media who can immediately jump on an opportunity or tackle a problem.

>> **A plan for every possible situation — good and bad:** Preparation is at the root of success with all real-time engagement. You should have already planned how you'll deal with everything from customer service to real-time responses before you launch your communications program.

>> **Customer service that can take place online, preferably on social media:** Conventional customer service rarely works well with new media. For this

reason, you need to review your customer service processes to determine the kind of information your customers want to share to get their needs met.

Of course, some situations will require you to take the conversation offline. For example, you may need to have the customer share confidential information. However, the key to successfully handling customer service in real time is to determine whether new media provides enough of a platform for you to manage customer service online from start to finish.

Getting started with automated replies and bots

Facebook Messenger has become one of the most popular communications platforms for Millennials. Slowly, brands have begun offering real-time communication with customers on this platform. However, the issue that has arisen is that while Messenger provides a great way to communicate in real time, you can't always respond to a customer query right away. Your customer service team may not be available at that moment. This kind of situation is where bots or automated responses come in.

The two types of real-time communications are bots and automated replies. *Automated replies* are automated messages that you configure to respond to users when you are away. *Bots*, on the other hand, are far more customized and can assist with sales and communications. However, bots are quite a bit more complicated to develop.

You can set up both types by going to the Settings tab of your Facebook Page and selecting Messages. Both of these tabs are highlighted in Figure 14-6.

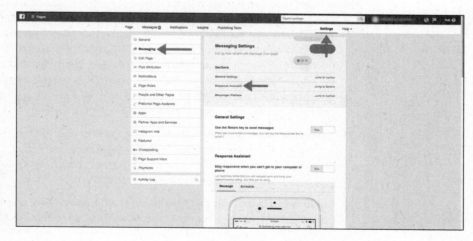

FIGURE 14-6: Automated responses in the Messages section of your Facebook Page Settings tab.

Automated replies

Here are the steps for setting up your automated replies:

1. **Under the Response Assistant section, start by creating your away message.**

The away message is a simple way to maintain a degree of real-time communication with your audience. This feature is particularly useful for small organizations or solo entrepreneurs. It's much harder for these businesses to be active online every second of every day. Even your demand economy audience knows that.

Provide an away message, preferably one with a degree of personalization, which is shown as an option under the text box, and one that will allow you to maintain a real-time communication even when you're not around (see Figure 14-7).

FIGURE 14-7:
Create a customized away message for your audience to receive when you're not available.

2. **Set up your Instant Replies to immediately respond to a user that contacts you.**

Instant replies, shown in Figure 14-8, let users know that they can always expect a response. It also reduces the pressure on you that comes from requiring an immediate response to every conversation.

WARNING

If you choose to activate this option, you can't set up replies and ignore conversations for hours or days. You still need to personally handle these issues and maintain regular conversations for the program to be effective.

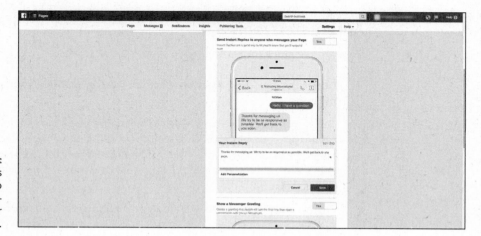

FIGURE 14-8:
Instant Replies allow you to start a conversation with a user right away.

3. **Create a Messenger Greeting to welcome users that open the Messenger app for your brand before they write a message.**

While this step is optional, it does show a user that you take your real-time engagement seriously. This message doesn't need to be complicated. It's a basic greeting for your audience (see Figure 14-9).

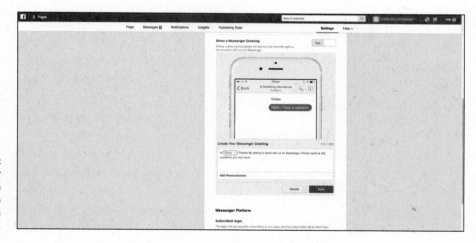

FIGURE 14-9:
Greet your audience when they decide to chat with you on Facebook.

Bots

When it comes to Messenger bots, things get a little more complicated. You need to develop and load your bot through the Facebook Developers portal, which you can find at http://developers.facebook.com.

TIP

For more information on the development of your bot and integration of your bot on your Facebook Page, visit Facebook's Quick Start guide here: (`https://developers.facebook.com/docs/messenger-platform/guides/quick-start`).

You can derive two main benefits from developing a chat bot:

>> **Customization:** Chatbots are fully customizable so that you can design them to help you achieve objectives with users as part of your real-time communications strategy. Bots function on Messenger, which Millennials primarily use on mobile devices.

>> **Variety:** You can set up chatbots to offer newsletters, conduct polls, answer customer service queries, or even sell products to users engaging with them. This variety dovetails perfectly with the demand market's characteristics because it takes place on the go. Whenever the demand economy audience is ready to engage or even make a purchase, a bot can give you a leg up over the competition. The demand market will look for the most readily available options, and your chat sales bot may fit the bill.

If you're unable to code the bot yourself or prefer to save money hiring a developer, you can use products and services, such as Botsify (`https://botsify.com`), to take care of the development and integration of this process.

Leveraging alternatives to popular platforms

While Facebook Messenger and Twitter are the most widely used platforms for real-time engagement with the demand economy, you can use three additional means to communicate with your audience in real time:

>> **Website Live Chat:** Offering a live chat feature on your website is a great way to cater to an audience that is already engaged with your brand and wants to find out more information. If a prospect with values aligned with those in the demand economy has made it to your website and can't locate the information he or she is looking for, a live chat can provide additional answers.

>> **Live Video Streaming:** Video streaming is about as live as it gets. If you're comfortable enough on camera and are prepared to accept the uncertainties that result from live video streaming, then letting your audience ask questions or communicate via live video is a great way to drive up engagement and build relationships. Video content is a powerful force when it comes to Millennial relationship development. I cover this topic in Chapter 15.

>> **Ask Me Anything:** An Ask Me Anything–styled session on a media platform like Reddit (the world's largest user-generated content aggregator and general discussion forum) or on a forum you control, like your website, is another excellent way to engage your audience in real time and provide answers. Ask Me Anything events allow participants to ask questions related to your industry, your product, or your brand and then allots you time to provide as many answers as possible. It helps to bolster relationships and provide a transparent view of your organization and industry.

REMEMBER

The one thing to keep in mind with an Ask Me Anything session is that you may receive such a massive outpouring of questions and comments that you won't necessarily be able to get to all of them in the allotted time. In this type of case, you want to inform your audience that you'll try your best to answer the most relevant or popular questions, and that you'll attempt to respond to any additional questions in some other form such as a blog post or perhaps even a video Q&A session.

Building Out the Components of Your Real-Time Strategy

Before you launch your real-time communications strategy, you need to consider several components. Considering the overall objective covered in this section is the acquisition of an audience with an interest in the demand economy, your strategy will consist of the following components:

>> Audience identification

>> Primary objectives

>> Secondary objectives

>> Opportunity indicators

>> Social care

>> Real-time communications playbook

Audience identification

As you prepare your real-time communications strategy, start by defining the audience you want to reach. In Chapter 3, I detail the process of developing a targeted audience cluster. This is the exact process you should follow to build your real-time communications audience. This audience is a subset of the demand economy audience you want to reach.

Primary objectives

One of your primary objectives is the acquisition of prospects that fall into the demand-economy audience. These individuals have chosen one brand over another because their need to have instant access to the product is met. Converting these prospects falls into your primary objective category. Additional goals, such as the growth of your brand's share of voice in industry conversations, may also be an objective of yours.

Share of voice is the ratio of industry conversation owned by a particular brand. For example, suppose that you sell office supplies online and 100 mentions of office supplies appear across various digital media. If your brand is mentioned ten times in those conversations, then your share of voice is 10 percent. As you build your share of voice, you build your brand recognition and, ultimately, your business.

Secondary objectives

Secondary objectives don't drive your decision-making. They can be considered more of a wish list rather than a list of objectives you work toward.

An example of a secondary objective may be a higher number of backlinks or links to your website that are generated by third-party publications as a result of your increased real-time activity.

Opportunity indicators

In your real-time communications strategy, you need to define exactly what constitutes an opportunity to engage in real time. These opportunities can include increases in industry conversations or increased mentions of a particular keyword. When looking for opportunities to share the kind of content Oreo shared during the 2013 Super Bowl — when the brand's real-time "Dunk in the Dark" tweet in response to the power outage at the game was the talk of the Internet — you need to know what data indicators to look for. You won't necessarily have the exact content ready to go, but you should monitor online trends and conversations that allow you to adapt your templated content.

Templated content is the basic framework of content that you can customize to match any scenario that helps you respond to the situation faster than your competitors.

Social care

You need to carefully plan your real-time new media customer service strategy (see Chapter 15). It must include responses and step-by-step instructions on how to handle any customer service query that may come up.

Managing a crisis (see Chapter 15) will take a different approach. In the case of real-time customer service, you want to have your processes carefully laid out so that your team can address any issue online in a very short time frame.

Real-time communications playbook

Your communications playbook should outline the various scenarios in which real-time engagement comes into play. It should include detailed plans for

>> Participating in events like breaking industry news

>> Following global stories like major, international sporting events

>> Dealing with brand-relevant or brand-involved stories (both positive and negative)

>> Handling competitor-involved stories or announcements

TIP

Make an effort to carefully think about all the scenarios where real-time engagement could benefit your brand. Then plan out the steps to approach each situation and document it in your playbook. If you don't have to make things up as you go along, you'll get much better results.

Chapter **15**

Adjusting Strategies for Millennial Consumption Habits

illennials are partial to certain types of media over others. To quickly capture their attention, you need to use these media types more frequently than others. To facilitate the process of grabbing Millennials' attention, you can analyze your target audience's media consumption habits to determine which platform investments will be the most successful.

After your media is in the format that appeals to a Millennial market, you should spend some time building out additional strategies that cater to the way Millennials do business. A central theme of those strategies is the growth of relationships. Relationships are at the root of any successful brand strategy.

Looking at Crucial Media Types

New media is where you find your Millennial audience. You can use certain media strategies with this group to produce exceptional results. The use of these strategies will also lead to the furthering of your relationships with Millennial consumers. These media types are designed to cater to the consumption habits that Millennials exhibit.

For more about Millennial habits, see Chapter 1.

Examining video's impact on consumer brands

YouTube reaches more Millennials than any major cable outlet. What's more, according to Google, mobile YouTube sessions last an average of 40 minutes. The fact that video content attracts Millennials is good for brands because research conducted by Animoto, an online video creation and editing platform, has found that about 76 percent of Millennials follow brands on YouTube.

To put it simply, you need to find a way to use video if you want to capture the attention of your Millennial audience.

Creating your video content

When building out a video strategy to cater to a Millennial audience, you should avoid making the mistake of creating videos simply for the sake of creating videos. Your video strategy needs to be intentional. Your audience needs a reason to watch your videos.

The following sections describe the things you should consider when creating video content.

Identify the best ways to provide value to your audience

Your audience could be doing an endless number of things online instead of watching your video content. For example, they could be watching other videos, reading articles, taking quizzes, or playing games.

If you expect an audience with limitless alternative options to pay attention to what you're sharing, you to need to give its members a reason to do so. Find a means of providing these users with value to keep them around. That value can take many forms. For example, you can provide them with a laugh if you're creating a series of funny videos or useful tips to help them save money every month. Whatever it is, think about having your audience walk away with something of value.

Create videos that have a purpose

Stuffing a YouTube channel with as many videos as possible is the video marketing equivalent of the boy who cried wolf. If your videos serve no purpose, it won't take long for Millennials to realize that they have no reason to watch them. This characteristic of Millennial video-viewing habits doesn't necessarily mean that you should create videos sparingly. If you have a reason to create videos and your audience is benefitting from watching them, then keep doing what you're doing. Just remember that you should have a reason for your audience to view the video, which means you should have a reason for making the video as well.

Get to the point quickly and keep your videos short

The use of rich media may extend the time a Millennial devotes to your content before moving on to something else, but you still need to get to your point quickly.

Exceptions exist, of course, such as when you're sharing detailed instructions for users to follow. This type of video will cause them to stick around as long as necessary. But when you're trying to engage a first-time prospect, the shorter and more direct your video is, the greater likelihood that it will encourage engagement.

Don't take Millennials for granted

Millennials have grown up in the era of camera phones and live video. Brands don't need to spend millions to produce high-quality videos to capture their attention and business — but don't take that fact for granted. Even though Millennials may not be as concerned with picture clarity and flawless audio as consumers once were, it doesn't mean that you can completely abandon the delivery of high-quality video.

TIP

Allocate some of your budget to improving the quality of your videos because it reflects well on your brand. Improved quality also means you'll have a better chance of keeping your audience around for longer periods of time.

Maintain a tone that is consistent with your brand on other media

Consistency is always an important aspect on which to focus. There is a vast amount of content and a limited amount of time your audience has for each piece of content. For this reason, you need to maintain brand consistency throughout your video content so that your audience recognizes your brand right away.

Make your branding clear and incorporate subtle calls-to-action

Just as you need to maintain consistency with your tone and brand, you need to ensure that your branding is clear from the start. While branding doesn't need to be center stage and overtake the video's content, your logo, brand colors, or other brand elements should be apparent.

Don't wait until the very end to implement a call-to-action. A call-to-action can be inserted at any point during the video or placed on the video as an overlay.

A *call-to-action* is a piece of content, such as a phrase or button, that invites your audience to take some sort of action. Typically, a call-to-action is used to encourage users to move to the next step in the buying journey or to provide you with some valuable information.

TECHNICAL STUFF

A *video overlay* is a technical term that refers to a button, ad, or call-to-action layer that is placed on top of a video and remains in place as the video continues playing. You can implement video overlays manually using either third-party tools or tools available on a video hosting service, like YouTube, or you can use an ad server, such as Google, to place them automatically.

REMEMBER

Not everyone will make it to the end of your video, so if you save your call-to-action for the very end, you could be losing out on several potential clicks, visits, or follow-ups from people who didn't make it to the last few seconds.

Don't push the sale too aggressively

Your brand and the presence of a clear call-to-action will take care of the selling for you. If there's one thing that Millennials don't want, it's a commercialized video whose only purpose is to make a sale. This kind of approach negates the critical objective of providing your audience with value.

Utilizing top video types

The video types and themes in the following list are among those that provide the most value to an audience. They're also associated with the highest retention and completion rates.

>> **Instructional videos:** When you provide viewers with an answer to a common industry question, you're not only providing them with something of value, you're showcasing your own expertise. Instructional or informational content is generally regarded as some of the most valuable video content you can provide. It's easily digestible by your audience. As long as you have helpful

information to share, producing and distributing short, branded videos is a good idea.

>> **Time-saving videos:** Tips and tricks videos provide your audience with value. You can expand this theme to include any material that saves resources. For example, money-saving tips are always highly engaging. These video types establish your brand as an industry leader and demonstrate that you're capable of creative thinking.

>> **Live videos:** The rise of live-streamed video on social networks like Facebook has shown marketers that Millennial consumers' level of interest in this format is particularly high. A live video taps into the demand economy by being a part of the action in real time. Live video strikes a chord with Millennials. Use a live video to answer questions, showcase a process as it's happening, or provide behind-the-scenes insight into how your organization works. (Chapter 14 covers the value of real-time communications.)

Running Social Care Programs on Various Media

Social care is the marketing industry term that refers to the handling of customer service requests via social platforms like Facebook or Twitter. Social care can take place on virtually any new medium and can be broad or narrow. If you want to use social media to respond to customers, you need to decide how comfortable you are with the public handling of customer issues. Things may not always go according to plan.

Dealing with assumptions about your social care program

If you're thinking about launching a social care program, you need to be aware of certain factors before pulling the trigger.

If you're there, Millennials will come

Whether or not you've planned to execute your social care strategy on a network like Instagram, it won't stop Millennials from reaching out to you on that platform. When you establish a social care strategy, it's important to determine exactly when and where you plan to execute it. If Instagram isn't a platform where you plan to engage in social care, you need to make that clear to customers. Your customer service needs to be executed from within a chosen framework.

While some people may still ignore this structure and reach out to you wherever they see fit, you would be doing yourself and your customers a disservice by trying to cater to anyone on any channel where you find a comment or question. When a customer or prospect reaches out to you on a medium that you're not using for customer service, refer them to your most centralized customer service outlet, such as your website, live chat, or ticketing system (Zendesk, for example) with a link to a form or chat section of your website.

Expectations for immediacy are high

Millennials want their issues addressed quickly. When you put a social care strategy into effect, you should have your staff ready to execute it. You can't fail to live up to the expectations Millennials have about social care.

At the same time, you also need to maintain the boundaries you set for your social care strategy. If you offer real-time assistance and engagement during certain hours, then you need to stick to those hours and limits because it may be cost-prohibitive to provide this kind of care around the clock. You don't want your audience to feel as though they can abuse your offer to provide customer service in real time. That creates a slippery slope that can lead to the breakdown of your social care program.

A lack of planning clearly shows

If you're not prepared to handle the volume, manage a broad variety of customer service issues, or respond in a short time frame, your audience will take note. A social care program may be a great way to cater to a subset of your Millennial consumers, but a lack of preparation can turn a potentially helpful idea into an unmanageable crisis.

Arguments are not customer service

Handling customer complaints in an open forum shows prospects that you care. But when a consumer is angry and wants to vent, you need to recognize when to quit. In any customer service situation, regardless of whether you're correct, you're going to look like the bad guy. That's just the way the world of customer service works.

WARNING

Avoid all cases where there is no alternative to an argument. It won't solve a problem and may turn away potential customers.

Not everything can be handled through social care

It's great to offer a public, third-party forum as a starting point for customer service, but some issues won't be able to be resolved on social media or within the private chat sections of social networks. These problems often include confidential information or data that may pose a security risk to either you or your customer if it's shared on a public forum.

When building out your social care strategy, take some time to identify the issues that can be handled on social media and the ones that need to move to a more controlled environment, such as your website or the phone. Plan exactly how you want to handle those problems and the subsequent transitions to a new medium.

Several platforms are ideally suited to assist you in the execution of your social care program. However, if you have a presence on multiple social platforms and offer social care, there is a distinct possibility that your Millennial audience will still reach out to you wherever they find you. Be prepared.

Choosing networks

To maintain control over your social care initiatives, it's important to concentrate on only a handful of networks. Twitter and Facebook will help you provide the best social care.

In the case of public social care, the definition is limited to public interactions (at least first interactions) and third-party platforms. This definition doesn't include a branded website where the entire process is under your control.

Twitter

Short-form, public communication directly to a brand's account is the most logical place to start when it comes to social care. Twitter has long been the launch point for a social care strategy because it's a favorite of Millennial consumers. Traditional, slow-moving outreach mechanisms like the phone or email just don't satisfy the traits of the demand economy members. They want answers fast, and Twitter is as fast a medium as any other social network.

During a crisis, Twitter can easily become overloaded with requests and comments from customers. Create a strategy that details the best way to approach these comments. Make sure to prioritize your social care comments on Twitter so that you can handle a lot of queries with less manpower.

Facebook

The options on Facebook are quite a bit more robust than they are on Twitter, but Facebook isn't yet as popular a choice for cold outreach among Millennials. For existing customers, however, Facebook is regarded as a powerhouse in the world of social care. Private communications exist within Messenger, but in a public forum, fans can comment on posts or post directly to your page if they don't want to reach out to you on Messenger. Either one of these post types is a good jumping off point. The ability to build out your Facebook Page in a modular fashion so that you can integrate customer service applications makes it a pretty appealing option for social care.

REMEMBER

There are, of course, other means of conducting social care, like live chat services embedded on your website. However, these private interactions are generally customized to fit your brand's customer service process.

Considering elements that go into a social care strategy

If you plan on using Facebook and Twitter to build out your social care strategy and you understand the public's expectations, then you're ready to start developing your program. You need to include a number of elements to ensure that you're covering all bases.

Broad scope situational planning

If you assume that every interaction in your social care strategy is going to be the same, you're making an incorrect assumption. A lot of inquiries may fall under the same category of requests, but you need to be prepared to deal with every possible situation a Millennial customer may present on social media.

Keep in mind that an inquiry and a customer service ticket both fall into the category of social care, but the methodical, step-by-step approach to handling requests from a customer should be planned for in great detail. Start by considering all the reasons why someone may reach out to you on social media, and then list all those situations in order of importance.

REMEMBER

Social care can be something as simple as a customer reaching out to you because she's happy with her transaction and wants to thank you. Not all interactions on social media are going to be negative. Plan responses to serve happy customers as well. These responses can be a little more conversational and don't need quite as much preparation. The thing to remember with positive interactions is that you want to maintain a consistent brand voice.

Ordering priorities

There's no doubt that every customer matters to your business. In this part of your strategy, the question isn't how much each query matters, but rather how important each situation is to the overall happiness of your customers and the maintenance of your brand's reputation.

For example, a request on Twitter about the release date for a new product isn't as urgent as a request from a customer whose product arrived damaged and late. Both issues need to be resolved, but clearly one is far more pressing than the other. As you develop your strategy, take some time to identify the order in which queries will be addressed.

Multiscenario road map

With each of the scenarios you outline, you can create a step-by-step guideline that walks you through the initial contact to resolution.

Of course, not every situation is going to work out exactly as you planned on paper, but the more prepared you are, the easier it will be to handle every situation as it arises.

Preemptive content development

After you design a road map to guide you through each situation, develop sample content that you can adapt for each of them. Content development will cut down on response and resolution time.

Crisis management strategy

One or two customer complaints are easily handled when you follow your road map. Things become far more challenging when your brand finds itself in hot water. On social media, you can find far too many examples of situations spiraling out of control. Remember Amy's Baking Company and the Facebook nightmare that took place after an episode of Gordon Ramsay's *Kitchen Nightmares*? In case you're not familiar with the scenario, Figure 15-1 shows you the epic meltdown that led to the eventual closure of the business.

FIGURE 15-1: Amy's Baking Company in Arizona saw a social media crisis turn into a failed business.

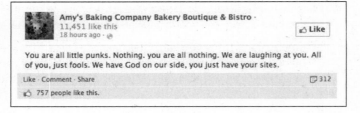

To avoid these issues, it's crucial for brands to prepare a crisis management strategy. The last section of this chapter covers the details involved in how to handle a crisis and build out that strategy.

Integrating email into your marketing strategy

You may think that email is no longer a viable tool to use when it comes to Millennials. The truth is that Millennials are still very active on email — they just use it in a different way than dictated by conventional marketing tactics.

To properly leverage email marketing to Millennials, think of it as part of your nurturing strategy. This approach means that email needs to be something used in the context of the relationship development process. You shouldn't try to send emails to Millennials who are not familiar with your brand.

Keep the following key points top of mind when leveraging the power of email to convert Millennials from prospects to customers and from customers to brand advocates:

>> **Have something to say.** Sending a holiday greeting or checking in with your audience members to let them know you have new stock is fine every once in a while, but you should have a good reason for sending a daily or weekly digest. Just sending an email for the sake of getting your brand in front of Millennial consumers isn't going to produce great results. Just like they do with your video and social content, Millennials need to derive value from email content you send.

>> **Share content that's worth your recipient's time.** Sharing offers via email or giving users an exclusive deal if they're on a particular list is a great way to drive action. Millennials love the concept of exclusivity, and once again, delivering a perceived value will lead to increased action like clicks and conversions. This type of offer will cause Millennials to open emails every time they receive them.

TIP

Make it clear in your subject line that the email itself contains something worthwhile. Hiding behind an obscure or cryptic subject line like "You Won't Believe What We're Offering!" does little to entice Millennial users to click. Telling them exactly what to expect when they open the email will lead to more positive action, and your campaign results will improve as well.

>> **Personalize everything you can.** When you can personalize elements like the subject line or body text of an email, it catches the eye of your recipient. Millennials like to believe that a brand is talking specifically to them and not

blanketing all users with the same content. It's not a secret that an email is going out to many individuals, but the feeling of personalization leads to a greater degree of action.

>> **Don't bombard inboxes.** As you know, an inbox is personal. When users look through their emails, the personalized component of a message is the first thing they pay attention to. If you continually send a barrage of emails, users will ignore everything you send, even the valuable ones designed to drive action. The last thing you want is to makes users blind to even your most enticing shares.

>> **Think mobile first.** Think mobile first with regard to Millennials. The value of using email is that the message is the only thing a recipient looks at when he opens it. On a mobile device, this focused attention is even more valuable. The email is literally the only thing the recipient sees on a hand-held screen. You have the complete attention of your audience for a brief moment in time, so everything you include in your email, from the structure to the links to the landing pages, needs to be mobile first.

Building Lasting Relationships

Relationships are the key to building a successful brand both now and in the future. Millennials may take a little longer than previous generations to make a purchasing decision, but they're fiercely loyal after they do. Big brands and flashy names are no longer the appeal. When Millennial consumers feel a connection to a brand and the brand produces a high-quality product, they're much more likely to choose that brand over one with a recognizable name or logo.

Building relationships takes time and planning, however. You have to get to know your audience and develop content uniquely geared toward them. If you maintain consistent communication both before and after the conversion takes place, you grow and strengthen that relationship. You can go about this process in several ways:

>> Running multiple audience analyses

>> Building out smaller audience segments

>> Creating content strategies based on audience traits

>> Running an ongoing, automated audience audit

Running multiple audience analyses

Chapter 3 covers the process of running an audience analysis. This analysis is a cornerstone element of any successful Millennial acquisition strategy. It's impossible to appeal to a Millennial audience if you don't take the time to get to know it.

One thing that becomes apparent as you begin your audience analyses is that not all Millennials are the same. It's a mistake to group them all together based on some superficial characteristics.

It's true that Millennials share traits about buying behaviors, like the desire for access over ownership. However, the content designed to appeal to their personalities should change from one group to another. This content development process is where running multiple audience analyses will come in handy.

To accomplish your audience analysis using Facebook Audiences, select your general Millennial custom audience or a general audience that you've created in the dashboard, as shown in Figure 15-2.

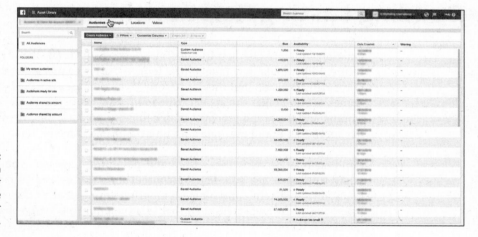

FIGURE 15-2:
Choose an audience or create a new one to begin your segment analysis.

To conduct analyses on multiple segments, start by selecting the particular element that you'll isolate, such as

>> **Location:** The place your audience lives may influence how it engages with brands online. When you start with a general Millennial audience, consider breaking the members down by region or even to a particular city.

>> **Age range:** Just because the term Millennial is often defined by age doesn't mean that every individual within a 20-year span will interact with you in the same way. They're certain to have different buying habits, spending abilities, aspirations, interests, and behaviors online. Segment your general Millennial audience into small groups of users broken down by age ranges closer together — maybe separated by 2 or 3 years as opposed to 20.

>> **Gender:** The way you engage with your Millennial audience may vary significantly from men to women. As you separately analyze these two groups, you may find that content strategy designed specifically to appeal to men or women will be necessary to improve the results of your campaigns.

Within these segments groups, start analyzing your audience to identify some of the criteria that make them tick (see Chapter 3). You can look at some of the interests and behaviors exhibited by members, showcased in the Audience Insights dashboard in the backend of Facebook, as shown in Figure 15-3.

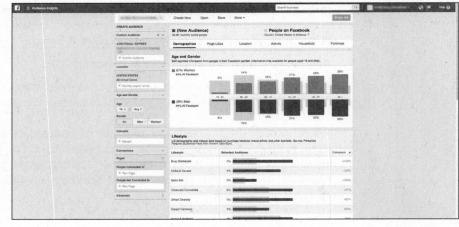

FIGURE 15-3:
Analyze your segmented audience's interests and behaviors in the Audience Insights dashboard on Facebook.

Building out smaller audience segments

After you run multiple audience analyses, you're ready to start building out smaller audience segments that you can target with much more tailored content. Building an audience of Millennials on Facebook can take place in one of two ways. The first is a broad location and/or age restricted starting point. The second is by using your existing database and narrowing your audience through the use of additional parameters.

The steps to run through this process with a more generalized audience are as follows:

1. **Begin by identifying age ranges.**

Marketers make the common mistake of defining Millennials using only age parameters. However, it's a good starting point when you're building out a new audience. In your analyses, you may have already looked at some smaller age clusters. Begin developing your target audiences by establishing small age ranges.

2. **Select a specific location for your audience.**

Next, include location parameters for your new audience cluster. The more that you narrowly target each of your audiences, the more likely the content you develop for them will resonate.

3. **Build out the base of interests these users possess.**

During your audience cluster analyses, you should have picked up on some of the tastes and preferences shared by a particular group. At this stage, you're going to begin including those interests as a means of narrowing the audience cluster even further. Focus largely on the elements that make these users tick.

4. **Define some of the behaviors your audience exhibits.**

Dig deeper into the details that make up your audiences. Make sure to include the behaviors you've noted in your individual audience analyses.

The second process begins with the audience of Millennials you have already cultivated, perhaps on your page or with an email database. The steps to building out this audience follow the same path as those detailed for the general audience. Just remember to begin the process by first selecting an audience that you've already saved on Facebook.

Creating content strategies based on audience traits

After you run multiple audience analyses and build out small audience pockets, your next goal should be to develop objective-oriented content that appeals to a particular subset. As you apply this process to each of the identified audience clusters, you'll start to see engagement and conversion rates spike. This engagement will further the process of building a personal relationship with your Millennial prospects.

While Chapters 6, 7, and 8 cover the detailed process of developing content strategies, you need to do specific things when hyper-targeting your content strategies for particular audience clusters:

>> **Create variations for every viable cluster.** You will notice while building out your audience clusters that they each exhibit unique personality traits that determine how best to capture their attention. Identify the attributes that are most pertinent to their engagement. These attributes are often showcased in the lifestyle categorization of an audience, as seen in Figure 15-4. Develop content that appeals to those traits.

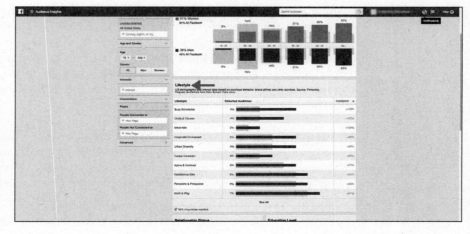

FIGURE 15-4: Determine the key qualities of your target audience by analyzing their lifestyle categories on Facebook.

>> **Focus your content variations on rich media.** If you want to capitalize on the small traits that your audience has exhibited, you can do so by leveraging the asset that is most noticeable in your content: rich media. If you're sharing a photo or video in your campaign, then that is the media you should vary to appeal to a particular Millennial audience.

>> **Maintain brand consistency.** Even if you're changing several details about your content when appealing to a specific cluster, be sure that your branding is consistent. While these variations are great tools for building relationships with Millennials, your audience needs to know who you are.

TIP

Keep your branding clear and noticeable so that members of any cluster will know exactly what brand they're dealing with when they come across your content, regardless of how it's structured.

REMEMBER

You don't have to create content for every trait that you identify in your audience. In the case where an audience cluster doesn't need to have a customized set of content, you should have some general content ready to share that relays your message in a clear fashion that's consistent with your branding.

Running an ongoing, automated audience audit

One of the benefits of using Facebook Audiences for the development of your audience clusters is that you can regularly use it to analyze your audience subsets. As long as you've saved an audience in Facebook Audiences, you'll be able to access it whenever you need to run a micro-analysis.

As a marketer, it's important to remember that your audience traits may change from time to time. When you're trying to build and maintain a relationship with your Millennial audience, you should stay on top of these changing qualities and adapt your strategies accordingly. You won't necessarily need to run an analysis on your audience the same way you did when you first starting developing it. However, you need to pay attention to certain criteria that tell you if you need to change your approach for a specific cluster:

>> **Lifestyle:** When lifestyle categories shift, you're definitely going to need to make some changes to the types of content you develop for a specific cluster. Pay close attention to these categories on a regular basis. Ideally, you should review the lifestyle categories of a particular audience cluster on a monthly basis.

>> **Job Title:** On Facebook, an individual's career field can be useful for framing content. Job Title isn't a category that changes often. When it does change, the shift usually isn't dramatic, so you can note changes in this group every few months. Figure 15-5 shows you an example of this audience criteria.

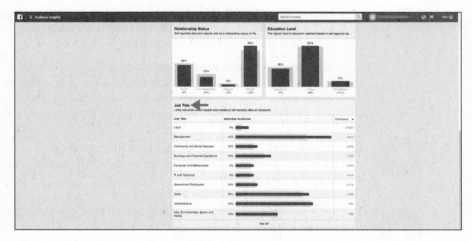

FIGURE 15-5:
Use your audience's career field as a means of developing targeted content.

>> **Page Likes:** Your Page Likes tab tells you about the brands or page themes in which your audience cluster is interested. When Page Likes change, it may be time to start shifting some of your targeting as well as your content. You can analyze page likes along with lifestyle categories every month.

>> **Purchase Behavior:** You can learn two things if you know where people spend their money. First, you can determine how receptive they may be to your product or service. You can base the likely receptiveness on whether or not the members of an audience cluster are buying similar products. Second, it highlights their priorities. Understanding their preferences allows you to improve your content to cater to them.

>> **Frequency of Activities:** Under the Activity tab, you want to pay close attention to how frequently your audience's activities shift, as shown in Figure 15-6. Identifying this behavior can help you develop your content or your next campaign based on what you see changing.

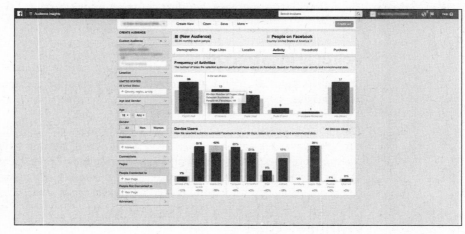

FIGURE 15-6: Determine what your audience is doing on Facebook to determine how to structure your next campaign.

If a particular audience is more engaged with ads than they once were or if they've been redeeming offers more frequently, you may be able to find some inspiration for your next initiative.

Managing a Brand Crisis

No marketer likes to think about the dreaded brand crisis, but as the saying goes, those that fail to plan, plan to fail. Developing a social media brand crisis strategy is crucial to communicating effectively with Millennials. It's all too easy for bad press to spiral out of control on social media. Without a proper plan in place, stopping the escalation of a bad situation is virtually impossible.

A brand crisis on new media can take many shapes, that's why developing several strategies is key to your effective management of one of these issues. There's no telling when or where it may come from. It may not even have anything to do with your brand specifically. Preparation is the name of the game.

Creating multiple strategies

The unfortunate reality is that managing a crisis doesn't have a one-size-fits-all approach. To adequately prepare, you need to create a variety of strategies. Brand crises can result from any number of factors. While you can follow certain steps, the implementation will vary from one situation to the next.

The following sections list the most common brand crises for which you should prepare.

Political incorrectness

On today's Internet, political incorrectness is the most common example of a brand crisis.

TIP

The general rule that you should adopt is that unless you've built a reputation as a tongue-in-cheek social operator, you should avoid sharing anything that leads customers to question or misconstrue your comment or post. Of course, you can't always be sure, so brands find themselves on the wrong end of an angry mob that has taken offense to something posted to a social feed.

Product issues

In some instances, such as a recall or a service failure, your product is to blame for the barrage of negative comments you receive. Sometimes, you can easily fix these issues with an apology and a repair, but, when you work in a field like the produce industry, a recall could mean lives at risk. You need to prepare for every possible outcome and determine how you'll respond if the worst happens.

Customer service failure

A good rule to live by about customer service comes from marketing consultant Jay Baer. He says, "If you, the brand, send a third reply to a complaining customer, then it's an argument."

WARNING

Don't send a third, contentious reply. There's no version of the customer versus brand story where the brand looks good getting into an argument with a customer. And today, where everything you share in writing is saved for all to see, it doesn't look good when one of these arguments is posted to a forum like Reddit. When that happens, you don't have much choice but to admit a mistake and apologize.

In some instances, you'll find yourself dealing with a *troll,* which is a common web term used to describe a customer, prospect, or social media user who is simply engaging with a brand with the goal of causing problems or getting under their skin.

Data breach

According to Breach Level Index, an online service that tracks global data breach statistics, nearly six billion data records have been lost or stolen since 2013. You can plan and protect all you want, but there are some instances where a breach occurs and your customer data is at risk. Taking the offensive and attacking the situation by highlighting how you're taking steps to remedy the issue is going to be your best course of action.

Untruthfulness

Don't lie to your customers. Don't lie to your prospects. Go one step further: Don't lie as a brand. You'll almost certainly be caught, and there is no benefit to falsifying information.

If the key to Millennial customer acquisition is relationships, then breaking their trust is the fastest way to lose them. If you're caught in a lie, the only hope of saving your brand from extinction is to admit guilt, apologize, and demonstrate absolute transparency moving forward. Even then, it's a steep hill that you have to climb to get back into the good graces of the Internet.

Internal scandal

Whether your CEO has been stealing funds or your latest product has been copied from a rival, you need to make some major changes. If a scandal is uncovered, you also need to let your audience know that you're working to prevent anything like that scandal from happening in the future.

Again, an internal scandal is an issue where trust is lost. And it can be very hard to build those relationships back up after they've fallen apart.

Detailing the components of a crisis strategy

While your approach to handling a crisis may differ based on the kind of crisis you're facing, each strategy you develop will contain a number of standard components:

>> Crisis outline

>> Initial response

>> Response type

>> Individual prioritization

>> Content templates

>> Remedy action strategy

>> Fallout planning

Crisis outline

The first component of any crisis management strategy is going to be the outlining of the crisis itself.

TIP

It may be helpful to think of a real-life scenario that fits into one of the situations detailed in the previous section and write it out as a narrative. When you can contextualize the crisis and think about it in real-world terms, the development of the remaining parts of the strategy is much easier.

Initial response

When a crisis first strikes, you need to provide the public with an immediate initial response. As you begin working on your strategy, think about how you'd respond when you're at the center of the action. This reply may be an apology, or you could acknowledge the problem and inform the public that you're looking into it. Either way, silence isn't an option, so plan your response accordingly.

Response type

You can either take an offensive or defensive stance when a crisis strikes. An offensive position is one where you get out ahead of the problem, letting people know that an issue has occurred and that you're aware of it. This position may also include an admission of guilt or an apology. This is the kind of response you take when the brand is clearly at fault. A defensive stance is a little less common, and it needs to be carefully thought out.

Using a defensive stance, you may initially stand by the actions of your company or be slow to admit guilt. In the case of a perceived data breach, you might begin by letting people know that you're looking into the matter, but that your systems are secure and until you know the cause and extent of the problem, you'll refrain from commenting. Again, this stance needs to be approached with caution. It isn't always the safest way to calm an angry public.

Individual prioritization

Will you be reaching out to the community as a whole or responding to individuals? Who should get the first outreach from your brand? These are the questions you need to answer at this stage of your strategy. If you're dealing with a product recall, then, of course, you're going to reach out to the public first before engaging with individuals. Then, you should assign priority rankings to different individual complaints.

For example, those directly impacted by the recall will be answered first, while those seeking information will be marked as a lower priority. In the case of a customer sharing a negative experience, you may not need to engage the public, as this approach can sometimes backfire.

WARNING

Be careful; if you decide not to engage the public, you risk looking like you either don't pay attention to what's being discussed, or you don't care. Both situations make you look bad, so it's almost always a better option to make some public comment.

Content templates

Things happen fast when a crisis strikes, so you may not have time to develop content and standardized responses on the spot. While your content should be genuine, some of your responses can be standardized.

Take the case of a data breach. When your brand pages are flooded with questions about the breach, it may be tedious to respond to each one with the same message that you're looking into it. In this case, you can develop a standardized response that you share to users when they ask. Remember, however, that Millennials appreciate personalization, so use the person's name or handle when you respond.

Remedy action strategy

In this part of your plan, you should detail how you may make it up to your audience. Some cases, like a scandal or fraud, will require shameless apologizing and efforts to rebuild trust. Product recalls and similar crises, however, may be remedied with special offers to those who were impacted. Again, you should observe the temperature of the audience before putting this plan into action.

Fallout planning

If all else fails, you may need to make some drastic moves, like rebranding. Of course, you won't plan to include a rebranding in your strategy, but in this section of the plan, you should outline what the worst-case scenario may look like.

REMEMBER

During major crises, you need to mobilize quickly. A fallout plan will help speed the implementation of the process.

Managing a crisis

After you have a series of crisis strategies in place, you should familiarize yourself with the four steps involved in handling a crisis:

1. **Figure out what happened.**

When you first notice the barrage of negative comments or interactions coming from an online audience, it can be a little overwhelming. The key is to stay calm and avoid making an early misstep by tracing the situation back to its roots.

REMEMBER

It's very possible, particularly when you're not engaged in round-the-clock monitoring, that the comments you're seeing are a byproduct of some secondary issue. You need to take some time (but not too much) to determine the cause of the crisis.

2. **Assign key roles**

A major brand crisis means that you stop business as usual. Now, it's all-hands-on-deck. You can't expect departments or employees to continue functioning normally when a crisis threatens your business, so you need to determine the responsibilities of your team members. At this stage, you should have figured out what went wrong, the severity of the situation, and the strategy you'll apply to address the problem. Your plan should contain components that you can delegate to your team, and the delegation process takes place at this point.

3. **Prioritize responses.**

You might like to think of your audience members as all being equal, but when you're faced with a crisis, that notion goes out the window. When you're under fire, getting to every individual complaint promptly, if at all, may not be possible. Therefore, you must decide the order of your responses. For example, do you reach out to high-value fans and followers first, then make a public statement, and then begin personal outreach? Influencers have significant power in the Millennial market, and they may need to take a priority spot in your outreach strategy.

4. Take ownership.

Whether you choose to take an offensive or defensive position, acknowledging the feelings of those impacted by the situation is important. Millennials want to be heard; ignoring the situation is perilous. Take a moment to reach out to the public (assuming that's part of your strategy) and let your audience know that you're listening.

TIP

Recognize when you can't win. There are going to be instances when a customer is simply fed up and angry and wants to argue with your brand. While they may not be right, it will look worse for you if you participate beyond a reasonable point. Of course, if someone is voicing displeasure, take it seriously, but you need to know when someone is looking to troll or vent and avoid engaging beyond an apology or sympathetic response. You can't win them all.

Chapter 16

Cause Marketing with Millennials in Mind

Cause marketing isn't a new concept, but it's one that has received a significant amount of attention in recent years, thanks in part to the Millennial market. Social consciousness is a characteristic that many Millennials possess, so brands have found a way to provide social utility by aligning with a cause.

Several brands, though, have hopped on the cause bandwagon only to find themselves on the receiving end of a barrage of negative publicity. For example, in 2013, Kellogg's UK told the world that for every retweet they received, a meal would be donated to a needy child. The problem here, as you may have already guessed, is that this seems like a lazy PR stunt that cares more about exposure than it does about the cause it's promoting.

This chapter introduces the concept of cause marketing and covers the integration of this popular strategy into your Millennial marketing initiatives. This chapter helps you align with the right cause to reach a Millennial audience that wants to connect with a socially conscious brand.

Recognizing Opportunities to Align with a Cause

Cause marketing strategies don't need to run in perpetuity. However, some brands have decided to permanently align with a particular cause or charity. Take, for example, the clothing company Gap's Project (RED), which has partnered with the Global Fund to combat AIDS in Africa. This ongoing initiative has yielded amazing results and raised awareness for both the cause and the brand. But many cases are simpler, less robust examples of cause marketing where a cause is simply adopted based on its popularity or virality on social media.

Virality refers to the rapid sharing of a particular trend on social media. An example of a popular cause-related trend was the Ice Bucket Challenge, in which participants dumped buckets of ice on themselves to raise awareness for ALS by challenging others to do the same and make a donation.

Making the right choice

Before you start monitoring web and industry content for an appropriate cause, you should review the following list so that your efforts won't backfire:

>> Relevance

>> Participation

>> Opportunism

>> Complexity

>> Turnaround time

REMEMBER

Millennials may feel drawn to a brand that aligns with a cause, but they are put off by a brand that is clearly leveraging the popularity of a cause to work toward a business goal.

Relevance

You need to first ask yourself whether the cause that you're considering is relevant to your industry, brand, and, perhaps most importantly, your brand voice. Two of the elements that Millennials look for in a brand are consistency and authenticity.

Choosing to adopt a cause that doesn't fit your persona, brand, or mission statement will be all too apparent to your Millennial audience. In this case, the best-case scenario is that your participation goes largely ignored. The worst-case scenario is that your audience picks up on your participation and questions its legitimacy.

Participation

Conduct a bit of research before diving into a cause. See whether it's something in which other brands have decided to participate. Some causes focus on the individual, so the participation of a brand may not be appropriate. For example, if part of a campaign's structure is to share a personal story about the issue in question, it's much more appropriate for individuals to participate. Unless your brand has humanized its online persona enough to provide something that fits this structure, you should skip this particular campaign.

Opportunism

Opportunism is the greatest factor you need to guard against. Spend time determining how much of risk there is in your participation being perceived as a business initiative. There is almost always a slight risk when a brand jumps on a cause bandwagon, so the real consideration should be whether the cause in question is one you truly care about.

If you find yourself thinking about participating in a cause that doesn't directly relate to you, the risk of perceived opportunism is high, and you may want to reconsider your involvement.

Complexity

Will the participation in a particular cause be overly complicated? Are a number of steps involved in the creation of a particular cause-driven campaign?

You should answer these two questions at the outset. If you discover an initiative that you believe in but find that participating in one of the more viral components is overly complex, you may want to consider only associating with the cause directly as an individual or brand.

Turnaround time

If your participation in a viral stunt is going to take too long to set up or execute, you may miss the opportunity to publicly align with the cause. Evaluate the turnaround time and then determine your best course of action considering the short life span of some Millennial-driven cause campaigns.

TECHNICAL STUFF

A characteristic of cause campaigns is that their shelf life isn't particularly long. This short duration doesn't mean that your brand doesn't have an opportunity to align with a cause. You simply need to determine whether a cause's viral exposure campaign is one that will exist long enough to warrant your involvement. If not, you may be better off publicly aligning yourself with the cause after the viral campaign has quieted down.

Looking for cause affiliations in an audience analysis

When conducting your audience analysis, analyzing cause affiliations is helpful. Millennial audiences are unusually public about the causes they support. This openness gives you insight into how actively your Millennial audience participates in causes and the kinds of causes and organizations it feels a connection to. (Chapter 3 covers audience analysis.)

After you create your Millennial audience on Facebook, you should take a few additional steps to determine its cause affiliations:

1. **Select the audience you'd like to analyze in your Audience Insights dashboard.**

   After your audiences have been loaded to your backend, you can begin the process of digging into their cause associations by selecting a custom audience in your Audience Insights dashboard, as shown in Figure 16-1.

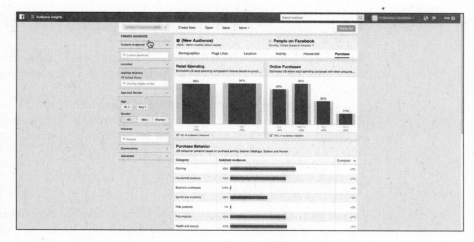

FIGURE 16-1: Select the audience you would like to analyze further in your Audience Insights dashboard.

2. Note the monthly active users within your selected audience.

Pay close attention to the active users in your selected Custom Audience so that you can compare the number of users actively associated with a particular cause. After you move on to the next step of the process, you can see the number of active users in the top bar of the dashboard, highlighted in Figure 16-2.

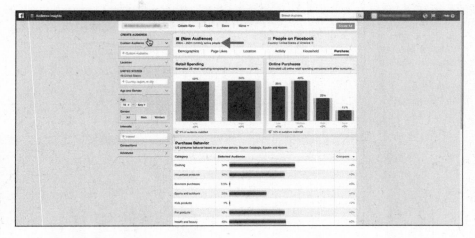

FIGURE 16-2:
Take note of the number of active users in your selected Custom Audience.

3. Select the relevant category or cause that you'd like to assess.

In the Interests box, shown in Figure 16-3, select the cause associated interest categories or associations, like charitable or not-for-profit organizations, that your audience may be interested in. This list can be fairly extensive and can either be unique to a single cause or can be very broad, covering a general base of cause-associated interests. You can use the latter option to simply get a feeling for how receptive your selected audience may be to your affiliation with a cause.

4. Note the ratio of the existing audience that fits this cause association.

Compare the number of original users in your custom audience to the number of users that have an interest in either your selected cause or causes in general. This comparison can give you a good idea of how viable this audience is and how responsive it will be when it comes to developing campaigns associated with your chosen cause. You can find this number in the same location as the original active audience total. An example is shown in Figure 16-4.

5. Repeat the process for other causes or charitable organizations.

If you plan on getting into the specifics of a cause, you may want to consider repeating this practice with the same audience for several causes of interest to you. The one with the largest audience ratio will be the one that has the best chance of generating interest and engagement.

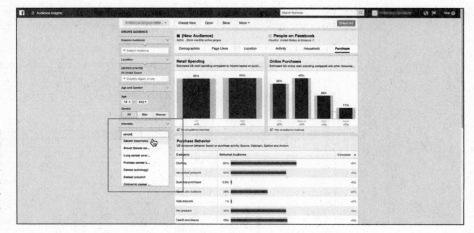

FIGURE 16-3: Select the cause associated interest categories or associations that your audience may be interested in.

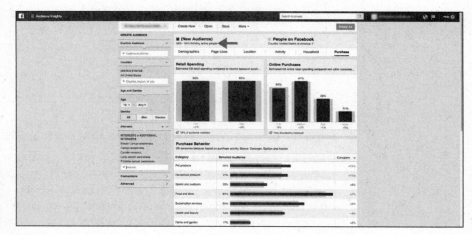

FIGURE 16-4: Determine how viable your selected audience is.

Identifying a cause that aligns with your brand

When the synergy between a brand and the cause is clear to everyone, the choice is a success. When choosing a cause, take a step back from your personal affiliations and ask yourself what causes would best align with your brand's industry or product. You should also ask which causes match the brand voice you've worked hard to cultivate.

To determine which causes best fit your brand, ask the questions in the following sections.

Is your audience currently engaged with a particular cause?

In your audience analysis, review your selected groups to see whether they currently align with a cause in which you're interested. Then, examine your broader analysis to determine whether they're interested in other causes that you may not have considered.

TIP

Take the time to review every possible cause, both general and specific. Then compile a list of all the causes your audience has shown an interest in at relatively strong ratios, such as those above 10 percent.

What is directly associated with this identified cause?

After you identify a cause that a majority of your audience is interested in, take the time to consider products, organizations, and initiatives that are directly associated with that cause. For example, world hunger is associated with a not-for-profit cause like Stop Hunger Now. Many companies have chosen to associate with this cause by offering small accessories, such as bracelets, bumper stickers, or pins.

TIP

When you've identified a cause that fits well with your brand, evaluate the different ways you can integrate this cause into your products or marketing, and determine how best to begin showcasing the cause and driving audience engagement with it.

Are there any indirect associations you can pinpoint?

Consider whether any indirect associations exist between the cause and your brand. In this case, you're going to need to think outside the box. This creative thinking will allow you to properly align your brand with your selected cause, as it won't always be obvious how your brand connects with the cause or organization you're trying to support. In this particular case, you should consider some of the ways in which a cause fits into your industry, or into your audience, rather than thinking about how it relates directly to your brand.

You won't always need to have a direct link between the cause you support and your brand. Sometimes you will simply support a cause because it's one you feel strongly about. As a brand, however, it will always be easier to integrate the cause into your communications strategy when a clear linkage exists between your brand and the cause in question.

For example, suppose that you're an online sporting goods retailer who supports a cause that provides sporting equipment to children who can't afford them. Your audience can easily see the connection. This apparent linkage also makes it easier for you to integrate the initiative into your marketing communications.

Your brand's passion for your cause needs to shine through in all your communications. This passion is the driving force that will help you build support for the cause you're promoting and will also build Millennial audience engagement and loyalty.

Marketing Your Brand with a Cause

After you determine the cause that will associate with your brand, you're ready to start developing the materials that will work with your cause marketing. Remember that cause marketing can be something that is associated with your brand in perpetuity, or it can be something that your brand is participating in while it's relevant to the community. Regardless of the approach, you need to put together a strategy that aligns your brand with the selected cause.

Establishing objectives associated with your brand and the cause

The cause marketing strategy you develop can have both short- and long-term objectives. These objectives may vary from one campaign or cause to the next. For example, a primary objective in participating in a viral cause, such as the Ice Bucket Challenge, may be entirely altruistic. You may simply want to raise awareness and money for a good cause, so your objective is to participate in the campaign to do exactly that. This motivation is the kind you need to have for any cause marketing initiative in which you participate if you want it to have an impact from a business standpoint.

The primary objective of any cause-related campaign is to benefit the cause. The short- and long-term business goals should be secondary to the greater good. This primary objective should be obvious to your Millennial audience.

Considering your business goals regarding cause alignment is also important. The following sections describe the objectives you should consider when planning a cause-related campaign.

Brand awareness

Cause marketing provides you with an entirely new theme around which to create content that you know interests your audience. Creating this kind of relatable content bolsters your brand's exposure in key Millennial markets. It also has the potential to significantly increase brand awareness among audience members participating in that conversation.

Relationship nurturing

If you've already cultivated a Millennial audience and you want to build on key relationships, then cause marketing may help you achieve that goal. According to a study by PR firm Cone Communications entitled "Cause Evolution," 85 percent of consumers think more highly of a brand that supports a cause that matters to them. By showcasing your support for a particular cause, you'll nurture relationships with your key demographic. (I cover the topic of relationship building in Chapter 15.)

Decreased conversion time

One of the strategies that online auction and retail giant eBay has implemented to prevent *cart abandonment* (when potential shoppers fill a cart online with goods and then leave the website before completing the purchase.) is the integration of donation options at checkout. According to the eBay study entitled "Integrating Cause and Commerce," when buyers are given the opportunity to donate during checkout, they're more likely to complete their transactions. In fact, these sellers see a 29 percent increase in sales in the same period as those without the option to donate to a cause.

TIP

Shortening the buying cycle by introducing a cause is a particularly valuable tactic to use in both the short and long term. This technique can be particularly useful to brands that have long buyer journeys.

Growth of customer loyalty

In the eBay study entitled "Integrating Cause and Commerce," the organization found that sellers saw a 50 percent decrease in churn rate. This reduction represents people who left from one transactional period to the next when a cause was integrated into the buying journey.

Churn rate is the rate at which customers stop buying from a brand or terminate their subscription. It is an important metric of customer loyalty and value.

As you know, Millennials in particular prefer to associate with brands that align themselves with important causes. Doing so not only means that your brand is helping a particular initiative that matters to you, but it also benefits you in the long run by improving customer loyalty.

Leveraging cause marketing for brand growth

Building your brand around association with a cause can be a useful strategy, but it can mean inextricably linking your brand to the cause. Some of the largest companies in the world build their brands without associating directly with a cause. Global retailers like Gap and Nike approach cause marketing from the perspective of associating with a cause only in some key areas as opposed to making it the focal point of the organization (like TOMS, which is covered in Chapter 17).

For example, Gap owns several brands, including Banana Republic and Old Navy, and isn't necessarily associated only with cause marketing efforts. The majority of Gap customers, however, are familiar with the brand's association with the Product (Red) initiative, which aims to help eradicate AIDS in Africa. Several brands, including Nike, American Express, Converse, and others have licensed the Product (Red) theme and linked their brands to the cause.

The strategy of associating your brand with a cause greater than your industry, as those big, public companies have done, is a good way to achieve a few objectives related to brand growth:

>> **You enter into a group with big players.** When it comes to a cause, big organizations like Gap or American Express may be participating, as well as smaller ones, like the entrepreneur's small business association. The size of the players may change, but the league in which they're playing remains the same. Leveraging a cause that is nationally or even globally recognized means increased exposure, and that exposure is certainly useful when it comes to building your company's presence.

>> **Your product line or service offering expands.** In the case of Livestrong or other causes that have a product or service that you can sell, it allows you to expand your offerings. While this expansion not be a primary source of revenue, you can be assured that the potential for discoverability by a target audience is improved.

>> **You reach new markets that may have otherwise been unreachable.** With so much online marketing noise, traditional marketing campaigns may understandably not reach a lot of prospects. So much is going on that a brand can easily be ignored, even if the prospect is a perfect fit. Aligning yourself with a cause can rescue lost prospects by appealing to them from a different angle.

Using Your Cause to Build Relationships with Millennials

Relationships drive Millennial buying decisions and inspire loyalty. The price may have a lot to do with the timing of the buying cycle, but ultimately a relationship can be the deciding factor. When you tie in the importance that Millennials place on cause affiliation, you can say with certainty that cause marketing can push your relationships with Millennial consumers forward.

You can leverage your cause in your communications strategies to build your relationships with Millennial consumers:

>> **Integrating the cause message on your website:** Consider calling attention to the cause from a stand-alone section on the website that your audience can access from the main menu or from embedded links in your home page content. You also want to feature your involvement with the cause wherever you can on your site content. If you have a scrolling home page banner, you can dedicate one of the slides to the cause you're working with.

>> **Adding donation options across multiple channels:** You can place donation options on your website in email forms using a tool like Constant Contact (http://constantcontact.com), shown in Figure 16-5, or on social channels, such as Facebook. The more you showcase the option to donate, the clearer you make it to your audience that you're invested in the cause and aren't being opportunistic.

FIGURE 16-5: Constant Contact allows users to create donation campaigns.

- » **Developing a cause-specific content strategy:** While you may have ongoing elements, such as donation buttons, running across various media to call attention to your selected cause, a content strategy that pushes the cause is a useful way to move your cause marketing efforts forward. This content needs to be the ultimate in soft-selling strategies. Tips on running a successful campaign that leverages this soft-selling approach and avoids hurting your image are covered in the following section, "Avoiding Damage to Your Brand."

- » **Participating in trending movements or events that call attention to a cause:** When you participate in a trend, it humanizes your brand. When you determine that your brand's participation would be acceptable and welcomed, you can bolster your relationship with other participating Millennials by showcasing that you're more than a profit-centric organization.

Avoiding Damage to Your Brand

While cause marketing can be hugely useful in building up relationships, you want to avoid being perceived as an opportunist at all costs. This perception is a surefire way to break your trust with the Millennial consumer. It can be detrimental to your audience's permanent perception of your brand.

Make sure that you take the following actions to avoid doing damage to your brand:

- » **Evaluate your participation in a trend.** Trends and Internet stunts can be great ways to humanize your brand and connect with Millennials. The wonderful thing about these simple campaigns is that they don't need to be extensively planned out or integrated into your day-to-day communications. However, you still need to consider whether it's appropriate for your brand to participate. More often than not, brands getting involved is a great addition, but in certain cases, such as campaigns where participants share personal stories to raise awareness for a particular cause, your brand's involvement isn't appropriate.

- » **Avoid asking for engagement in exchange for your donations.** In 2013, Kellogg's showcased an example of how brands can miss the point of cause marketing when it offered to exchange engagement for donations. Essentially, offering to donate to a cause only in exchange for a like or a share of its content told audiences that the company was only interested in the cause if it received something in return. The key point that this highlighted was that asking for donations in exchange for retweets shows that your involvement is entirely rooted in professional gain. Donating a portion of sales or matching donations or simply providing the option to donate are great ways to showcase your honest involvement. Holding your donations hostage in exchange for some benefit from consumers is not a good way to go.

>> **Avoid all cases of hypocrisy.** You should really give thought to how the public may perceive your involvement with a particular initiative when you're involved in an industry that has experienced controversy. If you're in the oil and gas business, for example, you may not want to align with a cause that is trying to help the environment. The irony won't be lost on your audience, and the response will be negative.

>> **Aim to be authentic.** Whatever you choose to do, the most important thing to remember is that authenticity is at the core of successful cause marketing. Millennials don't want to see brands capitalizing on a good cause for personal gain, and they're perceptive enough to catch onto this scheme. If you craft a strategy to help a cause that you truly believe in, that passion will shine through.

4

The Part of Tens

Discover campaigns that successfully connected with Millennials.

Avoid mistakes and assumptions that marketers make when it comes to Millennials.

Find out tips that will help you develop more successful programs and campaigns.

Chapter **17**

Ten Successful Marketing Campaigns That Won Over Millennials

n this chapter, you look at some of the ways brands have converted Millennials into loyal, lifelong customers. Every brand case study covered in this chapter has achieved success by leveraging different strategies, platforms, or audience characteristics. While not every strategy will be appropriate for your business, you can certainly discover some lessons from each of these examples.

Domino's Tackles Snapchat

Domino's is no stranger to cutting-edge social media campaigns. The fast-food pizza chain has conducted a number of very successful campaigns that have reinvented the pizza ordering process and garnered interest from Millennials who live on social media and mobile devices. Before launching its Snapchat initiative, Domino's UK recognized an interest in participating in brand experience campaigns when the pizza chain offered users a chance to turn the pizza customization process into a social, shareable experience. Domino's Pizza Legends immersed customers in the brand experience, so Domino's decided to tackle a new platform: Snapchat.

Using the Snapchat story feature, Domino's set a date, informed its loyal fans, and created a story that lasted 24 hours. This story followed a driver on his delivery route as he faced several major obstacles. Every so often, these stories would produce part of a secret discount code that the audience could use when ordering a pizza. This strategy created an immersive brand experience that catered to a young demographic, active on mobile devices, who were interested in opportunities to save money.

Nike's Experiences on Instagram

Instagram is a visual medium. There's no getting around the fact that without visually appealing content, a brand will fail on Instagram. Nike, a major shoe and sporting retailer, could have taken the easy route on Instagram by showcasing its product line. But instead, the brand decided to focus on lifestyle. The addition of an enormous audience of followers (more than any other brand on Instagram) proves that the company made the right move.

If you scroll through Nike's Instagram feed, you'll notice something interesting about the photos it shares: The images are rarely used to call attention to a particular product. Nike knows that the Millennials using Instagram are familiar with the brand. Nike doesn't want to see the product; it wants to see the lifestyle that the product is used for.

This savvy tactic has helped Nike build its content strategy. The retailer uses Instagram as an association tool for Millennials. By showcasing athletic, active individuals using Nike gear to engage in a healthy lifestyle, Instagram users associate Nike with healthy living.

Nike's use of its fans' state of mind and interests is a prime example of a brand that understands its audience on a very intimate level and uses that to craft a successful content strategy. Nike recognizes that Millennials are familiar with its globally recognized brand and are quite possibly ready to buy. Understanding the state of mind of its audience in this way allows Nike to maintain its brand's share of voice about healthy living without ever having to push a product.

Chipotle and Digital New Media

Chipotle is a multibillion-dollar fast-food chain that sells burritos. Not too many people would have guessed that burrito money would stack so high, but Chipotle leveraged Millennial preferences, communication habits, and cause marketing to build a burrito business that rivals some of the largest fast-food chains in the world. On top of that, Chipotle has achieved all of its success by spending virtually nothing on direct advertising. Compare this approach to the enormous ad spends of their competitors. How did Chipotle do it?

First, Chipotle knows its customer. Research allowed Chipotle to understand that Millennials wanted food quickly, but its customers also wanted it to be healthy, delicious, free of GMOs, and from a socially conscious institution. This research meant that Chipotle knew exactly how to frame its product to appeal to Millennials. It also knew how to leverage social media and Millennials' penchant for sharing to get the word out fast and effectively. Chipotle built its brand on healthy, non-GMO ingredients and an environmentally conscious mission statement. By putting a focus on the environment, cause marketing and social sharing came into play.

Millennials love the concept of buying from a brand that cares about more than the bottom line (see Chapter 16). Chipotle made its environmentally conscious approach a highlight of its media initiatives. The approach was largely video-based, as video is a Millennial's favorite medium. The results were staggering.

Unfortunately, Chipotle has recently faced issues with regards to food safety that hurt the brand, but its unconventional use of new media and audience preferences provides a blueprint that brands with even the smallest budgets can follow.

TOMS Focuses on a Cause

If you're unfamiliar with TOMS, it's a for-profit shoe company that reinvented the concept of cause marketing when it introduced its One for One mission statement. For every pair of shoes the company sells, it donates one pair to a child in need. The company provides shoes to children all over the world, and to date, it has provided more than 35 million pairs of shoes to children that need them.

So how does a for-profit company operate this way? TOMS makes no secret of the fact that the cost of a free pair of shoes is built into the price of the shoes. And despite this transparency and the openness about the fact that the price includes an additional pair of shoes, the company does exceptionally well, particularly with Millennials. TOMS Millennial audience and engagement on social media are sizeable, primarily due to the transparency on which the company built its brand. Customers can watch their purchases translate into donations to help children by following the TOMS brand.

Unlike so many of the checkout charity structures where customers are asked to donate to a cause at the checkout counter, TOMS shows its customers exactly how their purchases make an impact. This kind of cause marketing is extremely effective when it comes to building relationships with Millennials. Millennials want to see how their charitable contributions are being used. Giving a dollar at checkout is a somewhat passive act that yields no additional utility once the act is complete. When a customer is wearing TOMS and follows the story of what TOMS is doing for children, the feeling of having done something good for those less fortunate carries on.

What TOMS does is part of a broader industry category called *idea brands.* Idea brands are companies that reshape the business-as-usual model for various industries by integrating new components and reimagining how existing elements can be used.

Dollar Shave Club Picks Price and Viral Videos

Dollar Shave Club built a billion-dollar company delivering cheap razors and other grooming products to customers' homes on a monthly basis for a subscription fee. Dollar Shave Club built its business using viral videos and direct messaging to capitalize on Millennials' desire for on-demand products and their appreciation of unique marketing techniques.

One thing was clear to the heads of Dollar Shave Club from the beginning, Millennials would reject luxury-level pricing for disposable products. Instead of creating his and hers disposable razors with advanced technologies and other high-end reasons for charging a higher price, Dollar Shave Club played on the desire Millennials have for ads to be direct and funny. It worked.

According to research from market intelligence agency Mintel, roughly 70 percent of Millennials want ads to be funny. Over half of those not only want ads to be entertaining, but they also didn't want the ads to feel like advertising. This task isn't easy, but Dollar Shave Club found a way to deliver a video that went viral by throwing caution to the wind. It used outlandish, deadpan humor to deliver a clear-cut message to prospective buyers about what they would receive and how much it would cost. The ad was distributed via social networks like YouTube and

Facebook and promised a low-priced product without any games or gimmicks. The result was that Dollar Shave Club built a loyal following and an ongoing relationship with Millennials.

Understanding the audience was the key to Dollar Shave Club's success. Simply setting a low price isn't always the right option. For Dollar Shave Club, the key was to take it a step further and pair its low-price approach with a low-pressure marketing campaign. The authenticity of the brand and consistency in its messaging helped grow the company to the point where it was acquired by Unilever for $1 billion.

Uber Develops Millennial-Friendly Campaigns

Uber, an on-demand car service and ride-sharing application, has proven two things to the world. First, Uber has shown that when you provide a solution to a problem that consumers didn't even realize they had, you stand to find an incredible amount of success. Second, Uber has proven that when it comes to the sharing economy, Millennials epitomize the concept of pursuing access over ownership.

Uber recognizes that Millennials want to be a part of an experience. It has managed to consistently create marketing campaigns that keep the brand relevant and prevent it from becoming just another service offered to mobile users.

Capitalizing on the share economy was Uber's first goal, but the marketing around Uber has been largely tailored to the Millennial's desire for an experience. Before Uber, the black car experience was reserved for the ultra-elite. The average Millennial would never have thought of having a private black sedan chauffeur them a few city blocks. By creating the Uber experience and labeling it "Everyone's Private Driver," the experience was encapsulated in the mission statement of the company.

To keep the marketing fresh, Uber has consistently introduced new products and launched short-term campaigns to keep Millennials coming back to the app, even when they don't need a car. In campaigns such as #UberIceCream, users can call an Uber during a specified period for a chance to have ice cream delivered to their location. Another example was #UberKITTENS, launched on National Cat Day, which allowed users to use Uber to have kittens brought to their workplaces for a visit. These activities have kept Millennials engaged with the product beyond simply using it to hail a car.

Coca-Cola Plays the Name Game

In 2015, beverage giant Coca-Cola launched a campaign that put 250 of the most popular names for Millennials on bottles of Coke. The idea was to provide consumers with a reason to go searching for a bottle of Coca-Cola with their name on it. It also created a personalized, social, shareable experience for Millennials.

Coca-Cola understands that Millennials appreciate personalization. They also know that they like to use their mobile devices to share these personalized experiences on social channels. As a result, Coca-Cola created a campaign that produced a notable rise in U.S. sales. To add to the experience, Coca-Cola offered users an online component. The company provided a way for customers to research their name to learn about its history and etymology.

This brand experience is an excellent case of crossover between the real world and the digital one. Coca-Cola realized that the desire for personalization is not one rooted in Millennials' vanity, but rather one that speaks to the disconnectedness Millennials feel from some of the largest brands in the world. This small gesture is something that adds to the brand's relationship with its customers. It also helps foster loyalty among a Millennial audience that may feel forgotten or ignored by major retailers and brands.

Adblock Plus Identifies a Need

Millennials around the world have expressed a desire to remove advertising from their standard browsing experience. Despite Google's best efforts to personalize the ad experience and tailor it to the interests of a consumer, ads are often seen as ruining the browsing experience. When Adblock Plus rolled out its option to remove ads from browsers, Millennials went on an installation frenzy. Whereas Uber identified a problem that Millennials didn't realize they had, Adblock developed a solution to a problem that Millennials had been voicing for some time.

Shortly after reaching a critical mass of installs, Adblock announced that it would begin showing ads from approved (read: paying) advertisers. This change undermined its own product, but it did build a successful company by meeting the needs of its audience. This lesson is one worth noting.

Millennials are very open about their wants and needs, and they have made it clear to the world that ads are a distraction and often irrelevant, and that they would prefer a web without them. It's a marketer's job to listen to Millennial consumers when they share these kinds of struggles or problems, and either develop the solutions to the problems, or frame already existing solutions as the answer. Listening and reacting is an essential part of marketing to Millennials, and the creators of Adblock listened to what the market was telling them and reacted. Tools like Brandwatch or Mention facilitate this listening process for brand owners and marketers.

Hendricks Makes Gin Cool

Millennials largely ignored competition in the world of high-end spirits. Hendrick's, a high-quality, high-end gin, found itself competing for their attention, but Millennials were more interested in purchasing the cheapest option and ignoring the top shelf. Instead of trying to appeal to Millennials by showcasing its better quality and taste, the marketing team at Hendrick's decided to turn the gin into a component of a greater experience. It wanted to let the experience lead consumers to taste the product for themselves. This strategy caught the attention of Millennials.

Hendrick's made a conscious effort to appeal to the oddball or hipster movement by creating strange, Monty Python–esque videos. The company engaged in witty back-and-forth exchanges on social media, hosted curiously themed events, and opened pop-up bars and speak-easies ideally suited for sharing on social media.

Creating an experience has helped make Hendrick's one of the most popular and recognizable gins among Millennial consumers — even those who did not previously drink gin or know much about it.

Best Western Caters to One Group

As far as Millennials were concerned, staying at a traditional Best Western (BW) hotel was never considered an Instagram-worthy experience. The hotel chain realized that this coveted demographic was looking for something more than just a simple hotel stay, so it developed a pilot program at one of its locations in Missouri that catered exclusively to Millennial business travelers.

Research into Millennial business travelers' tastes and preferences revealed a desire for convenience and access. As a result, BW altered its rooms to provide only the basics in a stylish, minimalist setting. In addition, the hotel amenities were given a significant upgrade. Understanding the on-the-move lifestyle of Millennials meant integrating a grab-and-go station, which provides food that you can quickly access and take with you. The desire for healthy living provided the hotel with an incentive to build a more comprehensive exercise facility.

Now, Best Western International has also been using this research and customer insight to evolve its entire brand. It recognizes that Millennials want to garner utility beyond the basic transaction when they travel.

Chapter **18**

Ten Mistakes Marketers Make When Marketing to Millennials

I n this chapter, you may find yourself nodding your head each time I cover a particular mistake. That's because the majority of marketers have either made or might make these missteps when building out a Millennial marketing strategy. (If you have, don't worry; you're not alone!)

Not all these mistakes are necessarily going to lead to a failed campaign, but they can make achieving your objectives more difficult or increase the cost of running a campaign. Simply taking note of these common blunders and keeping them top of mind as you build out your Millennial marketing strategy is a good step in the right direction toward achieving your goals with the fewest hurdles possible.

Assuming Laziness

Baby Boomers often have the opinion and perception that Millennials are spoiled, entitled, and lazy. That last trait is the result of the growth of the demand economy among Millennial consumers. Millennials want access to goods and services at a moment's notice, and they don't want to have to go very far to get them. They also would much prefer to open an app and press a button or access a store online for these goods and services. For a generation that didn't grow up with this kind of accessibility, behaviors like these and the sense that access should be made easy translates into laziness — a major misconception.

A study by the professional services firm Ernst & Young found that Millennial managers voluntarily add hours to their workweek at a faster rate than the two generations that preceded them. Another study by Project: Time Off, which promotes and advocates for vacation time, found that half of all Millennials in the workforce strive to be considered *work martyrs,* which are employees that forego personal time, early work days, and paid time off in exchange for additional work hours. Millennials want to work, but their connectedness and buyer personas are often mistaken for laziness.

In order to avoid making the mistake of perceiving Millennials as lazy, recognize that what may seem like laziness is actually a byproduct of shifting market trends. For example, Millennials want accessibility because it fits in to a busy schedule, not because they want to avoid doing something on their own.

Framing your communications around the idea of making life easier as opposed to ignoring the demographic that finds the demand economy appealing will allow you to cater to an even broader range of consumers.

Assuming Selfishness

Millennials are driven and, like any consumer, consider a degree of self-interest in their decision-making processes, but that doesn't mean that Millennials are particularly selfish in their pursuits. They do have a degree of entitlement that comes from an upbringing during an economic boom, a high-level of education — the highest ratio of educated consumers of any generation in history — and from coming into buyer maturity during the Great Recession. However, to simply think of Millennials as selfish ignores a much greater, pertinent characteristic: They care about social good.

Cause marketing, a topic covered in detail in Chapter 16, is a field that has seen explosive growth over the last few years. Between 2000 and 2016, the funds raised from cause marketing initiatives have grown from $700 million to nearly $2 billion. This increase has been driven in large part thanks to Millennials. The Barkley American Millennials Report noted that more than 40 percent of Millennials prefer to give to a cause they care about through a business, rather than donating directly, and a study from the MSLGROUP found that nearly 70 percent of

Millennials want businesses to work toward addressing social issues instead of focusing solely on profit maximization.

Millennials care about society, and a brand's involvement in a cause is more than a kind gesture; it's a viable business tactic. Millennials will choose to buy from a brand that they feel does good as opposed to only buying from the brand that has a recognizable or impressive logo.

Aligning yourself with a cause or leveraging cause marketing when you have an opportunity to do so will help you avoid making the mistake of assuming that Millennials don't care and can actually lead to the development of new business from socially conscious Millennial consumers.

Assuming Vanity

It's all too easy to assume that Millennials are obsessed with vain. When you scroll through the Instagram feed of the average Millennial user or observe the selfie-obsessed habits of a Millennial on Snapchat, it seems almost safe to make the assumption that vanity plays a major role in the day-to-day lives of Millennial consumers. And while it may be true that you can observe a degree of narcissism or self-obsession in the sharing habits of Millennial consumers, to assume that these characteristics are only telling you that Millennials are egotistical is, in itself, an ironically superficial observation.

Millennials care about the experience, and they care about sharing that experience. While Millennial consumers may be a fairly price-sensitive generation (see next section), they're willing to spend when the transaction isn't the only part of the deal. Millennials spend on experience. The obsession with sharing, which comes off as pure vanity, is a consumer habit that has evolved with the growth of social media as an integral part of consumers' everyday lives. That habit needs to be a primary consideration whenever you're developing a Millennial-centric marketing strategy or campaign.

Think about the brand or transactional experience (see Chapter 13) when crafting a campaign designed to appeal to Millennials. Millennial consumers don't want the story to end at the point of conversion or payment. Do you have an opportunity to integrate an Instagrammable moment? Can you carry over the experience onto social channels? How can you garner additional value or utility from the transaction? These are things that Millennials weigh — consciously or not — when making a purchasing decision. Adding additional value — whether tangible or not — to a transaction will appeal greatly to Millennial consumers in search of an experience.

Assuming Frugality

With Millennials coming into their consumer maturation years during the Great Recession, it's easy to see why the assumption about Millennial frugality is made. The demand economy, access to information at a moment's notice, and the nature of social media has resulted in marketers and business owners assuming that Millennials seek everything they can for free and are rarely willing to pay for a product or service.

While Millennials as a consumer group are over-indexed when it comes to price sensitivity — that is, they consider price when making a purchasing decision ahead of all other factors — they will spend more than other consumers as a result of perceived value and utility. A study by DunnhumbyUSA, which handles loyalty programs in the United States, found that Millennial consumers are far more price-sensitive deal seekers than average consumers and will use coupons on a far more regular basis. The total of purchases for Millennial deal seekers, however, will be consistently higher than the average full-price customer, and they will return to a specific brand's store more loyally than the average customer.

Instead of simply assuming that Millennials are frugal and unwilling to spend, consider the fact that Millennials are often after more than just the product; they're after value. Value-seeking consumers, which includes those in pursuit of an experience on top of a transaction, will spend more and remain more loyal when you can provide that value to them. It can be in the form of deals, discounts, bonuses, giveaways, or other value-added components included in a transaction. For example, if a customer's name is entered in a weekly drawing to win his next purchase, he has a greater incentive to come back to that store or website and complete a transaction every week.

Assuming Ignorance

If you think traditional sales tropes will be the deciding factor in a Millennial's buying decision, think again. When you, as a brand, make first contact with a Millennial prospect, he has already progressed through a significant portion of the buying cycle. You're one of the last stops on the tour, so if you assume that the prospect is unfamiliar with your product, your quality, or your other customers' experiences, you're making a dangerous mistake. Treating a Millennial prospect the way a stereotypically shady used car salesman would treat unassuming, uninformed patrons (before all of that changed, of course) is one of the easiest ways to lose prospective business.

When engaging directly with a Millennial prospect — either online or in person — your approach should be one that allows the customer to share what she already knows, has researched, or would like to know. Comparison and peer review is a major part of the Millennial buying process, and there is a distinct possibility that by the time a prospect is contacting you, she has gone through several of those steps. While you also shouldn't assume that the prospect has all the information on hand when she first reaches out, the approach you may want to take is one of learning a little bit about where she is in the buying process before moving into the sales pitch. The assumption that you're dealing with an ignorant prospect that will respond to a one-way pitch will almost certainly end without a conversion.

Focusing on Age

Assuming that all Millennials are alike because they fall into the age parameters that statistically denote a Millennial is no different than assuming that a wealthy 50-something-year-old professional living in Manhattan and a 15-year-old high school student living in Missouri are alike because they both live in the United States. Consumers are all unique, and to lump a group together based on something as superficial as age and market to them all in the same way will yield subpar results and leave the majority of Millennial consumers with little to no impression of your brand.

While age may come into play when building an audience, you're going to want to take the time to develop hypertargeted audience segments that focus more on interests and behaviors as opposed to looking at only age or location. This process will help you develop more relevant content strategies and campaigns, which in turn will result in improved engagement and far above average conversion rates.

Chapter 3 covers the process of developing these narrowed, hypertargeted audience clusters.

Ignoring the Mindset

Age, or birth date range, is a relevant criteria when looking purely at statistics or sector studies. However, when it comes to marketing, the focus on a range of years as the enclosing parameters of a target audience is a practice that many marketers adopt without realizing how much missed opportunity they're leaving to a competitor as a result.

Millennials may possess certain traits and habits when it comes to their buying behavior, but they're not alone in possessing these traits. The Millennial mindset is one that has largely transcended generations, particularly as the adoption of mobile technology and integration of social media into the day-to-day lives of consumers from other generations has come to pass. When you develop a hyper-targeted audience around tastes and preferences and launch a campaign, you'll want to consider expanding that campaign's target audience over time to include consumers of other ages that fit the same interest and behavior criteria that you've outlined.

Once again, the Millennial mindset is one that isn't limited only to those born during a designated span of years. Take advantage of that when the opportunity to do so presents itself.

Focusing Only on the Campaign

When marketers are in the process of creating a campaign, they often tend to think about the campaign as if it will exist in a vacuum. Essentially, they develop the campaign while ignoring the ecosystem of initiatives, content, audiences, other campaigns, and advertising.

One element that Millennials are looking for when evaluating whether to buy from or work with a particular brand is how well the experience with the brand flows. This experience also contributes significantly to loyalty and assists greatly in the process of building relationships with your target Millennial audience.

When you develop a campaign, you need to think about it in terms of how it will fit in with all the active elements that currently exist around your brand. This thought process will not only assist in improving brand awareness with target Millennials because of the continuity from the campaign to your day-to-day content market-ing, but it will also create secondary benefits, such as audience growth or relation-ship nurturing, that extend beyond the original scope of the campaign.

Aggressively Selling

The pushy sales pitch was one that yielded some results in the early days of paid online advertising and affiliate marketing, but today, and particularly with Mil-lennial consumers, the aggressive sales pitch is one that results in zero engage-ment. In fact, this strategy is one that has more potential to damage your brand's reputation and your relationship with prospects than lead to conversions.

The soft sell may take a little bit more time, but during that time, you're cultivating a relationship with your Millennial prospects, which leads to loyalty. You may be able to entice quicker action by offering some sort of incentive, but if you ignore the process of getting to know your audience, crafting communications that appeal to their unique personalities, and developing campaigns that guide them along the buyer journey until they're ready to convert, then you won't find yourself succeeding when it comes to increasing your conversion rates.

Ignoring the Relationship

Aggressively selling is a part of a greater error that impacts your short-term gains and long-run success and survivability. When you ignore the importance of the relationship with Millennial consumers, you ignore the future of your business. Millennials may take a little bit longer to convert and may take a more convoluted buying journey that needs attention, but relationships mean loyalty, brand advocacy, and growth.

While Millennials may be price-sensitive, they're willing to spend when the transaction involves more than initial exchange of goods and services. Millennials want to work with a brand that has catered to their tastes, one that has shown it cares about more than just the sale, and one that won't quickly abandon its customers after a conversion. The development of relationships needs to be a central theme in the creation of both your overarching strategies and objective-specific campaigns.

Chapter **19**

Ten Quick Tips to Keep Top of Mind

In this chapter, I present some simple but effective tips to help keep you on the right track when crafting a campaign or acquisition strategy. While I cover the step-by-step approaches for each of these strategies throughout this book, I list them here to serve as a checklist when you're working on a strategy.

Start with Data

Data should drive everything you do. Data will prevent you from operating in the dark and basing your decisions on unfounded assumptions. Data can help you determine which decisions to make when you're first building your strategy, and it can help you improve your operations at various points in your audit.

Ultimately, using data will result in more effective programs, greater results, and shorter goal completion timelines. It will also help you maintain relevance with an evolving audience over time, which leads to stronger relationships and significant long-term growth.

For more information on the use of data, take a look at the strategies covered in Chapter 4.

Remember the Psychographics

The Millennial mindset needs to be the focal point of any initiative, campaign, program, or analysis. Simply thinking about your audience in superficial constructs, such as age or location, can cause you to completely miss what makes this audience so unique. The designation as a Millennial originally defined people in a specific age bracket. However, this term is quickly becoming one definition of a modern consumer. For this reason, you need to get to know these customers on a much more personal level.

See Chapter 2 for a more detailed look at the Millennial mindset.

Evaluate Additional Age Brackets

Don't limit yourself to a year range when you market to Millennials. You wouldn't limit your targeting and audience segmentation to age alone, so you shouldn't exclude audiences from different age demographics that fit particular interest and behavior targets. Consumers in every demographic are evolving and adapting.

Along with that evolution is a transcendence from one demographic to another. As you realize this and expand your targeting over time, you will build your business to greater heights.

Chapter 3 covers the creation of narrowed, highly detailed audiences, and Chapter 2 expands on the notion that your marketing tactics don't need to be restricted by the age of your audience.

Establish Demographic-Specific Objectives

As you build various audience segments and clusters, you need to clearly state the objectives. You need to clearly state a process for long-term objectives as well. For example, ask yourself, "What do you hope to achieve with the cluster that is made up of professionals over 35 versus the cluster that is only now completing their college years?" You need to consider this question because not every cluster will necessarily be suited for the same objective.

For more on the creation of targeted campaigns on new media and the development of highly focused objectives, visit Chapter 6.

Choose Your Causes Wisely

Cause marketing has the potential to be a tremendous asset, but you need to be very careful so as not to appear opportunistic. Brands that seem to be taking advantage of a particular cause or trend for personal gain will lose the respect, trust, and business of a socially conscious Millennial. Choose a cause that you care about, that makes sense for your business, and that your audience can relate to. That approach will benefit you much more than simply jumping on the bandwagon without giving thought as to how that cause may be perceived.

To find out more about the value of cause marketing, see the strategies in Chapter 14.

Identify the Foundation of Your Relationships

As you determine how to connect with Millennials, you need to clearly identify what the root of your brand's relationship is going to be with each of your clusters. To make the experience as personal as possible, identify a foundation and build out from that foundation with content, campaigns, and conversation.

Discover more about the importance of relationships in Chapter 13.

Focus on the Experience

Millennials want more than a simple transaction. When you observe their habits, you realize that the experience is crucial to the buying decision. The weight Millennials place on the experience also relates closely to the Millennial pursuit of value. Millennials may not be willing to spend quickly and are sensitive to price. However, they may be ready to pay a little bit more and become brand advocates when they perceive value in a greater brand experience.

You can find out more about the creation of a brand experience by reading Chapter 13.

Regularly Audit Your Performance

New media is in constant motion; it evolves, and consumers adapt. As a result, your audience will shift in real time, and you need to change with them. Audit your performance regularly to identify opportunities, optimize campaigns, or revise program structure. If you forget to move with the times, your audience may leave you behind.

Chapter 11 covers the steps and strategies of conducting an audit.

Keep Your Voice Genuine

Authenticity is key to the success of so many initiatives with Millennials and a key component in the development of relationships with Millennials. When developing content to appeal to their tastes and preferences, you want to ensure that you're genuine. Your audience should feel as though you're interested in building a relationship and not focused solely on the next sale. Create an authentic, tailored voice in your marketing materials to get this point across.

The importance of sincerity in your actions is a theme that is touched on in Chapters 6 and 16.

Go Mobile First

Millennials live on their mobile devices. If you want to reach them where they are, you need to think mobile first. Thinking mobile doesn't preclude you from focusing on other platforms. Plenty of other media may work better on a desktop than on a mobile device, like individual components of a membership backend.

The thing to remember is that mobile will be a key element in any Millennial's day-to-day life. If you want to build that relationship, consider mobile as a fundamental pillar of your overall marketing strategy.

You can find out more about the components of a mobile strategy by visiting Chapter 10.

Index

click-through rates, 91
CLV (customer lifetime value), 13
Coca-Cola, 304
cold emails, 225
color scheme, 169
communication
  with audiences, 215, 250–252
  with audiences in real-time, 250–252
  with detractors, 15
  habits of Millennials, 11
  identifying opportunities for, 249
  for Millennials, 17
  real-time, 250–252, 258
  regularity of, 229
community, in communications, 229
community conversations, integrating, 214
community forum, active, 210
competitive data, 62–64
complexity, cause marketing and, 285
Compress JPEG, 176
consideration stage, of buying process, 156, 158
consistency, 112
Constant Contact, 44, 90, 293
consumer brands, 260
consumption habits
  about, 259
  building lasting relationships, 269–275
  managing brand crisis, 275–281
  media types for, 259–263
  running social care programs, 263–269
content
  branded, 124
  choosing, 125–126
  conversational, 227
  creating, 160
  creating seamless experiences, 169
  for display advertising, 181
  evergreen, 128, 129
  Instagram, 190
  mobile-friendly, 249
  personalizing, 169–170
  preemptive development of, 267

promotional, 129, 130
repurposing, 127
segmenting, 229–233
for social media, 178
themed, 127
third-party, 124, 130–131, 228–229
Twitter, 129–131
unifying across channels, 232–233
content and creative split testing and
    optimization, 61
content engagement half-life, 164
content receptiveness, as a category for
    segmented audience pockets, 34–35
content requirements and access, evaluating, 30
content strategies
  about, 100
  building for Twitter, 120–121
  creating, 211, 213–215, 272–273
  developing hypertargeted content, 109–110
  editorial calendar structure, 102–107
  planning segmenting, 123–125
  thematic, 107–109
  tone of voice outline, 100–101
content templates, 38, 278–279
content-media alignment, 39
control group, 118
conversational content, 227
cooked data, 58
correlations, 67, 68, 204
cost per acquisition (CPA), 162
cost per click (CPC), 162
cost per lead (CPL), 162
cost per thousand impressions (CPM), 162
CPA (cost per acquisition), 162
CPC (cost per click), 162
CPL (cost per lead), 162
CPM (cost per thousand impressions), 162
creating
  brand experience strategies, 221–224
  components of real-time strategies, 256–258
  content, 160
  content experiences, 169

data (continued)
  post-level, 67
  from public channels, 75–76
  raw, 58
  segmentation of, 237
  small, 61
  social media user, 58–59, 73–75
  starting with, 315
  transactional, 64–65
  from Twitter, 74
  using as a strategy foundation, 69–70
  value of, 57–65
  visualized, 60
  from your owned media, 70–72
  from YouTube, 74–75
data breach, 276
data collection, 172–173, 187–188
deals, 228
debt, 10
decision-making, 18–19
decreased conversion time, cause marketing and, 291
demand
  about, 243
  building real-time response strategies, 250–256
  building real-time strategy components, 256–258
  catering to, 243–245
  creating on-demand services, 245–249
demographics, prioritizing target, 34
demographic-specific objectives, establishing, 316
deploying remarketing, 232–233
Desk.com (website), 173
determining KPIs, 161
detractors, communicating with, 15
developing
  brand experience strategies, 221–224
  components of real-time strategies, 256–258
  content, 160
  content experiences, 169
  content strategies, 211, 213–215, 272–273
  content strategies for Twitter, 120–121
  customer loyalty, 240

customer relationships, 227–229
demographic-specific objectives, 316
editorial calendars, 126–129
engagement goals by media, 158–160
experience-specific content, 230–232
Facebook content strategies, 100–110
hypertargeted content, 109–110
identifiable themes, 233–234
incentivized adoption schemes, 217
Instagram strategies, 142–147
loyalty programs, 12–13
mobile strategies, 171–192
mobile-specific content for websites, 174–177
mobile-specific goals, 172–174
multichannel media strategy, 153–170
multiple entry points, 223–224
multiple strategies, 275–277
objectives, 198, 290–292
on-demand audiences, 247–249
on-demand services, 245–249
real-time response strategies, 250–256
relationships, 240, 269–275, 293–294
relationships with Facebook audience, 111–113
segmented audience pockets, 50–53
segmented audiences, 239, 271–272
standalone landing pages, 214
strategy, 57–77
target audiences, 31–53
targeted content strategies, 99–100
timelines, 231
trust, 228–229
Twitter content, 129–131
unified omni-channel communications strategies, 155–168
unique assets, 233
unique messages, 232
video content, 136–137, 260–262
a voice, 211–215
digital access, offering to products/services, 244–245
Digital New Media, 301
discoverable assets, 234–235
display advertising, 87, 181–182

evergreen content, 128, 129

exclusivity, 111–112

experience. *See also* brand experience
  blending, 231
  focusing on, 317
  personalizing, 174

experience-specific content, creating, 230–232

expertise
  as a content type, 125
  highlighting, 227

F

Facebook
  about, 29, 40, 94, 266
  advertising on, 113–118, 182
  algorithm, 103
  analyzing your audience, 95–99
  building relationships with your audience on, 111–113
  creating content for, 178
  creating content strategies, 100–110
  data from, 73–74
  developing targeted content strategies, 99–100
  Insights tool, 45–48
  Quick Start Guide (website), 255
  utilizing features of, 94–95

Facebook Ads Manager, 114–116

Facebook Audience Network, 182

Facebook Audiences, 270

Facebook Business Manager (website), 45

Facebook Developers portal (website), 254

Facebook Messenger, 252

facilitating movement, 234

fallout planning, 280

fast sharing, of Millennials, 8

flexibility, of schedules, 127

followers, on Twitter, 134

freebies, 228

frequency of activities, audiences and, 275

frugality, assumptions about, 310

functioning, in real time, 245

Fung Business Intelligence Centre (website), 9

G

gaming, 103

gender, audiences and, 271

general interests, for target audience, 33

generalizations, making, 28

Goldman Sachs (website), 9

goodwill brand value growth rate, 168

Google AdWords, 179, 223

Google Alerts, 36–37

Google Analytics, 71–72, 219, 236

Google's Test My Site, 175

Google's URL building service (website), 236

H

half-life, 124

Hendricks, 305

highlighting
  benefits of sharing, 214
  expertise, 227
  share aspect, 214

high-value correlations, 204

How-To, as thematic content, 108

humor
  as a content type, 125, 137
  as a video content type, 137

hypertargeted content, developing, 109–110

hypertargeting, 111

I

icons, explained, 2–3

identifying
  brand advocates, 13–14
  brand defenders, 13–14
  communication opportunities, 249
  data sources, 70–76
  foundation of relationships, 317
  key influencers, 12–15
  new opportunities with data, 202–204
  opportunities by media type, 155–156
  preferred media, 29–30

S

Tip icon, 2

Tips & Tricks, as thematic content, 108

TOMS, 301–302

tone
  for videos, 261
  of voice, 100–101, 318
  of voice outline, 100–101

topical information, as a content type, 125

touchpoint attribution measurement model, 219

touchpoints
  about, 11
  elements for, 226–227
  identifying, 225–226

trackable links, 236–237

tracking brand experience, 235–237

tracking mechanisms, 234

TrackMaven, 62, 63

traditional media
  about, 35–39, 79
  email, 89–92
  print media, 86–89
  television, 80–85
  working with new media, 154

traditional TV, 80–81

transactional data, 64–65

trend setting, of Millennials, 8

troll, 276

trust, building, 228–229

turnaround time, cause marketing and, 285–286

tweet engagements, on Twitter, 133

Twitter
  about, 41, 119, 265
  advertising, 183–189
  algorithm, 128
  best practices, 134–135
  data from, 74
  developing content, 129–131
  developing editorial calendars, 126–129
  how it's used, 119–126
  reaching Millennial users, 131–135
  TV targeting, 83–85

Twitter Analytics dashboard (website), 121

Twitter cards, 183–185

U

Uber, 18, 303

understanding phase, of brand advocacy cycle, 13–14

unforeseen events, for second screen viewing, 83

unified omni-channel communications strategies, developing, 155–168

untruthfulness, 276

users, engaging, 227

V

valleys, 66–67

value
  about, 113
  of data, 57–65
  providing to audiences, 260
  of video, 136, 139

vanity, assumptions about, 309

variety, as a benefit of chat bots, 255

video overlay, 262

video views, on Twitter, 134

videos
  about, 135–136
  content types, 137
  creating content, 136–137, 260–262
  impact of on consumer brands, 260
  soft-selling your brand, 139–140
  tips for, 138–139
  types of, 262–263

virality, 161

visualized data, 60

visuals, as a content type, 125

voice, establishing a, 211–215

W

waiting game, Millennials and the, 10

Warning icon, 3

waste, 69

website goal conversion rate, 163

Website Live Chat, 255

website visitor volume, 162

website visits/conversions, 134, 188–189

About the Author

Corey Padveen is an industry-leading marketing data expert with extensive experience building strategies and working with brands in a variety of industries to execute measurable growth campaigns. He is a partner at t2 Marketing International (http://t2marketinginternational.com), an award-winning marketing consultancy that has worked with some of the largest brands in the world over its 30-year history.

Corey's background in economics is focused largely on econometrics — economic statistics — which has allowed him to develop unique, first-of-their-kind approaches to analyzing marketing data and identifying new opportunities for t2's clients. He has pioneered the concepts of social equity, which has provided a basis for an expansive study on new media measurability, and *Responsive Branding*, a proprietary concept that leverages vast amounts of market data to develop more effective strategies.

The highly in-demand nature of Corey's expertise has led to him speaking at conferences, summits, and corporate events all over the world. He contributes regularly to a variety of online and print publications, including *Search Engine Journal* and *Social Media Today,* and is the primary author for t2's corporate blog, as well as his personal blog, CoreyPadveen.com. He is Google AdWords and Analytics certified and received his BA in Economics from McGill University in Montreal.

On a personal side, Corey loves dogs, tries his best to impress the world with his cooking on Instagram, collects antique and handcrafted shoehorns (of all things), enjoys artisanal, small-batch gins, and like any good Montrealer, is a big fan of the Montreal Canadiens.

Dedication

To my family, who have all supported me in whatever pursuit I've chosen to explore.

To the partners and team at t2, who have provided me with an incredible series of opportunities and believed in me from the moment my career began.

Author's Acknowledgments

Writing this book has been an honor and a privilege. I would like to thank Wiley Publishing, Inc. for giving me a platform through which I could share my thoughts and insight. Specifically, I would like to thank the members of my creative and editing team: Amy Fandrei, Stephanie Diamond, Kelly Ewing, Mary Corder, and Michelle Krasniak. You've each contributed to making this process an easy one, and you've helped me turn this concept into a reality.

I would also like to thank you, the reader. It's humbling to me that you've decided to take the time to read my words, and for that I am truly grateful. I hope you learn something valuable, and I wish you luck and success putting these lessons into practice!

Publisher's Acknowledgments

Senior Acquisitions Editor: Amy Fandrei

Project Editor: Kelly Ewing

Copy Editor: Kelly Ewing

Editorial Assistant: Serena Novosel

Senior Editorial Assistant: Cherie Case

Reviewer: Michelle Krasniak

Production Editor: Vasanth Koilraj

Cover Image: © oneinchpunch/iStockphoto

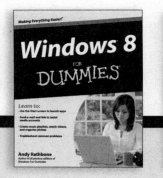

Math & Science

Algebra I For Dummies,
2nd Edition
978-0-470-55964-2

Anatomy and Physiology
For Dummies, 2nd Edition
978-0-470-92326-9

Astronomy For Dummies,
3rd Edition
978-1-118-37697-3

Biology For Dummies,
2nd Edition
978-0-470-59875-7

Chemistry For Dummies,
2nd Edition
978-1-118-00730-3

1001 Algebra II Practice
Problems For Dummies
978-1-118-44662-1

Microsoft Office

Excel 2013 For Dummies
978-1-118-51012-4

Office 2013 All-in-One
For Dummies
978-1-118-51636-2

PowerPoint 2013
For Dummies
978-1-118-50253-2

Word 2013 For Dummies
978-1-118-49123-2

Music

Blues Harmonica
For Dummies
978-1-118-25269-7

Guitar For Dummies,
3rd Edition
978-1-118-11554-1

iPod & iTunes
For Dummies, 10th Edition
978-1-118-50864-0

Programming

Beginning Programming
with C For Dummies
978-1-118-73763-7

Excel VBA Programming
For Dummies, 3rd Edition
978-1-118-49037-2

Java For Dummies,
6th Edition
978-1-118-40780-6

Religion & Inspiration

The Bible For Dummies
978-0-7645-5296-0

Buddhism For Dummies,
2nd Edition
978-1-118-02379-2

Catholicism For Dummies,
2nd Edition
978-1-118-07778-8

Self-Help & Relationships

Beating Sugar Addiction
For Dummies
978-1-118-54645-1

Meditation For Dummies,
3rd Edition
978-1-118-29144-3

Seniors

Laptops For Seniors
For Dummies, 3rd Edition
978-1-118-71105-7

Computers For Seniors
For Dummies, 3rd Edition
978-1-118-11553-4

iPad For Seniors
For Dummies, 6th Edition
978-1-118-72826-0

Social Security
For Dummies
978-1-118-20573-0

Smartphones & Tablets

Android Phones
For Dummies, 2nd Edition
978-1-118-72030-1

Nexus Tablets
For Dummies
978-1-118-77243-0

Samsung Galaxy S 4
For Dummies
978-1-118-64222-1

Samsung Galaxy Tabs
For Dummies
978-1-118-77294-2

Test Prep

ACT For Dummies,
5th Edition
978-1-118-01259-8

ASVAB For Dummies,
3rd Edition
978-0-470-63760-9

GRE For Dummies,
7th Edition
978-0-470-88921-3

Officer Candidate Tests
For Dummies
978-0-470-59876-4

Physician's Assistant Exam
For Dummies
978-1-118-11556-5

Series 7 Exam For Dummies
978-0-470-09932-2

Windows 8

Windows 8.1 All-in-One
For Dummies
978-1-118-82087-2

Windows 8.1 For Dummies
978-1-118-82121-3

Windows 8.1 For Dummies
Book + DVD Bundle
978-1-118-82107-7

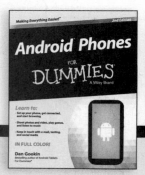   

e | **Available in print and e-book formats.**

Available wherever books are sold. **For more information or to order direct visit www.dummies.com**

Take Dummies with you everywhere you go!

Whether you are excited about e-books, want more from the web, must have your mobile apps, or are swept up in social media, Dummies makes everything easier.

For Dummies is the global leader in the reference category and one of the most trusted and highly regarded brands in the world. No longer just focused on books, customers now have access to the For Dummies content they need in the format they want. Let us help you develop a solution that will fit your brand and help you connect with your customers.

Advertising & Sponsorships

Connect with an engaged audience on a powerful multimedia site, and position your message alongside expert how-to content.

Targeted ads • Video • Email marketing • Microsites • Sweepstakes sponsorship

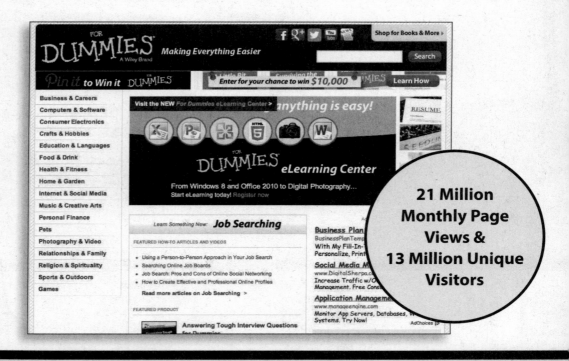